G000163306

THE GENERAL THEORY OF F

The General Theory of Profit Equilibrium

Keynes and the Entrepreneur Economy

Connell Fanning
Professor of Economics
National University of Ireland
Cork

and

David O Mahony
Emeritus Professor of Economics
University College
Cork

Consultant Editor: Jo Campling

First edition 1998
Reprinted (with minor alterations) 2000

Published by
MACMILLAN PRESS LTD
Houndmills, Basingstoke, Hampshire RG21 6XS
and London
Companies and representatives
throughout the world

ISBN 0–333–71669–8 hardcover
ISBN 0–333–77357–8 paperback

A catalogue record for this book is available
from the British Library.

This book is printed on paper suitable for recycling and made from fully managed and sustained forest sources.

Transferred to digital printing 2003

Printed and bound in Great Britain by
Antony Rowe Ltd, Chippenham and Eastbourne

Published in the United States of America by
ST. MARTIN'S PRESS, INC.,
Scholarly and Reference Division
175 Fifth Avenue, New York, N.Y. 10010

ISBN 0–312–21027–2

To Mary, Saranna and T.

C. F.

and to Moyra, Colm, Emer and Aonghus

D. OM.

Contents

Preface

The theme of this book is that the body of theory which Keynes propounds in *The General Theory* is based on an analysis of the decisions of individuals – producers, consumers and investors. We show how Keynes extended that analysis to the monetary-entrepreneur economic system as a whole in a simple unambiguous way which avoids the pitfalls of aggregation so as to provide a general theory by means of which questions relating to the employment of the available resources in such an economy can be addressed. We show, too, that the manner in which he devised this general theory was very much in the Marshallian tradition of theory conceived of as an apparatus of the mind. Thus *The General Theory* itself was new as to content but traditional as to the conception of theory that moulded it, and it is to be understood as a work dealing with the creation and formulation of theory rather than with economic policy in general or with macro-economic policy in particular.

Our interpretation of *The General Theory* stems from a critical reading of that book and from an examination of the other writings of Keynes that impinge upon it. We have made extensive use of quotations both to support our interpretation and to help our readers to read *The General Theory* for themselves. We have not made any direct use of the vast literature to which *The General Theory* has given rise. That is why almost all references are to the writings of Keynes himself. Nevertheless we have taken that literature into account, and we hope that this book will enable readers to see it from a different perspective.

CONNELL FANNING   DAVID O MAHONY

Acknowledgements

We wish to thank colleagues in the Department of Economics, UCC, who read various drafts: John Considine, Eleanor Doyle, Liam Gallagher, Catherine Kavanagh, Ella Kavanagh, Siobhán Lucey, Thomas McCarthy (now at Maynooth), Mary Maguire, Richard Moloney, Eoin O'Leary, Edward Shinnick, and William Sjostrom; and colleagues in other departments at UCC who gave their expertise: Professor Paddy Barry, Mathematics, John Curry, Accounting (now at University College Galway), Professor Shaun Doonan, Biochemistry (now at the University of East London), Professor Denis Lucey, Food Economics, Professor Michael Mortell, Applied Mathematics (now President of University College, Cork), and Professor Brian Twomey, Mathematics. Professor Garrett Barden of Philosophy deserves special acknowledgement for the particular help he gave us. Graduate students, in particular Brendan Kennelly and Donal O'Brien, deserve our thanks. Administrative colleagues who, not only for the technical support to produce the typescript, proofreading etc., but also for contributing to the everyday working environment without which the time and intellectual climate would not exist, are due our thanks: Daniel Blackshields, Margaret Clayton, Anne Delaney, Denise Keane, Patricia Kenny, Sheila O'Driscoll. Mary Maguire, the Department's Administrative Officer, deserves our special thanks.

Colleagues in other places who gave advice were Professors Philip Anderson of the University of St Thomas, Minneapolis, Tom Boylan of University College Galway, Gerry Hughes of the Economic and Social Research Institute, Dublin, and Frank Stephen of the University of Strathclyde. Tim Farmiloe, publishing director, Sunder Katwala, commissioning editor, at Macmillan, and Keith Povey, editorial consultant, were unfailing in their assistance, and encouragement. In a very special way we thank Jo Campling, our consulting editor who guided us through many difficulties and helped us to avoid many pitfalls – always with patience, sympathy and understanding.

In ventures such as this, families carry the greatest burden. They know what their sustained support has meant. Our dedication to them is a small token of our appreciation and thanks.

1 Introduction: The Keynesian Evolution

In *The General Theory of Employment, Interest and Money* (1936) Keynes set out to answer the question: what determines the employment of the available resources in the monetary- entrepreneur economy? Even to ask that question is to imply that the resources available at any particular time could be employed at different levels. If they could, the output of the economic system as a whole would not be fixed. Other things being equal, the level of output as a whole would correspond with the level at which resources were employed. Hence the question is synonymous with the question: what determines output as a whole? The answer to this question is what, as Keynes said, *The General Theory* purports to be (*CW, VII: xxvi*).[1] The question is a valid one because (i) we know from experience that the extent to which resources are employed varies from time to time; (ii) the assumptions required to support a theory that resources are normally employed fully or that general unemployment is merely a temporary aberration are not plausible, as is argued below. It is not, however, until the question is addressed in a methodical way that its validity can be fully appreciated. Up to Keynes's time the 'pure theory' relating to the question had 'seldom been examined in great detail' (*CW, VII*: 4). The issue was by no means totally 'overlooked', but 'the fundamental theory underlying it [had] been deemed so simple and obvious that it [had] received, at the most, a bare mention' (*CW, VII*: 4–5, *footnote omitted*).

THE 'CLASSICAL' ECONOMISTS

Keynes found that a new method of analysis had to be developed in order to address the question because economic theory, as it was in his time, did not provide a suitable means for doing so (*CW, VII: xxxv*). It took him many years to discover this. Much of his earlier work, as can now be seen with hindsight, was a search for the question itself. With hindsight too it can be seen that the question emerged clearly only in the process of formulating the method of answering it. It is clear that he was still searching for the question ever after he started on *The General Theory*.

1

As is shown in Chapter 2, Keynes understood economic theory to be the 'machinery of thought and knowledge', as Marshall (1920 : 779) put it or, as an 'apparatus of thought', in Keynes's own words (*CW, VII*: 340). It was very much in accordance with this view of theory that Keynes made his own contributions to Economics, original though they were in point of content.

In Keynes's opinion theory, in this sense, 'scarcely existed' before Adam Smith (*CW, XII*: 856). For Adam Smith the central issue or question in political economy related to something like the question that Keynes himself was concerned with, namely, the causes of the wealth of nations. Adam Smith's way of dealing with it hinged on the principle of division of labour which he used as a very powerful 'tool of thought'.

Ricardo changed the thrust of economic investigation, according to Keynes, by fixing on what determines the distribution of the produce of society amongst three social classes as his central question in place of that relating to the causes of wealth. Contrasting Malthus and Ricardo, he says

> Ricardo is investigating the theory of the *distribution* of the product in conditions of equilibrium and Malthus is concerned with what determines the *volume* of output day by day in the real world. Malthus is dealing with the monetary economy in which we happen to live; Ricardo with the abstraction of a neutral money economy (*CW, X*: 97, *footnote omitted*).

As Keynes saw it, it was Ricardo's question and, hence, his theory of political economy, stemming originally from Adam Smith, that dominated economic thinking from Ricardo's time to his own. The essence of this 'classical' or 'Ricardian' tradition, as he called it, was that '... Ricardo expressly repudiated any interest in the *amount* of the national dividend, as distinct from its distribution' (*CW, VII*: 4, fn.1). He cited a letter from Ricardo to Malthus, in support of this contention, in which Ricardo said

> Political Economy you think is an enquiry into the nature and causes of wealth – I think it should be called an enquiry into the laws which determine the division of the produce of industry amongst the classes who concur in its formation. No law can be laid down respecting quantity, but a tolerably correct one can be laid down respecting proportions (*CW, VII*: 4, fn.1).

The method Ricardo employed in addressing the question he posed was based on his theory of value and on two basic assumptions. The first of these assumptions was that resources were fully employed and, therefore, that total output was, in some sense, 'given'. The second was that money was merely a 'veil' covering, but not affecting, the 'real' transactions and relationships in the economic system. These assumptions are fundamental to Ricardo's way of reasoning and had far-reaching implications for the way in which economic theory evolved from Ricardo's time on. Although Ricardo changed the content or substance of economic theory and although his way of theorizing was highly abstract, as compared with that of Adam Smith and Malthus, nevertheless, what he did remained in the spirit of theory regarded as an apparatus of thought rather than, for example, as simplified description.

For their part the later economists, whom Keynes also included under the rubric 'classical' (*CW, VII*: 3), rejected what they considered to be Ricardo's theory of value on the grounds that the explanation of value which it offered was incomplete, being formulated in terms of cost only and, in particular, of labour costs. At the same time, however, they continued to follow Ricardo in seeing, explicitly or implicitly, the central question to be that of the distribution of a given output amongst the factors of production (Marshall, 1920: *xv*) and in seeing the development of theory as dealing with specific issues within that framework. They continued also to regard the theory of value as the framework within which the central issue was to be addressed. They reformulated the supply/demand-side concepts underlying the classical (in the strict sense) theory of value and extended it to explain the determination of factor prices and, thereby, the distribution of income. This reformulation is, perhaps, best exemplified in Marshall's *Principles*. The result of it was that the analytical apparatus based on supply-side and demand-side considerations became the outstanding characteristic of theorizing in the Marshallian tradition. Indeed economic theory became, in this tradition, virtually synonymous with supply and demand. Writers in the Marshallian tradition continued to follow Ricardo in assuming both that resources were fully employed and that money was 'neutral'.

Keynes was very conscious of this continuous evolution in the content of economic theory. He noted that 'between [Adam Smith's] time and this [1922], it has been steadily enlarged and improved' (*CW, XII*: 856). Even what he termed the Ricardian 'orthodoxy' had not stood still. 'On the contrary', Keynes declared, '[t]here has been a progressive evolution of the doctrine' but it was palpably a growth within a particular, easily identifiable, corpus of thought of which the 'presuppositions', the 'atmosphere', the 'method' have 'remained surprisingly the same, and a remarkable continuity has been observable through all the changes' (*CW, VII: xxxi*).

An example of the kind of evolution to which Keynes refers is Marshall's use of the idea of the margin. Another is his concept of the principle of substitution. Marshall's work, in Keynes's view, 'largely consisted in grafting the marginal principle and the principle of substitution on to the Ricardian tradition' (*CW, VII: xxv*). By so doing Marshall advanced the method of dealing with the central theoretical question as to the distribution of a given output amongst the factors of production. While this constituted a development of the theory considered as a method of thinking, the basic assumptions remained the same. Keynes recognized the great contributions Marshall had made to economic theory but saw him, in the last analysis, as a follower of Ricardo, in that he addressed the same central question and held the same assumptions.

Ricardo's theory was designed to deal with the question he chose to address and its presuppositions were appropriate, and indeed necessary, for the purpose of addressing that particular question. But in Keynes's opinion it was also used, or rather misused, for other purposes. Ricardo's successors, 'less clear-sighted' than Ricardo himself, he held, 'have used the classical theory in discussions concerning the causes of wealth' (*CW, VII*: 4, fn.1). He made the same point in reference to Marshall's 'immediate successors and followers' who had 'dispensed' with a theory of 'output and consumption as a whole' and had not 'apparently, felt the lack of it' (*CW, VII: xxv*). Thus, for example, Pigou in his *The Economics of Welfare* (1920) ignored the fact 'that some resources are generally unemployed against the will of the owners' because '*[t]his does not affect the substance of the argument*, while it simplified its exposition' (*CW, VII*: 5, fn.1). In other words, in dealing with the national dividend, Pigou did not see any difficulty of a theoretical nature arising from the possibility that some resources might be unemployed against the will of their owners. As he perceived it, the same theory would hold whether or not resources were fully employed. Or as Keynes put it

whilst Ricardo expressly disclaimed any attempt to deal with the amount of the national dividend as a whole, Prof. Pigou, in a book which is specifically directed to the problem of the national dividend, maintains that the same theory holds good when there is some involuntary unemployment as in the case of full employment (*CW, VII*: 5, fn.1).

Keynes was not sure if Marshall himself felt the need for a theory of supply and demand for output as a whole. What was certain, however, was that 'as distinct from his theory of the production and distribution of a *given* output, [such a theory] was never separately expounded' (*CW, VII*: xxv). Moreover, in Keynes's estimation, Marshall's '... old ideas were never repudiated or rooted out of the basic assumptions of his thought' (*CW, VII*: 20, fn.1). As evidence of the tacit assumption that output as a whole may be taken to be given he cited *The Economics of Industry* (1879) by Alfred and Mary Marshall, who claimed that

It is not good for trade to have dresses made of material which wears out quickly. For if people did not spend their means on buying new dresses they would spend them on giving employment to labour in some other way (*CW, VII*: 20, fn.1).

By Keynes's time then, economic theorizing, as he understood it, was still concerned almost exclusively with the allocation of resources and the distribution of a given total output. Keynes observed in this connection that

Most treatises on the theory of value and production are primarily concerned with the distribution of a *given* volume of employed resources between different uses and with the conditions which, assuming the employment of this quantity of resources, determine their relative rewards and the relative values of their products (*CW, VII*: 4, *footnote omitted*).

A TREATISE ON MONEY

In writing *A Treatise on Money*, Keynes came to grasp the purpose of 'classical' theory and to recognize what were its presuppositions. In that book, however, he had not yet become fully clear in his own mind either as to the nature of the particular question that still needed to be addressed or as to the limitations of existing theory as far as questions relating to the production of and demand for output as a whole were concerned.

Shortly after the publication of the *Treatise* he expressed his dissatisfaction with what he had done in that book in a number of letters. To Ohlin he said: 'My own feeling is that now at last I have things clearer in my own head, and I am itching to do it all over again' (*CW, XXIX*: 8); to Taussig: 'Before long I shall make an effort to express more fundamentally parts of the argument in another way' (*CW, XXIX*: 10); and to Kaldor: 'I must be more lucid next time. I am now endeavouring to express the whole thing over again more clearly and from a different angle; and in two years' time I may feel able to publish a revised and completer version' (*CW, XIII*: 243).

A Treatise on Money itself was in the tradition which assumed a given output. Keynes pointed out in the preface to *The General Theory* that in the *Treatise* his

so-called 'fundamental equations' were an instantaneous picture taken on the assumption of a *given output*. They attempted to show how, assuming the given output, forces could develop which involved a profit-disequilibrium, and thus required a change in the level of output (*CW, VII: xxii, emphasis added*).

He did, however, claim that in the *Treatise* he 'had made some progress towards pushing monetary theory back to becoming a theory of output as a whole' even though when he began to write it he was 'still moving along the traditional lines of regarding the influence of money as something so to speak separate from the general theory of supply and demand' (*CW, VII: xxii*).

PREMISES OF CLASSICAL THEORY

What rendered classical theory inappropriate for the analysis of 'output as a whole' was that its explicit and implicit premises were unsatisfactory for that purpose. They suffered from 'a lack of clearness and of generality' in Keynes's opinion (*CW, VII: xxi*). These premises or presuppositions were

(1) that resources are fully employed,
(2) that total output is given, and
(3) that the economic system is a real exchange rather than a monetary one.

As Keynes's interpreted classical theory, full employment was implied by Say's Law and by competition between profit-maximizing entrepreneurs for the available resources (*CW, VII: xxxv*; also 15, 25–6). Output, therefore, was the maximum attainable and in that sense was 'given'. As a consequence 'a new activity was always in substitution for, and never in addition to, some other activity' (*CW, VII: xxxv*).

The classical theorists, according to Keynes, in assuming a real exchange economy for the purposes of theoretical analysis, regarded money

> as a convenient means of effecting exchanges – as an instrument of great convenience, but transitory and neutral in its effect... as a mere link between cloth and wheat, or between the day's labour spent on building the canoe and the day's labour spent on harvesting the crop... [which] is not supposed to affect the essential nature of the transaction from being, in the minds of those making it, one between real things, or to modify the motives and decisions of the parties to it (*CW, XIII*: 408).

Thus money was seen as being used in the real exchange economy purely as a medium of exchange and so was 'treated as being in some sense *neutral'*. The real exchange economy, therefore, was one

> which uses money but uses it merely as a neutral link between transactions in real things and real assets and does not allow it to enter into motives or decisions...(*CW, XIII*: 408).

That is precisely what the earlier economists had in mind when they referred to the 'veil of money'.

By contrast, Keynes said in regard to what he himself was doing that

> The theory which I desiderate would deal,...with an economy in which money plays a part of its own and affects motives and decisions and is, in short, one of the operative factors in the situation, so that the course of events cannot be predicted, either in the long period or in the short, without a knowledge of the behaviour of money between the first state and the last. And it is this which we ought to mean when we speak of a *monetary economy* (*CW, XIII*: 408–9).

While Keynes accepted that everyone agreed that 'it is in a monetary economy in [his] sense of the term that we actually live' (*CW, XIII*:

410), he contended that the conditions 'assumed by the classical theory happen not to be those of the economic society in which we actually live' (*CW, VII*: 3). As a result, the conclusions which follow from the use of an analysis based on the assumptions of the existence of a real exchange economy may be seriously misleading when applied to the world as it is. Keynes believed

that the far-reaching and in some respects fundamental differences between the conclusions of a monetary economy and those of the more simplified real-exchange economy have been greatly underestimated by the exponents of the traditional economics; with the result that the machinery of thought with which real-exchange economics has equipped the minds of practitioners in the world of affairs, and also of economists themselves, has led in practice to many erroneous conclusions and policies (*CW, XIII*: 410).

In spite of its presuppositions traditional theory was sometimes used, as we have seen, in an attempt to analyze fluctuations in employment (*CW, VII*: 4). It did so by explaining the determination of the demand for labour as a whole in terms of an extrapolation from the case of the individual firm or industry (*CW, VII*: 258–9). It is for that reason that the theory underlying discussions concerning fluctuations of employment 'has been deemed so simple and obvious' (*CW, VII*: 4–5). Keynes regarded this approach as being utterly fallacious (*CW, VII*: 259). As a result of its presuppositions existing theory was 'clearly incompetent to tackle the problems of unemployment and of the trade cycle' (*CW, VII*: xxxv) since it 'has no method of analysis wherewith to tackle the problem' of the relationship between money-wages and employment (*CW, VII*: 260).

Keynes summed up his conclusions regarding the inapplicability of existing theory to questions relating to employment as a whole in his criticism of Pigou's *Theory of Unemployment* which he took to be the 'most formidable presentment' of 'the classical theory of unemployment' (*CW, VII*: 279). He said

Professor Pigou's *Theory of Unemployment* seems to ... get out of the classical theory all that can be got out of it; with the result that the book becomes a striking demonstration that this theory has nothing to offer, when it is applied to the problem of what determines the volume of actual employment as a whole (*CW, VII*: 260, *footnote omitted*).

Although emphasizing the incompleteness of traditional economic theory, as it was in his time, to address the issue of the actual employment of the available resources, Keynes never lost sight of its validity as a 'theory of the individual firm and of the distribution of the product resulting from the employment of a given quantity of resources...' (*CW, VII*: 339–40). In that context he stressed that 'the classical theory has made a contribution to economic thinking which cannot be impugned' (*CW, VII*: 340) and that it 'is impossible to think clearly on the subject without this theory as a part of one's apparatus of thought' (*CW, VII*: 340).

THE 'VITAL CHAPTER'

Having seen that the 'instantaneous picture', that is, the assumption of a given output, was an integral part of the theory of economics as he had been using it up to the time he wrote *A Treatise on Money*, Keynes realized that he had been using it for a purpose other than that for which it was suited. He therefore set about adapting that theory in such a way that the question as to the determination of the actual level of employment could be addressed properly (*CW, XIII*: 410). One of the most important steps towards his understanding of the limitations of traditional theory and towards the identification of the 'vitally important chapter of economic theory which remains to be written and without which all discussions concerning the volume of aggregate employment are futile' (*CW, VII*: 26) was the realization that traditional theory was based on the tacit assumption of the real-exchange economy. At that stage in the development of his thinking, as may be seen from an early draft of what later became *The General Theory*, he considered that 'the next task [was] to work out in some detail a monetary theory of production, to *supplement* the real-exchange theories which we already possess' (*CW, XIII*: 411, *emphasis added*; also *XIII*: 254).

In retrospect it is now obvious that Keynes saw himself not as debunking what he labelled 'classical' theory but rather as supplementing it by writing another, so far unwritten, chapter in the tradition of the supply and demand method of reasoning. Indeed, even for the purposes of the specific question he was addressing in *The General Theory*, he recognized that essential elements of the traditional theory as well as one of its crucial postulates remain valid and relevant to the methods he forged to address that question. In the preface to the

French edition he was quite explicit about this. He remarked that as far as those 'looking from outside' were concerned he probably still belonged to 'that orthodoxy... that continuous transition' in which he 'was brought up' and which he learnt, taught, and wrote. He thought that '[s]ubsequent historians of doctrine will regard this book as in essentially the same tradition' (*CW, VII: xxxi*). Keynes saw the development of his thinking from *A Treatise* to *The General Theory* as 'a natural evolution in a line of thought which [he had] been pursuing for several years' (*CW, VII: xxii*). At the same time he admitted that this line of evolution was 'probably clearer to [himself] than it will be to others' (*CW, VII: xxii*). Equally, we can now see the outcome of this development in Keynes's thinking, namely, *The General Theory* as the 'vital chapter' in the tradition to which he belonged. This 'chapter' explicitly added a question to the body of questions underlying classical theory and provided the means of addressing that question. Thus *The General Theory* is part of the 'continuity' to which Keynes refers. It is an extension of the old edifice which does not require the destruction of any part of what was there before. Rather it releases the old part for the purposes for which it was originally designed.

THEORY OF OUTPUT AS A WHOLE

Essentially, what Keynes did in *The General Theory* was to devise a method of addressing the question he posed by extending the supply-side/demand-side analysis of the Marshallian tradition from commodities and factors of production to output as a whole. He succeeded in doing this without extrapolating from the individual firm or industry in the fallacious manner, which, as we have seen, he criticized some of his contemporaries and predecessors for doing, and also without falling into the trap of using the notion of the general level of prices as the device for tying together the demand for and the supply of output as whole. The method he devised was based on a new generalization of an old concept. This new generalization, the pivotal one in his analysis, is that of profit-equilibrium at the level of the economic system as a whole (*CW, VII: xxxiii*). Its role is to serve as the organizing principle on the basis of which the formal statement of the general theory of employment is made.

As we shall see, the method of analysis which Keynes devised involves a number of elements. The most important of these are

(1)   the formulation of the theory of the supply of output as a whole in terms of the concepts of (i) the aggregate demand function; (ii) the aggregate supply function; and (iii) paradoxically perhaps, effective demand, which together encapsulate the fact that employment and output are determined by what entrepreneurs perceive to be the level of activity at which they expect to maximize their profits;

(2)   the formulation of the theory of demand, demand being understood to be for a newly produced output, in terms of the two concepts – propensity-to-consume and marginal efficiency of capital;

(3)   the concept of profit-equilibrium, which is an adaptation of the concept of the equilibrium of the firm to the economic system as a whole, as the organizing principle;

(4)   the use of logically consistent quantitative foundations for all the aggregates arrived at so that the transition from the individual level to the economy as a whole is made unambiguously;

(5)   the analysis of the meaning of money and of the particular part played by the own rate of interest on money;

(6)   an explanation of the nature of *involuntary unemployment* and of how this type of unemployment may arise by reason of the monetary nature of the economic system.

Many of the ideas and concepts embodied in *The General Theory* are new. They did not come to Keynes ready-made, so to speak. Rather, he discovered them in the very process of theorizing. This process threw up many questions related in one way or another to his central question. It was in trying to answer these secondary or derivative questions that he devised these ideas and concepts and turned them into essential parts of the machinery of thought that he formulated.

NATURE OF *THE GENERAL THEORY*

To read *The General Theory*, as Keynes evidently intended it to be read (*CW, VII: xvi*), the reader must approach it first and foremost as a work of pure economic theory. But to do so the central argument of the book has to be disentangled from the web of controversies and polemics in which it is, to a greater or lesser extent, enmeshed. It is also necessary to grapple with the style of the book. Keynes's style is a reflection of the long process of development in his own thinking. It reflects too his understanding of the tradition in which he worked and his belief that economic theory is above all else a logical apparatus of thought. The book is the culmination of many years' work as an economist, the fruit of his attempts to formulate a new and crucial question clearly and to develop the method for answering it. Being, as it is, a highly original addition to the traditional body of economic theory (which at the time the book was written required, in its author's view, to be defended and to be offered in as persuasive a way as possible), it is a long book. Nevertheless, despite its length it is a concise, and sometimes unduly concise, statement of that addition to economic theory. Consequently, on occasions particular arguments are merely hinted at. These have to be elaborated upon so that their full import and their place in the overall argument can be seen. Our purpose is to reveal Keynes's method of reasoning by disentangling it from the obfuscations that surround it and by elaborating upon its argument where necessary.

Keynes's conception of economic theory and his understanding of the tradition to which he belonged, his solutions to certain problems inherent in that tradition and his concept of profit-equilibrium are the ultimate keys to an understanding of *The General Theory*. Once these key elements in the book are grasped and, in particular, once the pivotal role played by the concept of profit-equilibrium in the organization of the overall argument is appreciated, all the elements of that argument fall into place and *The General Theory*, as a whole, can be seen to constitute in itself an integrated, coherent and logical argument.

Each element of that argument is directly or indirectly connected with every other element. To understand any one element fully it is necessary to understand how it fits into the whole argument. Indeed the elements of the argument are so interrelated that the parts cannot be understood without understanding the whole and the whole cannot be understood without understanding the parts. Consequently, it is very useful when embarking on a study of *The General Theory* for the first time to have some idea, however sketchy, of the general thrust of the argument.

THE ARGUMENT

The question as to what determines the employment of the available resources naturally suggests the further question: who employs resources? The answer, obviously, is the entrepreneur. The entrepreneur and the resources so employed together constitute the firm (Kirzner, 1973: 52).

The conventional theory of the firm is primarily about the identification of the level of output at which profit is maximized. Though costs enter into the theory explicitly the extent to which resources are used is left implicit.

Given his question, what Keynes did was to adapt the theory of the firm in such a way that the employment of resources is dealt with explicitly and directly while output is dealt with indirectly.

The hypothesis that businesses maximize profit is retained but it too is interpreted in a somewhat different light from the traditional one in that it is recognized that firms act on the basis of expectation rather than on the basis of certain knowledge as was normally assumed.

The recognition that firms act on the basis of expectation leads to the making of a distinction between the various possible hypothetical demand schedules that the entrepreneur might envisage, on the one hand, and the demand from the buyers' perspective, on the other.

As Keynes's formulation of the theory of the firm is made in terms of units of quantity (to be considered in Chapter 3) which can be added without ambiguity, that theory can be extended to the economic system as a whole. The system as a whole can then be treated as if it were one firm without, however, having to make the implausible assumption that it is one firm.

The extended or generalized theory of the firm constitutes the theory of the supply of output as a whole. Output as a whole is to be understood as a set rather than an aggregate. The theory of the supply of output as a whole expressed in terms of the employment of the resources required to produce the output as a whole constitutes the supply side of Keynes's theory of employment.

Keynes could not build on traditional theory in order to formulate the demand side of his theory of employment as he had done in the case of the supply side. Instead he developed a new theory of the demand for output as a whole. He did so by distinguishing the demand for goods and services into those purchased for consumption purposes and those purchased for investment purposes.

Up to Keynes's time the theory of consumption related to the allocation of expenditure on the purchase of individual goods and services on the basis of their relative prices. Keynes concentrated on what determines the total amount so allocated. By converting this total into the amount of labour required to produce the goods and services devoted to consumption the implications of consumer-expenditure for the employment of resources emerges.

Keynes formulated his theory of the demand for capital goods in terms of the sums which the investor-entrepreneur allocates for investment as determined by the expectations of future returns in relation to the rate of interest. The sums so allocated can also be expressed in terms of the labour required for its production.

The theory of demand for consumption purposes and the theory of demand for investment purposes are the two aspects of Keynes's theory of the demand for output as a whole. Taken together they constitute the demand side of his theory of employment. Being expressed in terms of the labour required to produce total output, it can be compared directly to the supply side.

Keynes's theory of investment necessarily leads to an examination of (a) the nature and the determinants of the rate of interest and (b) the role of money considered as an asset.

The theory of aggregate supply, the theory of aggregate demand and the theory of money and interest constitute the basic elements of Keynes's general theory of employment. Its equilibrium condition is analogous to the equilibrium condition of the theory of the firm and is encapsulated by the term 'profit-equilibrium'.

THEMES OF *THE GENERAL THEORY*

There are three interwoven themes in *The General Theory*. The first is the exposition of the answer to the question: what determines the employment of the available resources in the monetary-entrepreneur economy? As the next Chapter shows the answer is set out in general terms which can be summarized in the form of a schema with the help of which questions relating to the employment of resources in particular instances can be addressed. The second theme is the critique of 'classical' theory. Its purpose, as we have seen, is to discover the presuppositions of classical economic theory and thereby to show that a new component had to be added to the body of economic theory if the question, which Keynes posed, was to be addressed in a manner that was both relevant to the facts and internally consistent. It is evident that this second theme also served to clear Keynes's own mind in regard to his understanding of theory as he knew it and in regard to the way in which he worked out his own theory. His reflections on possible 'cures' (or policies) for what he regarded as the economic ills of his time in the light of the theory he was working out are the subject matter of the third theme.

The chapters which follow concentrate on the first theme, namely, the extension of the supply and demand method of reasoning to the analysis of the economy as a whole. The second and third themes are touched on only in so far as they elucidate the first.

In reading *The General Theory* it must be remembered that it is primarily a book of pure theory, as we have already stressed. To the extent that it includes applied theory it does so only in the final sections of the book where a number of topics suggested by the pure theory are treated briefly.

2 Keynes's Way of Theorizing: The Marshall Connection

The General Theory amply demonstrates that Keynes took his ideas about economics in general and about economic theory in particular seriously and followed them conscientiously. Hence, if that book is to be understood, it is essential that his conception of the nature and purpose of economics be appreciated. Although he did not write a systematic account of his views in this connection a reasonably clear picture of his thinking may be gleaned from various passages scattered throughout his writings and his correspondence.

THE MARSHALLIAN TRADITION

Keynes perceived himself to be part of an intellectual tradition which he traced back to John Locke. He referred to this tradition as the 'Locke Connection' (*CW, X: xix*), and conceived it to be one of what he called 'humane science' (*CW, X*: 86). He described it as

> that tradition of Scotch and English thought, in which there has been ... an extraordinary continuity of feeling, ... from the eight-eenth century to the present time – the tradition which is suggested by the names of Locke, Hume, Adam Smith, Paley, Bentham, Darwin and Mill, a tradition marked by a love of truth and a most noble lucidity, by a prosaic sanity free from sentiment or metaphysic, and by an immense disinterestedness and public spirit (*CW, X*: 86, *emphasis omitted*).

As far as economics was concerned Keynes was, and saw himself to be, in the tradition of Marshall. His manner of addressing the questions he posed was imbued by the way in which he interpreted the Cambridge or Marshallian approach to economics.

His intellectual background predisposed Keynes to regard economics both as a moral science and as a branch of logic. For Marshall, as he said in his inaugural lecture in 1885, economics was 'a science of

16

human motives' which 'could not be better grouped than with the other Moral Sciences' (1885: 171). For Keynes economics deals with motives, expectations and decisions and with the psychological uncertainties that pervade our lives. Being a 'moral' as opposed to a 'natural' science it 'employs introspection and judgements of value' (*CW, XIV*: 297). Unlike the natural sciences its subject matter is neither constant nor homogeneous. All aspects of economic activity from the motives that give rise to it to the consequences that follow from it are part of history. Marshall made the same point in contrasting the physical sciences on the one hand with the biological and human sciences on the other

> At the beginning of the nineteenth century the mathematico-physical group of sciences was in the ascendant. These sciences, widely as they differ from one another, have this point in common, that their subject-matter is constant and unchanged in all countries and in all ages. The progress of science was familiar to men's minds, but the development of the subject-matter of science was strange to them. As the century wore on the biological group of sciences were slowly making way, and people were getting clearer ideas as to the nature of organic growth. They were learning that, if the subject-matter of a science passes through different stages of development, the laws which apply to one stage will seldom apply without modification to others; the laws of the science must have a development corresponding to that of the things of which they treat. The influence of this new notion gradually spread to the sciences which relate to man (1885: 154).

For his part Keynes summed up his views of economics as a moral science (that is, one which deals with decisions) in a letter to Harrod in which he said

> I also want to emphasise strongly the point about economics being a moral science. I mentioned before that it deals with introspection and with values. I might have added that it deals with motives, expectations, psychological uncertainties. *One has to be constantly on guard against treating the material as constant and homogeneous.* It is as though the fall of the apple to the ground depended on the apple's motives, on whether it is worthwhile falling to the ground, and whether the ground wanted the apple to fall, and on mistaken calculations on the part of the apple as to how far it

was from the centre of the earth (*CW, XIV*: 300, *emphasis added*; also *CW, XXIX*: 294).

Keynes tended to distrust some of the work being done in economics in his time because he feared it would obscure the moral science nature of the subject. He saw that work as leading to the view that economics could be treated as if it were more in the nature of a physical or natural science than a moral science and so could not be conducive to the attitude of mind required of an economist. 'The pseudo-analogy with the physical sciences', he said, 'leads directly counter to the habit of mind which is most important for an economist proper to acquire' (*CW, XIV*: 300).

ECONOMIC THEORY

Keynes's primary purpose in writing *The General Theory*, as we saw in Chapter 1, was to develop traditional economic theory in a particular direction. He repeatedly emphasized that the book is a theoretical one. In the preface, for example, he says 'its main purpose is to deal with difficult questions of theory, and only in the second place with the applications of this theory to practice' (*CW, VII*: *xxi*; also *CW, XIV*: 14–15). He did not see it as part of his immediate purpose to pursue 'the detailed analysis of the general ideas' he was setting forth (*CW, VII*: 42, fn. 2). Nor did he enter 'into statistical enquiry as to the actual value of the propensity to consume', for example, because it was not his 'job in a theoretical discussion' (*CW, XIV*: 274). Again about a year before the publication of the book he said in the course of correspondence with Dennis Robertson that 'this book is a purely theoretical work, not a collection of wisecracks. Everything turns on the mumbo-jumbo' (*CW, XIII*: 520). He pointed out to Joan Robinson after publication that '[t]here is a considerable difference between more or less formal theory, which my existing book purports to be, and something which is meant to be applied to current events without too much qualification by people who do not fully comprehend the theory' (*CW, XXIX*: 186).

In the Introduction to the Cambridge Economic Handbooks, which he wrote in 1922, Keynes very briefly set out the idea which is at the core of his conception of economic theory. He conceived of theory as providing the means by which we can think purposefully about actual economic problems. As he put it

[t]he theory of economics does not furnish a body of settled conclusions immediately applicable to policy. It is a method rather than a doctrine, an apparatus of the mind, a technique of thinking, which helps its possessor to draw correct conclusions (*CW, XII*: 856).

He held to that view of economic theory throughout his life. As late as 1939 he declared in a letter to Robertson that the Introduction 'remains more up to date than one might have expected' and agreed that it could be retained in new additions to the series which were about to appear (*CW, XIV*: 251). This view of economic theory as being the particular logic applicable to economic issues and problems derives from Marshall's concept of its being 'the machinery of thought' to which we have already alluded. The same idea was also expressed in Marshall's assertion that 'Economic science is but the working of common sense aided by appliances of organized analysis and general reasoning' (Marshall, 1920: 38). It also reflects Marshall's way of explaining the rôle of economic theory as an 'engine' of analysis in the following well-known passage. For Marshall

> that part of economic doctrine, which alone can claim universality, has no dogmas. It is not a body of concrete truth, but an engine for the discovery of concrete truth, similar to, say, the theory of mechanics.
>
> The theory of mechanics contains no statement of fact as to the greatest strain which bridges will bear. Every bridge has its peculiarities of construction and material: and mechanics supplies a universal engine, which will help in determining what strains any bridge will bear. But it has no universal dogmas by which this strain can be determined without observation of the particular facts of the case. (1885: 159).

In the tradition of Marshall, Keynes sees a theory as a general explanation in the sense that it is a general answer to a question of a general, rather than a specific, nature. As such it provides the 'method', as Keynes puts it, or 'organon', as Marshall puts it (1885: 160), by which specific questions belonging to the class of questions to which the theory itself is the general answer may be addressed. In that sense it is a logic. From this view of theory arises the distinction between 'pure' and 'applied' theory (Marshall, 1920: 43) as exemplified by the first and second volumes respectively of Keynes's *Treatise on Money*.

The purpose of theory is to help us to think in an orderly way but not to do our thinking for us, so to speak. Pure theory must be applied carefully and must not be thought of as a way of automatically coming to conclusions and reaching solutions. Of its nature a theory must be a general method of approaching a problem. It does not and cannot include all the details and complexities of a specific problem under examination. In Keynes's own words

The object of our analysis is, not to provide a machine, or method of blind manipulation, which will furnish an infallible answer, but to provide ourselves with an organised and orderly method of thinking out particular problems; and, after we have reached a provisional conclusion by isolating the complicating factors one by one, we then have to go back on ourselves and allow, as well as we can, for the probable interactions of the factors amongst themselves. This is the nature of economic thinking. Any other way of applying our formal principles of thought (without which, however, we shall be lost in the wood) will lead us into error (*CW, VII*: 297).

So, applied theory or the application of pure theory is itself a theoretical activity. In this connection also he said that

what I am primarily interested in supplying is a sound and scientific way of thinking about our essential problems. Before this way of thinking can be *translated into practice it has to be mixed with politics and passions just like any other way of thinking,* and the nature of the outcome is something which I cannot foresee in detail (*CW, XXI*: 348, *emphasis added*).

Keynes refers to the propositions in which a theory may be summed up as a 'schematism' (*CW, VII*: 249). Schematisms may be expressed in words only or in the form of what he calls 'schematic equations' the 'only purpose' of which is 'to elucidate general ideas' (*CW, XIII*: 484; also *CW, XIV*: 219). They provide a convenient framework for the examination of particular questions, that is, for the application of pure theory. Keynes usually writes schematic equations in functional form to remind the reader that, *ceteris paribus*, the variables on the left-hand side is governed by the variable on the right-hand side. Schematic equations, irrespective of the form in which they are expressed, are subject to the proviso that other things are unchanged. These equations are not intended to be estimated nor are they to be seen as the general form of a type or class of equation.

Keynes explains the use of schematic summaries of arguments by reference to *The General Theory* itself as follows

> If we examine any actual problem along the lines of the above schematism [his 'summary of *The General Theory* '], we shall find it more manageable; and our practical intuition (which can take account of a more detailed complex of facts than can be treated on general principles) will be offered a less intractable material upon which to work (*CW, VII*: 249).

Cannan's explanation of the basic apparatus of supply and demand conveys the essence of this approach to the application of economic theory. He says

> I have used what will perhaps appear a somewhat clumsy phrase in place of the more familiar 'Laws of Supply and Demand', or even the 'theory of the relation of demand and supply to value', because I think it desirable to suggest that 'Supply and Demand' are heads of arrangement rather than the name of a doctrine. When we say that the value of a thing depends on supply and demand, we do not, or at any rate ought not, to mean more than that we think it will be convenient to arrange the causes of changes in value under those two heads (Cannan, 1921: 3).

Similarly, Robertson in discussing the schematic equation tradition-ally known as the Cambridge equation writes of it as being a con-venient framework for analysis. He says

> nobody, I think, has ever expected a little group of symbols to be a *substitute* for an argument! And to my mind one of the attractive features of the Cambridge equation is precisely ... its complete gen-erality, so that we can use it to order our thoughts about a great number of different sequences of events, some of them starting at one point in the causal chain and some at another (Robertson, 1959: 29).

Being a method of thinking or form of logic, economic theory is not to be thought of as being descriptive. It is rather as Marshall said 'the abstract of past experience' (1885: 181). As Marshall pointed out in relation to the theory of value

Thus it is not descriptive, nor does it deal constructively with real problems. But it sets out the theoretical backbone of our knowledge of the causes which govern value, ... It aims not so much at the attainment of knowledge, as at the power to obtain and arrange knowledge with regard to two opposing sets of forces (1920: 324).

Clearly then Keynes, in his conception of economic theory, was at one with Marshall and with his contemporaries in the tradition emanating from Marshall. He did not in any way depart from that tradition in his own work. Instead he developed it from within.

RÔLE OF MODELS

The purpose of economic theorizing is to produce theories which, as we have seen, are the 'method' or 'apparatus of the mind' or logic which the economist uses to think about particular economic phenomena and events. As we have also seen these theories are explanatory in the sense that they deal with the causes or determinants of these phenomena and events. Most of what Keynes wrote about the process of reasoning by which the theories are worked out relate to what he terms 'models' and to their purpose.[2]

The use of models according to Keynes is of the very essence of economic reasoning. But 'the art of thinking in terms of models is a difficult – largely because it is an unaccustomed – practice' (*CW, XIV*: 300).

The development of economic theory depends on the capacity of economists to devise 'new and improved models' (*CW, XIV*: 296). But the danger is that old models will be misused, as was the case with those economists who tried to use the model of the real exchange economy for a purpose for which it was not fitted. In this connection Keynes says

Progress in economics consists almost entirely in a progressive improvement in the choice of models. The grave fault of the later classical school, exemplified by Pigou, has been to overwork a too simple or out-of-date model, and in not seeing that progress lay in improving the model; whilst Marshall often confused his models, for devising which he had great genius, by wanting to be realistic and by being unnecessarily ashamed of lean and abstract outlines (*CW, XIV*: 296; also *CW, VII*: 3).

In the case of the 'natural' sciences a theory is a general hypothesis and is usually expressed in the form of an equation. Often, particularly when so expressed, it is referred to as a 'model'. Experiments, which almost invariably involve measurement, are carried out in an artificially created environment in the laboratory in order to discover the magnitudes of the variables in the equation. Sometimes the subject-matter under investigation can be observed and measured directly with the appropriate measuring instruments. Sometimes it cannot and the measurements have to be made indirectly. But provided measurements can be made, it may be possible to identify relationships between the variables and to express them in the form of a quantitative or numerical 'law'.

The 'motives, expectations, psychological uncertainties' (*CW, XIV*: 300) with which economics deals are not observable. Moreover, the economic activities which result from these motives and expectations and the consequences of these activities are ever changing. Hence, the subject-matter for economic theorizing is neither constant nor homogeneous, as we have already observed.

For these reasons the economic theorist has to reason in terms of a typical general 'case' exhibiting what is 'normal' as distinct from all the complexities and changes inherent in actual situations. Such a general case is what Keynes means by a model. The model is, therefore, a construct or abstraction from reality created for the purpose of formulating theory. Keynes holds that

> *Economics is a science of thinking in terms of models joined to the art of choosing models* which are relevant to the contemporary world. It is compelled to be this, because, unlike the typical natural science, the material to which it is applied is, in too many respects, not homogenous through time (*CW, XIV*: 296, *emphasis added*).

Occasionally, to avoid confusion with contemporary usage of the term 'model', we use the term 'setting' instead.

The economic system is not only highly complex it is also highly interdependent. Any one phenomenon or event may be affected by many different and interrelated causes. To deal with this problem 'it is usual . . . to regard as the *causa causans* that factor which is most prone to sudden and wide fluctuations' (*CW, XIV*: 121). Echoing Marshall's use of the principle of *ceteris paribus* Keynes says that the object of a model is to segregate the semi-permanent or relatively constant factors from those which are transitory or fluctuating so as to develop a logical way of thinking about the latter, and of understanding the time sequences to which they give rise in particular cases (*CW, XIV*: 296–7).

Thus, as Keynes sees it, the model, or setting, is to economic theorizing what the controlled conditions of the laboratory are to the physical sciences. Its rôle is analogous to that of these controlled conditions though the model itself is very different from them.

In *The General Theory*, Keynes refers to the semi-permanent or relatively constant factors as the 'given factors' (*CW, VII*: 247; also 245) and points out that they are not to be taken as constant in any absolute sense. As he says

This does not mean that we assume these factors to be constant; but merely that, in this place and context, we are not considering or taking into account the effects and consequences of changes in them (*CW, VII*: 245).

He subdivides the transitory, or fluctuating, factors into the dependent variables, which are the objects of his concern, and the independent variables, which are the determining or causal factors. But the distinction between them is not to be taken to be absolute. It must rather be based on experience and judgement in the light of what the particular question at issue is. In this connection he says

The division of the determinants of the economic system into the two groups of given factors and independent variables is, of course, quite arbitrary from any absolute standpoint. The division must be made entirely on the basis of experience, so as to correspond on the one hand to the factors in which the changes seem to be so slow or so little relevant as to have only a small and comparatively negligible short-term influence on our *quaesitum*; and on the other hand to those factors in which the changes are found in practice to exercise a dominant influence on our *quaesitum* (*CW, VII*: 247; also *CW, XXIX*: 265).

The answer to the question under investigation is arrived at by means of a process of reasoning involving both induction and deduction. In Keynes's view the reasoning should not involve many steps.

Marshall too favoured the 'short chains and single connecting links' rather than 'long chains of reasoning' (1920: 773). He observed that 'even in mechanics long chains of deductive reasoning are directly applicable only to the occurrences of the laboratory' (1920: 771).

The model or setting must be a general case representative of the reality that the economist knows rather than a fanciful ideal derived from his imagination. Accordingly, though the setting must be an abstraction from all the details of an historical situation, it must also remain close to reality in that it must avoid all arbitrariness. Keynes agreed with the view expressed by Harrod that a 'vigilant observation of the actual working of our system' is necessary (*CW, XIV*: 296) and commented that '[t]he specialist in the manufacture of models will not be successful unless he is constantly correcting his judgment by intimate and messy acquaintance with the facts to which his model has to be applied' (*CW, XIV*: 300).

Keynes's clearest and most compelling statement of his position is to be found in his essay on Malthus. The general thrust of that essay is highly favourable to Malthus. He explicitly approved of Malthus's method as one 'which to me is most sympathetic, and, as I think, more likely to lead to right conclusions than the alternative approach of Ricardo' (*CW, X*: 87). Malthus and Ricardo personified for Keynes what he considered to be the two alternative approaches to economic theorizing

> In economic discussions Ricardo was the abstract and *a priori* theorist, Malthus the inductive and intuitive investigator who hated to stray too far from what he could test by reference to the facts and his own intuitions (*CW, X*: 95; also *CW, VII*: 32–3; 362–4).

As Keynes saw it, Ricardo's 'line of approach' dominated economics and impeded the progress of the subject (*CW, X*: 98). Keynes agreed both with the substance of Malthus's thinking and with his method of approach and quoted the argument he put to Ricardo in this regard

> Besides I really think that the progress of society consists of irregular movements, and that to omit the consideration of causes which for eight or ten years will give a great *stimulus* to production and population, or a great *check* to them, is to omit the causes of

the wealth and poverty of nations – the grand object of all enquiries in Political Economy. A writer may, to be sure, make any hypothesis he pleases; but if he supposes what is not at all true practically, he precludes himself from drawing any practical inferences from his hypotheses (*CW, X*: 98).

Thus a good model is one which provides the appropriate setting in which the general answer to a general question may be sought. It permits the permanent and semi-permanent features of the phenomenon or phenomena under investigation to be distinguished from those which fluctuate in such a way that the latter lead to the answer to the question.

The answer is usually reducible to a number of propositions the rôle of which we have already referred to. The propositions are connected to each other. They and the reasoning by which they are derived and which connects them constitute the 'theory' which, as we have seen, is used as a 'logic' for the purpose of examining particular cases (as distinct from the model or general case) and for answering questions relating to particular cases. These particular cases are always more complex than the general case but can be made manageable when under investigation by means of the method developed on the basis of the general case.

The particular cases compared with the general case are examples of what Marshall referred to as the 'many in the one' (1892: 379; also 421, 423). The 'one' is the general or model case. The many particular cases have enough in common to enable their relationship to the one to be discerned or rather their commonness with the 'one' to be seen. Keynes's own model, which we discuss in Chapter 4, is a typical or normal example of the kind of economy in which we live in that it is representative of the features that all examples of the monetary-entrepreneur economy have in common.

In view of what Keynes understood the purpose of a model or setting to be, it follows that attempts to quantify models as such are misdirected. He asserts that

it is of the essence of a model that one does *not* fill in real values for the variable functions. To do so would make it useless as a model. For as soon as this is done, the model loses its generality and its value as a mode of thought (*CW, XIV*: 296).

To purport to quantify a model in the sense in which Keynes uses the term is to subvert it from performing the function for which it is intended, namely, to aid in the formulation of a theory. The attempt to discover quantitative formulae or laws in economics is doomed to failure because of the non-constant and non-homogeneous nature of the subject matter of economics and is the very antithesis of what a model is for. As Keynes saw it, such attempts would transform the model from being a general case, on the basis of which a process of reasoning leading to general conclusions could be conducted, into a particular case which could not be analyzed until the general case had first been investigated. In the natural sciences, according to Keynes

> the object of experiment is to fill in the actual values of the various quantities and factors appearing in an equation or a formula; and the work when done is once and for all. In economics that is not the case, and *to convert a model into a quantitative formula is to destroy its usefulness as an instrument of thought* (*CW, XIV*: 299, *emphasis added*).

Although, in Keynes's view, the quantification of models with a view to the discovery of quantitative formulae or laws on the basis of which forecasts could be made was inadmissible there is, nevertheless, an important rôle to be played by statistics in the process of economic reasoning. That rôle is 'to test the relevance and validity of the model' (*CW, XIV*: 296) by means, for example, of historical statistics. Such testing is necessary in order to ensure that economists know what they are talking about, and that they are not like the 'professional economists, after Malthus [who] were apparently unmoved by the lack of correspondence between the results of their theory and the facts of observation' (*CW, VII*: 33). Related to this view of the rôle of statistics is Keynes's concern that the relative sizes and importance of the causal factors and of various possible results be established. He thought 'it most important, for example, to investigate statistically the order of magnitude of the multiplier, and to discover the relative importance of the various facts which are theoretically possible' (*CW, XIV*: 299).

The 'variable functions' in a model do, of course, relate to quantities. But the quantities in question are abstract or general ones rather than 'actual values'. As they are used for analytical purposes they must be precise in principle. Keynes's concern is always with logical or conceptual exactness rather than with precision in counting and measurement. We return to the matter of quantitative analysis in the next chapter.

Keynes insisted that in economic reasoning we must always be aware of the highly interdependent nature of the economic system. It was for this reason that, like Marshall, he mistrusted the use of mathematics as a method of discovery. Marshall's maxim was 'use mathematics as a shorthand language, rather than as an engine of inquiry' (1901: 427). To follow mathematical rules in an attempt to discover the meaning of some aspect of economic activity is to ignore that each step in economic activity involves the making of decisions. Mathematical steps do not correspond to the interlinked network of causes and effects in the real world. Mathematical rules have meaning only within mathematics itself. They are rules which must be followed not choices that may be made. Hence the use of mathematics as 'an engine of inquiry' may be said to involve 'blind manipulation' and so cannot capture the choices and decisions which underlie economic activity.

Keynes categorically rejects what he refers to as 'symbolic pseudo-mathematical methods of formalizing a system of economic analysis' (*CW, VII*: 297) and asserts that

> It is a great fault of [such methods] . . . that they expressly assume strict independence between the factors involved and lose all their cogency and authority if this hypothesis is disallowed; whereas, in ordinary discourse, where we are not blindly manipulating but know all the time what we are doing and what the words mean, we can keep 'at the back of our heads' the necessary reserves and qualifications and the adjustments which we shall have to make later on, in a way in which we cannot keep complicated partial differentials 'at the back' of several pages of algebra which assume that they all vanish. Too large a proportion of recent 'mathematical' economics are merely concoctions, as imprecise as the initial assumptions they rest on, which allow the author to lose sight of the complexities and interdependencies of the real world in a maze of pretentious and unhelpful symbols (*CW, VII*: 297–8; also 305, 275, 280, fn.1; and *CW, XXIX*: 37–8, 265).

Keynes was indeed so sceptical about the use of mathematics as a method of discovery that he referred in *The General Theory* to those who '(rightly) dislike algebra' (*CW, VII*: 280, fn.1). Subsequently he said that when he came to revise the book 'properly' he was 'not at all sure that the right solution may not lie in leaving out all this sort of stuff [the algebra in section VI, Chapter 20 of *The General Theory*] altogether', because he was 'extremely doubtful whether it adds anything at all which is significant to the argument as a whole' (*CW, XXIX*: 246).

As Keynes saw economic theory and the process of theorizing, the theorist, if he is to be successful, could not be a narrow specialist. He would have to be many-sided and able to bring a range of talents and skills to his task. His description of the 'master-economist' epitomises his perception of the kind of subject economics is and of what kind of a mind the theorist needs to have. This description also provides an illuminating explanation of the diverse strands which make up *The General Theory* itself. Marshall personified the master-economist for Keynes. In his essay on Marshall he says

> The study of economics does not seem to require any specialised gifts of an unusually high order. Is it not, intellectually regarded, a very easy subject compared with the high branches of philosophy and pure science? Yet good, or even competent, economists are the rarest of birds. An easy subject, at which very few excel! The paradox finds its explanation, perhaps, in that the master-economist must possess a rare *combination* of gifts. He must reach a high standard in several different directions and must combine talents not often found together. He must be mathematician, historian, statesman, philosopher – in some degree. He must understand symbols and speak in words. He must contemplate the particular in terms of the general, and touch abstract and concrete in the same flight of thought. He must study the present in the light of the past for the purposes of the future. No part of man's nature or his institutions must lie entirely outside his regard. He must be purposeful and disinterested in a simultaneous mood; as aloof and incorruptible as an artist, yet sometimes as near the earth as a politician (*CW, X*: 173–4).

Malthus was certainly Keynes's favourite economist. He too exemplified the master-economist, at least at the pioneering stage of the subject. Keynes draws attention to the way in which Malthus's educational background peculiarly fitted him for the kind of work in economics that Keynes himself valued most highly – work that was intellectually rigorous but at the same time firmly grounded in historical experience. He says in his essay on Malthus

> Let us, however, think of Malthus to-day as the first of the Cambridge economists – as, above all, a great pioneer of the application

of a frame of formal thinking to the complex confusion of the world of daily events. Malthus approached the central problems of economic theory by the best of all routes. He began to be interested as a philosopher and moral scientist, one who had been brought up in the Cambridge of Paley, applying the *a priori* method of the political philosopher. He then immersed himself for several years in the facts of economic history and of the contemporary world, applying the methods of historical induction and filling his mind with a mass of the material of experience. And then finally he returned to *a priori* thought, but this time to the pure theory of the economist proper and sought, being one of the very first to seek, to impose the methods of formal thought on the material presented by events, so as to penetrate these events with understanding by a mixture of intuitive selection and formal principle and thus to interpret the problem and propose the remedy. In short, from being a caterpillar of a moral scientist and chrysalis of an historian, he could at last spread the wings of his thought and survey the world as an economist (*CW, X*: 107).

THE CONCEPT OF EQUILIBRIUM

True to the Marshallian tradition, Keynes's analytical apparatus is based on a supply-side, a demand-side and on a concept of equilibrium. He considered that Marshall had extended the 'general idea, underlying the proposition that value is determined at the equilibrium point of demand and supply...so as to discover a whole Copernican system, by which all the elements of the economic universe are kept in their places' (*CW, X*: 205). The problem facing Keynes was to develop this method of theorizing further so that it could deal with the particular question that he was addressing. In principle the choice of what would constitute the supply-side was straight-forward enough though, as we shall see, formidable difficulties had to be overcome in order to devise a satisfactory way of identifying supply in the economy as a whole in a way which is quantitatively precise in principle. Keynes had to break entirely new ground in developing the demand-side for the economy as a whole. The way he did so was logically inevitable once he had decided on his treatment of the supply-side. Equally inevitable was the particular concept of equilibrium that emerged. This concept of equilibrium involves the coincidence of the magnitudes on the demand-side and on the supply-side which determine the employment of the available resources in the economic system as whole.

As we have seen, Keynes is concerned with the monetary-entrepreneur economy. From this perspective the essential feature, and the one that provides the basis for the organization of the answer to the question he is addressing, is what he referred to in an early draft of *The General Theory* as the '*law of production in an entrepreneur economy*'. By this he means that '[a] process of production will not be started up, unless the money proceeds expected from the sale of the output are at least equal to the money costs which could be avoided by not starting up the process' (*CW, XXIX*: 78). As profit is the motivating factor in an entrepreneur economy any explanation of the determination of the level of activity in such an economic system must hinge on the rôle of profit in governing the decisions of entrepreneurs regarding their scale of operation given the capital equipment over which they have command. It was, therefore, inevitable that the concept of equilibrium would relate to profit just as it does in the case of the individual firm. This, as we have already said, Keynes refers to as 'profit-equilibrium' (*CW, VII*: *xxxiii*).

In the Marshallian tradition the statements or propositions which constitute an explanation are of a hypothetical as opposed to a descriptive nature. For example, a demand schedule is a set of hypothetical statements to the effect that if price were to be, let us say, x, then demand would be, let us say, y; x and y being any values over a given range in each case. The propositions in the formal statement of the general theory of employment are similar. Even though the argument underlying them is normally descriptive, as it has to be, in order to explain them and establish their plausibility, the actual theoretical propositions themselves must be hypothetical since they are couched in equilibrium terms. Equilibrium does not prevail in practice since reality is constantly changing through time. The only purpose of the concept of equilibrium is to aid the process of theorizing about certain aspects of reality. It does so because it is the *logical* (not the historical) outcome of the various forces which act on one another and so enables the process of theorizing to be brought to a determinate conclusion.

Keynes makes a clear distinction between his method of analysis and the sequential or process method (*CW, XIV*: 179; 181–3), which is essentially a stylized description rather than a method of thinking. In the process method, equilibrium is interpreted as the realization of what was intended by the participants in the sequence of activities which is being described. Equilibrium prevails when the outcome is what was anticipated in the sense that it is the consequence of the successful implementation of plans. In this way process analysis purports to take account of the passage of time. By contrast a formal statement of theory in the method followed by Keynes involves sets of hypothetical statements with equilibrium identified as the coincidence of two or more of these *statements*. For example, demand schedules and supply schedules represent sets of hypothetical statements. The interaction of these schedules implies the coincidence of an element in one set with an element in the other set in the sense that the variables in both are the same. Thus, the idea of a distinction between anticipated or *ex ante* conditions and realized or *ex post* conditions in process analysis as, for example, when there are unintended changes in stocks as a result of *failure* to implement plans does not arise in Keynes's concept of equilibrium. His method does not purport to be descriptive. It does not tell a simplified 'story', being concerned only with logical possibilities. Under conditions of profit-equilibrium the profit *implied* on the demand-side is the same as the profit *required* on the supply-side. Time does not enter into the formal statement of the theory and so the analysis does not involve assumptions about time. On the other hand process analysis involves the assumption of a standardized or 'definite unit of time' (*CW, XIV*: 184; also *CW, XXIX*: 131) as well as a concept of equilibrium which rules out the possibility of unanticipated happenings during the sequence of standardized units of time.

Even though time does not enter into Keynes's formal theory he claims that *The General Theory* 'is primarily a study of the forces which determine changes in the scale of output and employment as a whole' (*CW, VII*: xxii). The formal statement of the theory is organized around a particular concept of *equilibrium* which, superficially, might be characterized as a static one. Nevertheless, the theory is intended to direct our attention to those factors which cause the equilibrium to be in one position rather than another and which, therefore, remind us of what causes change. Hence in reading *The General Theory*, it is important to keep in mind that the use of the word 'changes' carries connotations of causality. Generally, the reference to changes in the causal factors is for the purpose of fixing our attention on the possibility of different equilibria rather than for the purpose of describing a course or sequence of economic events.

THE WRITING OF ECONOMIC THEORY

Marshall was very much aware of the difficulties encountered in the writing of economics. He pointed out, for example, that

> The conditioning clauses implied in a law are not continually repeated, but the common sense of the reader supplies them for himself. In economics it is necessary to repeat them oftener than elsewhere, because its doctrines are more apt than those of any other science to be quoted by persons who have had no scientific training (1920: 37).

He also adverted to 'the need under which economics, alone among sciences [has to make shift] with a few terms in common use to express a great number of subtle distinctions' (1920: 50).

Keynes too was highly conscious of these difficulties. In *Notes on Fundamental Terminology*, which he appears to have prepared for a lecture given in 1932, he set down his ideas regarding the proper scope of and limits to the way in which terms ought to be defined. He insisted, in particular, that the language in which theory is presented ought to permit of a certain flexibility of interpretation and that the reader, for his part, ought to approach what an author has written not only with intelligence but also with goodwill. As far as Keynes is concerned, in other words, the reader has to be prepared to make an effort to complement the author's work so that a legalistic style of writing can be avoided. In view of the importance of the passage in which he deals with the problems of expressing the theory of economics for an appreciation of the style of *The General Theory*, it is worth quoting it at length

> A definition can often be *vague* within fairly wide limits and capable of several interpretations differing slightly from one another, and still be perfectly serviceable and free from serious risk of leading either the author or the reader into error, provided that *any* of the alternative definitions will do so long as it is used consistently within a given context. If an author tries to avoid all vagueness and to be perfectly precise, he will become so prolix and pedantic, will find it necessary to split so many hairs, and will be so constantly diverted into an attempt to clear up some other part of the subject, that he himself may perhaps never reach the matter in hand and the reader certainly will not. *I believe, therefore, that it is*

necessary in writing economic theory for one's language to be less generalised than one's thought. It is often impracticable to discuss the most generalised case; and the author selects, therefore, a fairly typical case out of the genus which he is in fact discussing, and talks in terms of this – satisfied in his own mind the same argument applies *mutatis mutandis* to the other members of the genus, and that the task of mutating the mutanda is a merely routine one as soon as the argument in the particular case discussed has been fully grasped by the reader. This means, of course, intelligence and goodwill on the part of the reader. But an author is entitled to presume these qualities. At any rate if he tries to dispense with them by endeavouring to concoct a legal document which he is prepared to stand by literally and to suffer deprivation of rights if any case or contingency can be discovered for which he has failed to provide strictly and explicitly beforehand – then, I am afraid, he will never, if he has a thorough mind, reach the stage of publication (*CW, XXIX:* 36–7, *emphasis added, footnotes omitted*).

The same point emerges in a draft preface to *The General Theory* written in 1934 in which Keynes argues that economic theory, is written 'in a quasi-formal style'. He contends that it is

of the essential nature of economic exposition that it gives, not a complete statement, which, even if it were possible, would be prolix and complicated to the point of obscurity but a sample statement, so to speak, out of all the things which could be said, intended to suggest to the reader the whole bundle of associated ideas, so that, if he catches the bundle, he will not in the least be confused or impeded by the technical incompleteness of the mere words which the author has written down, taken by themselves (*CW, XIII:* 470).

Another 'problem of exposition which frequently faces the economist' is that of deciding to what extent possible objections to his argument should be anticipated. On the whole, Keynes held that there is little point in trying to forestall all criticism especially as much of it is likely to come from those who are not really following his argument in any case. 'How far is it worthwhile', he asked, 'to anticipate objections or difficulties which will only be raised by someone who has not really followed the argument or taken in the point?' And his answer was

Where such further explanations may help to clarify the argument itself, yes. But beyond that, no. For there is no reasonable limit to the objections which can be raised by someone, who has misunderstood the argument, and an author is unlikely to be successful if he tries to anticipate beforehand what points will be taken by a critic whose mind is really running on another track (*CW, XXIX*: 37).

If economic theory is what Keynes thought it to be it cannot borrow the methods of mathematics which seek total formal exactness and which are intended to exclude from consideration everything that is not specifically included. Economic theory has a substance or content, in the sense that it is about something real, in a way that mathematics has not. Consequently, attempts to make economics formal in the manner of mathematics tend to deprive it of substance because while mathematics is self-contained economics is not. The purpose of mathematics may be said to be mathematics itself. It has no direct purpose outside of itself. It is otherwise in the case of economic theory in Keynes's opinion. Economic theory is not an end in itself. The justification for its existence, as we have already observed, is that it helps us to think in an orderly disciplined way about certain aspects of reality. This seems to be the import of his assertion that

theoretical economics often has a formal appearance where the reality is not strictly formal. It is not, and is not meant to be, logically watertight in the sense in which mathematics is. It is a generalisation which lacks precise statement of the cases to which the generalisation applies.

Thus, it is exceedingly dependent on the intelligence and goodwill of the reader or hearer, whose object should be to catch the substance, what the writer is at. Those writers who try to be *strictly* formal generally have no substance (*CW, XXIX*: 37–8).

That *The General Theory* should appear to be written in a rather informal manner is not, therefore, surprising in view of these considerations. Nevertheless, Keynes is usually careful in his choice of words as well as in the logical construction of the book. In this connection, for example, the definitions of user cost (*CW, VII*: 66–73) and of the marginal efficiency of capital (*CW, VII*: 135–7), the consistent attention paid to the difference or 'gap' in absolute terms between income and consumption (*CW, VII*: 97) and the subtle contrast in terminology when he is referring to what is *spent* for consumption purposes and to what is *devoted* to investment (*CW, VII*: 29), may be mentioned. The style, though apparently casual, is quite deliberate. It is employed because Keynes considers it to be the one appropriate to economics since it presents the argument to the reader in such a way that its substance can be grasped directly at every stage and compared to the reader's own knowledge and experience.

THE STYLE OF *THE GENERAL THEORY*

The style of *The General Theory* is also a reflection of the difficulties facing an author when working in, what may be called, the 'mode of discovery' as distinct from the 'mode of exposition'. In a comment on a draft of *A Treatise on Money* contained in a letter to Keynes, Kahn put the difference between the two very succinctly. He said that 'the logical and time sequences which are appropriate to the conception of ideas are not always the best adapted for the purposes of exposition' (*CW, XXIX*: 4).

Keynes was very well aware of this distinction as several passages in his correspondence reveal. For example, in a letter to Taussig, written shortly after the publication of the *Treatise* he said

When I wrote the book many of the ideas were still too fresh in my mind for me to have thought of the clearest, most accurate or most convincing ways of expressing them (*CW, XXIX*: 10).

In the same vein, following the completion of *The General Theory*, he said

I should like some day to endeavour to restate the whole matter . . . simply as a positive doctrine.

Criticisms like yours [Townshend's] are mainly useful in helping one to get more fully emancipated from what one has emerged out of (*CW, XXIX*: 247).

Again, in the preface to the French edition he came back to the same point

Now three years later, having grown accustomed to my new skin and having almost forgotten the smell of my old one, I should, if I were writing afresh, endeavour to free myself from this fault [see below] and state my own position in a more clear-cut manner (*CW, VII*: xxxi).

Keynes released *The General Theory* for publication at the mode of discovery stage. This was consistent, to some extent at least, with his belief that the development of economics and its usefulness require that new ideas and insights should be made available as soon as possible rather than be kept long enough to be perfected. He made this point forcefully in criticizing Marshall's tardiness when it came to publishing *his* ideas

> An economic treatise may have great educational value. Perhaps we require one treatise, as a *pièce de resistance*, for each generation. But in view of the transitory character of economic facts, and the bareness of economic principles in isolation, does not the progress and the daily usefulness of economic science require that pioneers and innovators should eschew the treatise and prefer the pamphlet or the monograph?... Economists must leave to Adam Smith alone the glory of the quarto, must pluck the day, fling pamphlets into the wind, write always *sub specie temporis*, and achieve immortality by accident, if at all (*CW, X*: 198–9).

In the preface to the French edition Keynes also referred to what he regarded as 'certain faults in the book'. These faults were 'in particular its controversial note in some passages, and its air of being addressed too much to the holders of a particular point of view and too little *ad urbem et orbem*' (*CW, VII*: xxxi). They arose because, as he put it 'I was wanting to convince my own environment and did not address myself with sufficient directness to outside opinion' (*CW, VII*: xxxi). In a letter to Harrod written some six months after *The General Theory* was published Keynes observed that

> What some people treat as an unnecessarily controversial tone is really due to the importance in my own mind of what I *used* to believe, and of the moments of transitions which were for me personally moments of illumination. You don't feel the weight of the past as I do. One cannot shake off a pack one has never properly worn. And probably your ignoring [in an article entitled 'Mr Keynes and Traditional Theory', *Econometrica*, January 1937] all this is a better plan than mine. For experience seems to show

that people are divided between the old ones whom nothing will
shift and are merely annoyed by my attempts to underline the
points of transition so vital in my own progress, and the young
ones who have not been properly brought up and believe nothing in
particular. The portholes of light seen in escaping from a tunnel are
interesting neither to those who mean to stay there nor to those
who have never been there! I have no companions, it seems, in my
own generation, either of earliest teachers or of earliest pupils; I
cannot in thought help being somewhat bound to them – which
they find exceedingly irritating! (*CW, XIV*: 84–5, *emphasis added*;
see also letter to Robertson, *CW, XIV*: 87).

Keynes pointed out that *The General Theory* was 'chiefly addressed
to [his] fellow economists' with a view to persuading them 'to re-
examine critically certain of their basic assumptions' and that this
required 'a highly abstract argument' and 'much controversy' (*CW,
VII: xxi*). In part indeed the argument was with himself. He seems to
have been trying to justify his new insights to himself. For him the
writing of the book was 'a long struggle of escape' (*CW, VII: xxiii*).
For that reason he 'thought it important, not only to explain [his] own
point of view, but also to show in what respects it departs from the
prevailing theory' (*CW, VII: xxi*).

Keynes remarks that his 'book is couched in the form of being in
the main a criticism of the classical theory' (*CW, XIV*: 15). But
although it is certainly controversial in tone it should not be
approached as a negative book. It is concerned far more with establishing and clarifying new insights than with criticizing old ones.
Indeed the purpose of the disputation with the earlier economic
theorists of his tradition is more to identify the conditions under
which their conclusions hold logically rather than to demolish them.
They do, after all, hold under certain conditions in Keynes's view.

Keynes did not re-write *The General Theory* 'in a more clear-cut
manner', that is, in the mode of exposition. Even the article he
published in response to a series of reviews in the *Quarterly Journal
of Economics* in February 1937 under the title 'The General Theory of
Employment' is still in the controversial tone of *The General Theory*
itself, concentrating, as it does, on the points where it seemed to
Keynes that he is 'most clearly departing from previous theories'
(*CW, XIV*: 112). Consequently, it is neither a direct nor, because of
its brevity, a complete re-statement of the analysis contained in *The
General Theory*.

The nearest thing to a 'clear-cut' and non-controversial re-statement of the book by Keynes himself is to be found in the preface to the French edition, to which reference has been made already. That was written in February 1939 and was very largely ignored no doubt because of the war. By the time the war was over the controversies surrounding *The General Theory* were well under way and that preface did not play any rôle in them. In any case it became easily available in English only with the publication of *The General Theory* as Volume VII of *The Collected Writings* in 1973. Thus Keynes's use of the term 'profit-equilibrium' and consequently the implications of that term for an understanding of Keynes's argument went unnoticed in the innumerable interpretations, explanations, and re-statements of *The General Theory*.

CONCLUSION

The purpose of the body of theory developed in *The General Theory*, as of all economic theory in Keynes's view, is to provide a method of reasoning – involving concepts, ideas, definitions, observations and deductions – which draws our attention to what must be examined in any particular case out of the class of cases to which the theory relates. Economic theory is a method of discovery because its function is to direct attention to what has to be investigated in seeking answers to particular questions about reality. Keynes's view of theory, following as it does the Marshallian tradition, is not consonant with the view that the purpose of theory is to provide a description, or a 'model' to be quantified, or a doctrine to be propounded.

3 Foundations: Units, Expectations, Income

In the course of writing *The General Theory*, Keynes found that 'three perplexities' impeded his progress. He could not 'express [himself] conveniently' until he had found 'some solution for them' (*CW, VII*: 37). The three perplexities were 'the choice of units of quantity appropriate to the problems of the economic system as a whole; ... the part played by expectation in economic analysis; ... and ... the definition of income' (*CW, VII*: 37).

THE CHOICE OF UNITS

The unsatisfactory units of quantity 'in terms of which economists commonly work' (*CW, VII*: 37) and which Keynes sees as perplexing were probably those referred to as 'units of output', 'units of capital', 'units of product'. Designations such as these were widely used in economics especially in the context of the notion of 'real' income and of the general level of prices. They carried the connotation that it was possible in some way to add heterogeneous goods so that the total quantity of the goods in question could be expressed as a single physical quantity in some sense. Keynes reminds us that heterogeneous entities cannot be added. Homogeneous entities only can be added. He found it perplexing that economists should use such dubious units. They are vague at best and so, obviously, incompatible with logical analysis.

Units of quantity and units of measure

A unit of quantity is the unit in which items are counted. For example, watches may be counted in terms of 'a watch' as the unit, oranges in terms of 'an orange' as the unit, coal in terms of 'ton of coal' as the unit, cloth in terms of 'yard of cloth' as the unit. A unit of measure is the unit which is compared with (or counted against) a property of the entity which is being measured. For example, the property length is measured in terms of metres or feet, the property volume in terms of pints or litres.

Only items or entities can be counted. Properties of items or entities can be measured. Items or entities which can be regarded as

40

homogeneous, and these alone can be counted and, therefore, added. Judgements have usually to be made as to what can and cannot be regarded as homogeneous. For example, in some instances it might be sufficient to regard watches as homogeneous while in others it might be necessary to distinguish between gold watches and silver watches.

In some cases the appropriate unit of quantity for purposes of aggregation is the entity which is being added. For example, if spades are to be added the unit of quantity is 'the spade'. In other cases it is more convenient to take a property (for example, weight, length, volume) of whatever is being aggregated and to use the unit of measure appropriate to that property, in conjunction with the subject of the aggregation, as the unit of quantity. Thus, coal is aggregated in terms of kilograms, cloth in terms of metres, water in terms of litres and so on.

Items which are regarded as heterogeneous cannot be added so as to give a single total. For example, three watches cannot be added to five water melons so as to give a total of eight something. However, if both watches and water melons can be regarded merely as objects the three of the former and the five of the latter can be added so as to give a total of eight objects.

Complexes

The calculation of an average requires the components of that which is to be expressed as an average to be aggregated before being divided by the relevant number of components. It follows that only homogeneous entities can be averaged. When Keynes refers to the wage rate, the rate of interest, the rate of discount he is not to be understood as dealing with averages. He uses such terms merely for 'simplicity of statement' (*CW, VII*: 137, fn.1) to denote what he calls 'complexes' of rates of wages, discount, and interest. The constituents of such complexes are related to one another and so may be said to form 'structures' which, however, are capable of changing internally.

Quantitatively vague expressions

Keynes illustrates the unsatisfactory nature of the units he has in mind by reference to the national dividend (or income), the stock of real capital, and the general price-level (*CW, VII*: 37).

The national dividend as Marshall and Pigou understood it is 'the *volume* of current output or *real* income and *not* the *value* of output or *money-income*' (*CW, VII*: 38, *emphasis added*). There is, however, no physical unit of quantity in which the total of all the outputs of individual goods and services can be expressed. Keynes regards it as 'a grave objection' to the national dividend, as Marshall and Pigou define it,

> that the community's output of goods and services is a non-homogeneous complex [changes in] which cannot be measured, strictly speaking, except in certain special cases, as for example when all the items of one output are included in the same proportion in another output (*CW, VII*: 38).

The volume of current output as a whole can be thought of only as a set or array the elements of which are the outputs of individual goods and services. It could be expressed as a single numerical quantity only if it were to be measured in terms of a unit relating to some property common to all the elements. It is difficult to imagine a physical property common to all goods and services. Goods have the property weight in common. (Services, of course, do not.) Clearly, however, the total weight of all the goods currently produced would not make any economic sense.

Alternatively, the various elements could be regarded as 'objects' judged to be qualitatively similar to all the other 'objects' and so countable and addable in terms of a unit, 'object'. Again, however, such a procedure would be devoid of economic sense.

Attempts to measure the stock of real capital run into the same problems. Since the stock of physical capital assets, like the volume of current output as a whole, is a non-homogeneous complex there is no physical unit of quantity in which it can be expressed as a single numerical quantity. It follows that *net* output cannot be calculated either, even though the national dividend depends

> in some sense, on *net* output – on the net addition…to the resources of the community available for consumption or for retention as capital stock, due to the economic activities and sacrifices of the current period, after allowing for the wastage of the stock of real capital at the commencement of the period (*CW, VII*: 38).

Keynes sums up the problems associated with attempts to derive totals such as real income and the stock of capital by saying that

> The problem of comparing one real output with another and of then calculating net output by setting off new items of equipment

against the wastage of old items presents conundrums which permit, one can confidently say, of no solution (*CW, VII*: 39).

The concept of net output is a 'right and appropriate concept for economic analysis' (*CW, VII*: 39) but 'until a satisfactory system of units has been adopted, its precise definition is an impossible task' (*CW, VII*: 39).

The absence of a unit by which heterogeneous goods can be aggregated also vitiates the concept of the general price-level. In this connection Keynes remarks that

> the well-known, but unavoidable, element of vagueness which admittedly attends the concept of the general price-level makes this term very unsatisfactory for the purposes of a causal analysis, which ought to be exact (*CW, VII*: 39).

The price of a good or service is the sum of money paid for a unit of the item in question (for example, the price of a chair is money per chair, that is *money/chair*). The notion of a general price-level must refer to an average of all the individual prices in an economic system. To obtain such an average all the individual prices would have to be added and divided by the number of prices. But to do so is impossible because the denominators of the various prices are themselves heterogeneous. Thus it is not possible to add the prices of even two separate commodities. For example, if it is supposed that the price of an apple is 10p and that the price of an orange is 12p, the sum of their prices is 10*p*/1 *apple* + 12*p*/1 *orange*. This expression cannot be reduced to one numerical quantity since there is no common denominator in terms of which its components could be added. The sum of 10p can, of course, be added to the sum of 12p, giving 22p, but the 22p is merely a sum of money or quantity of money value. It is *not* the combined *price* of the two items.

The logical difficulties involved in trying to quantify the volume of output as a whole and the stock of capital assets as well as the inherent logical contradiction in the notion of a general price-level all flow from the fact that output as a whole is a heterogeneous complex. These difficulties, Keynes says, 'are rightly regarded as 'conundrums''. He points out, however, that

> They are 'purely theoretical' in the sense that they never perplex, or indeed enter in any way into, business decisions and have no

relevance to the causal sequence of economic events, which are clear-cut and determinate in spite of the quantitative indeterminacy of these concepts (*CW, VII*: 39).

What Keynes seems to mean in that passage is that people go about making business decisions without regard to the logical difficulties involved in the calculation of magnitudes purporting to involve the aggregation of heterogeneous entities. Rightly or wrongly, they make their decisions on the basis of the factors they deem to be relevant. It is most unlikely that logical problems are ever relevant to such decisions. Keynes is not to be taken as meaning that business people never take, for example, changes or expected changes in an index of prices into account in making decisions. Obviously, they do, just as they take rumours, feelings, weather forecasts, even political speeches into account.

The conclusion Keynes comes to is that the concepts he is discussing 'not only lack precision but are unnecessary' (*CW, VII*: 39). Quantitative *analysis*, as distinct from numerical description requires that the quantitative concepts which are used be internally consistent and exact in a logical sense. Expressions which are 'quantitatively vague' (*CW, VII*: 39) can play no part in a precise logical analysis. To employ such expressions would mean that the analysis itself would be vague. Quantitative vagueness means that a *concept* which relates to quantities is itself vague, not that actual numbers are imprecise. Estimates are to a greater or lesser extent imprecise. If the matter being investigated is itself logically self-consistent the imprecision of an estimate will affect the accuracy of a result but not its logical validity. To 'quantify' a concept which is logically inconsistent or incoherent cannot make that concept any more logical. It cannot save it from its internal defects. Quantitatively vague expressions are not used in the analysis of the behaviour of the individual consumer, factor-owner or firm. To use them in the analysis of the economic system as a whole would, therefore, mean that the analysis of individual units and of the system as a whole would be on different levels of logical rigour. Keynes, clearly, took it that the same standards should apply to all aspects of economic analysis.

Description and rough comparison

The concepts that Keynes rejects in the context of quantitative analysis may, however, be used 'for purposes of description or rough comparison' (*CW, VII*: 41). As he puts it:

The fact that two incommensurable collections of miscellaneous objects cannot in themselves provide the material for a quantitative analysis need not, of course, prevent us from making approximate statistical comparisons, depending on some broad element of judgement rather than of strict calculation, which may possess significance and validity within certain limits. But the proper place for such *things* as net real output and the general level of prices lies within the field of historical and statistical description, and their purpose should be to satisfy historical or social curiosity, a purpose for which perfect precision – such as our causal analysis requires, whether or not our knowledge of the actual values of the relevant quantities is complete or exact – is neither usual nor necessary (*CW, VII*: 39–40, *emphasis added*).

In the foregoing passage Keynes is evidently referring to the use of index numbers of prices and of quantities. Index numbers can be used in a rough and ready way to give an impression (but not an estimate) as to how broad ranges of prices and 'real' output change over time. Their use, however, must be confined 'to the occasions when we are attempting some historical comparison which is within certain (perhaps fairly wide) limits avowedly unprecise and approximate' (*CW, VII*: 43). Thus in Keynes's view the logical analysis of economic activity requires the use, in principle, of precise unambiguous magnitudes. Vague, quantitatively imprecise notions have no place in such analysis though they may have a place in historical description in which no more than an impression of orders of magnitude is required to convey such understanding as may be gleaned from historical description or narrative. In other words, analysis requires that the quantities be precise in principle though they may not be known (or knowable) in practice while historical description may require the use of figures though the logical basis for them may be vague.

Homogeneous units of quantity

In view of the foregoing considerations Keynes, in dealing with the theory of employment, makes use of only two 'fundamental units of quantity, namely, quantities of money value and quantities of employment' (*CW, VII*: 41). Units of money, he says, are 'strictly homogeneous' while units of employment 'can be made so' (*CW, VII*: 41).

The money-unit is ready-made and is naturally homogeneous. Quantities of money value can be aggregated in a logically precise way. The money-unit itself, however, possesses value. Its value may change over time. Indeed its value may differ from one person or one place to another person or place even at any particular time. Hence it is not analogous to homogeneous units of measure such as the yard or the gallon which are in principle invariant. Changes in the value of the money-unit cannot be measured in a logically precise way for the reasons given above and this must be allowed for in the formulation of the theory.

The labour-unit

Keynes defines the labour-unit as 'an hour's employment of ordinary labour' (*CW, VII*: 41). The money-wage of a labour-unit is a wage-unit (*CW, VII*: 41). If the wages paid to different types of labour are proportional to the productiveness or 'efficiency' of the different types of labour, the relative contribution of each type of labour to output will be reflected in its relative remuneration. Thus what Keynes refers to as 'an hour of special labour' will count as a multiple of an hour of ordinary labour. Accordingly, the different types of labour can be regarded 'as contributing to the supply of labour in proportion to their remuneration' (*CW, VII*: 42). Since each wage-unit is the price of a labour-unit it follows that the number of labour-units employed by a firm or in the economic system as a whole may be obtained simply by dividing the wage-bill by the wage-unit. Thus the labour-unit and the wage-unit can be used to provide the means of 'aggregating the activities of all firms' into a single numerical magnitude in terms of a quantity of employment (*CW, VII*: 40).

Keynes claims that the 'obvious fact' that individual workers may differ as regards their 'specialised skill' and in 'their suitability for different occupations', does not upset his 'assumption of homogeneity in the supply of labour' (*CW, VII*: 41) because

if the remuneration of the workers is proportional to their effi-ciency, the differences are dealt with by our having regarded indi-viduals as contributing to the supply of labour in proportion to their remuneration; whilst if, as output increases, a given firm has to bring in labour which is less and less efficient for its special purposes per wage-unit paid to it, this is merely one factor among others leading to a diminishing return from the capital equipment in terms of output as more labour is employed on it (*CW, VII*: 42).

In other words

> We subsume, so to speak, the non-homogeneity of equally remuner-
> ated labour units in the equipment, which we regard as less and less
> adapted to employ the available labour units as output increases,
> instead of regarding the available labour units as less and less adapted
> to use a homogeneous capital equipment (*CW, VII*: 42).

Keynes further argues that

> Even in the limiting case where different labour units were so highly
> specialised as to be altogether incapable of being substituted for one
> another, there is no awkwardness; for this merely means that the
> elasticity of supply of output from a particular type of capital
> equipment falls suddenly to zero when all the available labour
> specialised to its use is already employed (*CW, VII*: 42).

What ultimately justifies this approach is that

> the increasing surpluses, which emerge as output is increased,
> accrue in practice mainly to the owners of the equipment and not
> to the more efficient workers (*CW, VII*: 42–3, fn.2).

Summary

Total current output and total capital equipment in physical terms in the economic system as a whole must be interpreted as an array (or complex) of heterogeneous goods only. The only way that heterogeneous goods can be aggregated into a single numerical magnitude is in terms of money values. Employment can be aggregated, even though labour is heterogeneous, by means of the labour-unit.

EXPECTATIONS

What must have perplexed Keynes in regard to 'the part played by expectation in economic analysis' (*CW, VII*: 37), although he does not explicitly say so, is that, in his time, expectation did not play any part. Yet business decisions are inevitably made on the basis of expectations. As the future is not known, they cannot be made in any other way. Keynes, for his part, places expectations at the heart of his analysis both of production and of investment, as logically he must. By doing so he avoids the need to make implausible assumptions relating to knowledge of the future and, at the same time, avoids some of the analytical problems associated with the passage of time.

Short-term and long-term expectations

Keynes distinguishes between what he calls short-term and long- term expectations. The former underlie the making of decisions relating to the level of current output and thereby to the scale on which a firm's capital equipment is operated. The latter underlie the decisions relating to investment. The decision to produce goods to be used for investment purposes is based on short-term expectations while the decision to purchase these goods is based on long-term expectations. In Keynes's words,

> the behaviour of each individual firm in deciding its daily [see below] output will be determined by its *short-term expectations –* expectations as to the cost of output on various possible scales and expectations as to the sale-proceeds of this output; though, in the case of additions to capital equipment and even of sales to distributors, these short-term expectations will largely depend on the long-term (or medium- term) expectations of other parties. It is upon these various expectations that the amount of employment which the firms offer will depend (*CW, VII*: 47, *footnote omitted*).

Short-term expectations and long-term expectations are examined in Chapter 4 and in Chapter 6 respectively.

Expectation and the theory of the firm

From the analysis of the firm's production decisions in expectational terms the distinction between demand as *perceived* by the entrepreneur and the demand which the buyers decide upon naturally emerges. Time usually passes between the formation of the seller's expectations and the buyers' decisions to buy. For these reasons the two aspects of demand may be quite different. Whether they are or not, there is a clear conceptual distinction between them which is not made in the conventional theory of production but which must be made in any plausible theory of the firm.

This distinction, as is argued in Chapter 4, is the foundation upon which Keynes's concept of effective demand is based. It is also the foundation of the distinction between aggregate demand and effective demand and, therefore, of the essential character both of the demand-side and of the supply-side of his theory of employment.

The distinction between short-term and long-term expectations also serves to clarify the rôle of the firm on the demand-side as compared to its rôle on the supply-side. All firms are likely to engage in both supply-side and demand-side activities in the sense that they produce current output for sale or for their own use and buy goods for investment purposes. The two sides are, however, quite distinct and need to be analyzed in a manner which is appropriate to each rôle.

Expectations and time

The analytical use of expectation also has the advantage of enabling certain problems stemming from the passage of time and from the absence of a 'determinate time unit' (*CW, XIV*: 180) to be avoided for as Keynes says 'it is of the nature of expectation that it takes account of the time element' (*CW, XIII*: 512).

He introduces the concept of the 'day' in order to establish that there is no standard or determinate unit of economic time. He defines the 'day' as 'the shortest interval after which the firm is free to revise its decision as to how much employment to offer', and says that it is 'so to speak, the minimum effective unit of economic time' (*CW, VII*: 47, fn.1).

The 'day' differs from firm to firm and possibly even for the same firm over time. Days then are not homogeneous. As they cannot be standardized they cannot be aggregated. Moreover, as economic activity is continuous, production processes start and finish at different times in different firms. Thus it is not possible, for example, to compare inputs at one time with outputs at another time in respect of an aggregate of firms. In this connection Keynes said in a letter to Ohlin, written in 1937,

I used to speak of the period between expectation and result as 'funnels of process', but the fact that the funnels are all of different lengths and overlap one another meant that at any given time there was no aggregate realised result capable of being compared with some aggregate expectation at some earlier date (*CW, XIV*: 185).

What can be done, at least in principle, and what Keynes does, is to compare the receipts which entrepreneurs expect will accrue to them during any given period with the actual expenditure incurred during that period. It can be assumed without doing much violence to reality that the period is the same for all firms. Expectations covering any period can be formed and, if necessary, they can be revised. 'What primarily matters', according to Keynes, 'is the expectation of expenditure formed by the entrepreneur beforehand and secondarily by the gradual revision of this expectation in the light of experience' (*CW, XIV*: 181–2). Even if the original expectations are revised, the revised expectations still relate to the period in question. If the length of the 'day' permits, new decisions can be made and implemented during the period. Actual receipts over the period compared with the outlays incurred tell the entrepreneur whether or not the expectations are realized and form the basis for forming new expectations and making new decisions for the future. This seems to be the purport of Keynes's lecture notes (1937) in which he says

Employment is determined *solely* by effective demand which is influenced by realised results up to date irrespective of the date to which the decision relates (*CW, XIV*: 180).

The expenditure incurred during any period comes in part from the income generated during the period of the expenditure itself and is incurred, in part, on the output which generates the income. The difference between the income so generated and the expenditure out of it for consumption purposes is what Keynes calls the 'gap'. This is examined in Chapter 5.

Another possible way of interpreting what Keynes says about its being in the nature of expectation that it takes account of the time element may also be considered. In this interpretation it is assumed that all firms form their expectations as to the proceeds they receive at the same time. This may be justified on the grounds that all firms hold expectations at any given time about the future irrespective of when they formed them. The amounts of money relating to these expectations can be aggregated. When so aggregated the resulting sum is the expected value of the output which the firms decide to produce in the light of the expectations they hold. If expenditure on the output in question were to be what was expected the firms would be generating the factor incomes and earning the profit they planned. Consequently the total income generated would be equal to the expected value of the output. This is considered further in Chapter 4.

This interpretation is perfectly logical. But compared to the first interpretation it is rather artificial. In particular it implies a total income of which the time dimension of its components is not uniform. It is true that the money incomes expected to arise in the process of generating the expected output can be aggregated because, by definition, they are made up of units of money. But for a collection of separate incomes to constitute what could reasonably be regarded as a total income seems to require that they all relate to a given period of time – since income is a flow.

The first interpretation seems more natural as it is closer to what is ordinarily meant by income and by expenditure. Besides it more readily lends itself to the idea that expenditure for consumption purposes comes out of an income. Hence it seems to be closer to reality and to ordinary usage as well as to the normal practice of accountants than is the second interpretation. It also seems to be more in accordance with what Keynes says about the revision of expectations.

THE DEFINITION OF INCOME

The definition of income was a perplexity because there was no generally agreed definition available. There was a 'welter of divergent usages of terms' (*CW, VII*: 61). As a result there was a great deal of confusion to which Keynes himself contributed, as he admits, in regard to the definitions of income he used in the *Treatise on Money* (*CW, VII*: 61).

Income

In a letter which Keynes wrote to Hicks in September 1936 he said

I commenced with the conviction that one has in some way to identify income with the value of output. In calculating the value of output one has to make some allowance for pre-existing capital which is used up. Pre-existing capital seems to be capable of being used up in one or other of three ways, namely, (i) that part which is avoidable and depends on decisions as to what current output is

undertaken, (ii) that which is unavoidable but is quite in accordance
with expectations, and (iii) that which is neither avoidable nor in
accordance with expectations. In defining income I deduct the first
only; in defining net income the second also; whilst the third I do
not regard as occurring on income account, but as being a windfall
loss of capital (*CW, XIV*: 75).

That passage summarises Keynes's approach to and understanding
of what income is. In particular it reveals his concern with the problem of the treatment of the capital which exists at the beginning of
any period and the distinction he draws between income, or income
proper, and net income. His solution to the problem of pre-existing
capital and his distinction between income and net income all play a
rôle in his analysis.

During any period of time a firm sells output to consumers and/or
to other firms. Keynes designates the value of such sales as A. During
the period it buys finished output from other firms, the value of which
is designated A_1. At the end of the period the firm has capital equipment (including working capital and finished goods as well as fixed
capital) designated G in value. Part of what the firm sells and part of
what it retains at the end of the period less what it buys from other
firms, that is, part of $(A + G - A_1)$, is attributable to the capital
equipment which it had at the beginning of the period, and which it
may be thought of as 'inheriting' from the previous period, rather
than to its activities during the period in question. Hence in order to
identify the income of that period a certain sum must be deducted
from $(A + G - A_1)$ in respect of that part of its value which is
attributable to what was inherited from the previous period. Keynes
sees the problem of defining income as that of finding 'a satisfactory
method for calculating this deduction' (*CW, VII*: 52).

There are two ways of making this calculation. One leads to the
concept of 'income proper' and is what is significant for production.
The other leads to the concept of 'net income' and is what is significant
for consumption. Keynes intends his definition of these two concepts 'to
conform as closely as possible to common usage' (*CW, VII*: 60).

Income proper

The value of the capital equipment which the firm has at the end of
the period, namely G, is the 'net result' (*CW, VII*: 53) of (i) the money
spent on maintaining and improving it during the period, whether

involving purchases from other firms or on work done on it within the firm itself, and (ii) its exhaustion or depreciation arising from its use in production.

Even if the firm were not to use the inherited capital equipment to produce output there would, nevertheless, be 'a certain optimum sum' (*CW, VII*: 53) which it would be desirable to spend on it in order to maintain and improve it. Assuming B' to be this optimum amount, Keynes further assumes that the inherited capital equipment would be worth G' at the end of the period if B' had been spent on it. Thus $(G' - B')$ is the 'maximum net value which might have been conserved from the previous period' (*CW, VII*: 53) if the inherited capital equipment had *not* been used to contribute to the production of what was sold for A. The difference between this potential value of the inherited equipment, that is, $(G' - B')$ and $(G - A_1)$, is 'the measure of what has been sacrificed . . . to produce A' (*CW, VII*: 53).

The difference between these two magnitudes, namely $[(G' - B') - (G - A_1)]$, Keynes calls the *user cost of A* and abbreviates it as U. In other words, user cost is the difference between the potential value of the inherited capital equipment on the one hand and the actual value of the capital equipment at the end of the period less what was bought from other firms during the period on the other. If the value of the amount bought from other firms is greater than G, as is normally the case, $(G - A_1)$ is negative. Consequently, user cost is positive, as is to be expected. What that means then is simply that the cost of producing what is sold for A, apart, that is, from factor cost, is positive. Money paid to the factors employed by the firm itself with a view to the maintenance and improvement of its inherited capital equipment is, of course, included in B'.

What the firm pays to the factors of production (apart from the entrepreneur) Keynes calls the factor cost of A and designates it as F. The sum of F and U Keynes calls the *prime cost* of the output sold for A. The factor costs included in B' are automatically deducted from prime cost since B appears in U as a negative amount. Looked at from the perspective of the factors, the factor cost of A is the income of the factors themselves.

The income (or *income proper*) of the firm is thus $[A - (F + U)]$. It is identical to the gross profit of the entrepreneur and it is the quantity which 'he endeavours to maximise' (*CW, VII*: 53). It follows that the total income generated by the firm in producing its output is $A - U$, since profit plus factor cost is total income.

Expected income proper being what the entrepreneur tries to maximize, 'it is the quantity which is causally significant for employment'
(*CW, VII*: 54).

Since all the foregoing magnitudes are amounts of money they can
be aggregated from individual firms to the economic system as a
whole. Thus aggregate sales are ΣA, aggregate purchases from other
entrepreneurs are ΣA_1 and so on.

Net income

That part of the change in the value of capital equipment at the end of
the period as compared with its value at the beginning, dealt with
above, is due to the voluntary decisions of the entrepreneur (*CW, VII*:
56). But there may also be

> an involuntary loss (or gain) in the value of his [the entrepreneur's]
> capital equipment, occurring for reasons beyond his control and
> irrespective of his current decisions, on account of (e.g.) a change in
> market values, wastage by obsolescence or the mere passage of
> time, or destruction by catastrophe such as war or earthquake
> (*CW, VII*: 56).

Although such losses are involuntary and unavoidable they are not
'broadly speaking' (*CW, VII*: 56) unexpected. Keynes refers to them
as *supplementary cost* and designates them as V.

When supplementary cost is deducted from the income proper of
the firm the *net income* of the firm is obtained. At the level of the
economy as a whole net income is $\Sigma(A - U - V)$. The significance of
net income is that it is what the entrepreneur in his capacity as a
consumer sees as the income available to him out of which he can
spend money for consumption purposes. Thus, as Keynes puts it

> The *causal* significance of net income lies in the psychological
> influence of the magnitude of V on the amount of current consump-
> tion, since *net income* is what we suppose the ordinary man to
> reckon his available income to be when he is deciding how much
> to spend on current consumption (*CW, VII*: 57, *second emphasis
> added*).

The value of the equipment may also change as a result of involuntary and 'in a broad sense' (*CW, VII*: 57) unforeseen changes in, for

example, market value or because of exceptional obsolescence or destruction by catastrophe. Losses of this kind Keynes regards as windfall losses and considers that they ought not to be taken into account in calculating income but ought to be charged to capital account (*CW, VII*: 57).

The distinction between supplementary costs and windfall losses 'is partly a conventional or psychological one' (*CW, VII*: 58) and depends on how supplementary costs are estimated. There is no 'unique principle' (*CW, VII*: 58) by which such costs are estimated. Hence their amount depends on the particular accounting method chosen. Moreover, while the expected supplementary cost 'is a definite quantity' (*CW, VII*: 58) when the equipment was originally produced it may be revised subsequently. In this case, the windfall capital loss would be the difference between the original expectation of what supplementary cost would be and 'the revised expectation of the prospective series $U + V$' (*CW, VII*: 58).

Keynes distinguishes between *basic supplementary cost* and *current supplementary cost*. The former is 'the initial expectation of supplementary cost when the equipment is first acquired' while the latter is 'the same quantity recalculated up to date on the basis of current values and expectations' (*CW, VII*: 59). Keynes concludes that

> we cannot get closer to a quantitative definition of supplementary cost than that it comprises those deductions from his income which a typical entrepreneur makes before reckoning what he considers his *net* income for the purpose of declaring a dividend (in the case of a corporation) or of deciding the scale of his current consumption (in the case of an individual) (*CW, VII*: 59).

While net income is 'not perfectly clear-cut' (*CW, VII*: 60), income proper (A-U) is 'completely unambiguous' (*CW, VII*: 54). Accordingly, Keynes considers that 'it is a mistake to put all the emphasis on *net income*' (*CW, VII*: 60) as his contemporaries and predecessors had done (*CW, VII*: 59–60). Net income is relevant to decisions concerning consumption only. Income proper, on the other hand, is what is relevant to decisions concerning current production. Both are significant in an analysis of the determination of the employment of the available resources. Neither ought to be excluded from consideration.

Income and the value of output

Since at the level of the economic system as a whole the output of any period less what is consumed of that output is necessarily what is added to capital equipment during that period it follows that the value of what is consumed plus the value of investment are equal to the value of output.

Consumption is equal in value to total sales (ΣA) less what entrepreneurs buy from one another (ΣA_1). In symbols ΣC is equal to $\Sigma(A - A_1)$. Investment (I) is equal to what entrepreneurs buy from each other $\Sigma(A_1)$ less user cost (ΣU). Again in symbols ΣI is equal to $\Sigma(A_1 - U)$.

It follows that the total value of output in any period must be equal to $\Sigma(A - A_1 + A_1 - U)$ or $\Sigma(A - U)$ which is the income of the community. Thus income is equal to the value of output in any period.

4 The Supply-Side

The supply-side is as important as the demand-side in the general theory of employment. As in the general theory of value or price the two sides are as important as the two blades of a scissors (Marshall, 1920: 348). Yet Keynes says very little about his supply-side. The reason seems to be that he considers what he calls the aggregate supply function to involve 'few considerations which are not already familiar' (*CW, VII*: 89). 'The form', he says, 'may be unfamiliar but the underlying factors are not new' (*CW, VII*: 89). It may be taken, then, that Keynes did not see himself as making any fundamental additions to economic theory in his discussion of the supply-side even though he develops it in terms of the resources which firms employ and the expectations they form in a way which, in retrospect, seems to make a significant addition to the theory of the firm as it was in his own time.

THE MODEL

As we mentioned in Chapter 1, Keynes develops his ideas about the supply-side and about the operation of the economic system in general in the context of what he refers to as the *monetary-entrepreneur economy*. By that he means, as we also touched on in Chapter 1, an economy in which production is undertaken by firms with a view to the sale of the output ultimately to consumers and investors. By reason of the fact that firms produce in order to sell they can survive only if they make profit. Keynes is mindful of what motivates people to establish firms apart from the prospect of profit. Human nature is such that some people like to take a chance and derive satisfaction from setting-up productive enterprises (*CW, VII*: 150). The making of profit, is however, the necessary condition for the survival of any firm, unless it is subsidised by the taxpayer. But Keynes does not contemplate that possibility. He remarks that

> The firm is dealing throughout in terms of sums of money. It has no object in the world except to end up with more money than it started with. That is the essential characteristic of an entrepreneur economy (*CW, XXIX*: 89).

In an early draft of *The General Theory*, (written in 1933), Keynes sets out what he terms 'a simplified model of an entrepreneur economy' (*CW, XXIX*: 87). He supposes that production is organized by 'a number of firms which do nothing but exercise entrepreneur functions' in that 'they rent their fixed capital equipment from capitalists, in return for an annual rent, payable over the prospective life of the equipment ... and they hire labour, whenever they decide to use the capital equipment' (*CW, XXIX*: 87–8). He also suggests that 'it is convenient, though not essential, to assume that the firms own their own working capital' (*CW, XXIX*: 88). That implies that the firms

> find the cash to rent the capital equipment and to meet the variable costs incurred between starting up their capital equipment ... to produce output and the sale of this output for cash' (*CW, XXIX*: 88).

He adds that 'there is no impediment to partly finished goods changing hands for cash between firms' (CW, *XXIX*: 88).

In *The General Theory* itself Keynes enumerates what he takes to be the given factors and the factors which change for the purposes of his analysis. His treatment of these two sets of factors is strictly in accordance with his views as to what the purpose of a model is as outlined in Chapter 2 above. The given factors are

> the existing skill and quantity of available labour, the existing quality and quantity of available equipment, the existing technique, the degree of competition, the tastes and habits of the consumers, the disutility of different intensities of labour and of the activities of supervision and organisation, as well as the social structure including the forces, other than our variables set forth below, which determine the distribution of the national income (*CW, VII*: 245).

What the foregoing amounts to is that the resources (including the capital equipment) are given and that the determination of the distribution of the national income is not at issue. The former is logically required since the issue Keynes is addressing is the determination of the employment of the *available* resources. The latter is logically implied since the main issue, as we pointed out in Chapter 1, is nearly the same as the determination of the size, but not of the distribution, of the national income. The question as to the size of the national income is clearly different from the question as to why it is distributed in one way rather than another.

By capital equipment Keynes means 'fixed capital, working capital' and 'liquid capital' (*CW, VII*: 75). Working capital consists of goods used in the process of production. Liquid capital consists of the stock of unsold goods. Thus the 'partly finished goods' to which he refers are part of the working capital. That there is 'no impediment' to their changing hands for money simply means that they may be located in one firm rather than another for the time being. The important consideration is that they are somewhere in the economic system.

The independent variables 'in the first instance' (*CW, VII*: 245) are the propensity to consume (Chapter 5), the schedule of the marginal efficiency of capital (Chapter 6), and the rate of interest (Chapter 7). Keynes allows that the given factors influence the independent variables but 'do not completely determine them' (*CW, VII*: 246). Moreover, he points out that the given factors enable the shape of the aggregate supply functions to be inferred. In addition they furnish the supply functions of labour, or effort (*CW, VII*: 246).

The schedule of the marginal efficiency of capital depends partly on the given quality and quantity of equipment and partly on the 'prospective yield of capital-assets of different kinds' (*CW, VII*: 246). The rate of interest depends partly on the 'state of liquidity-preference', discussed in Chapter 7 below, and 'partly on the quantity of money measured in terms of wage-units' (*CW, VII*: 246). These considerations lead Keynes to conclude that

> we can sometimes regard our ultimate independent variable as consisting of (1) the three fundamental psychological factors, namely the psychological propensity to consume, the psychological attitude to liquidity and the psychological expectation of future yield from capital assets, (2) the wage-unit as determined by the bargains reached between employers and employed, and (3) the quantity of money as determined by the action of the central bank' (*CW, VII*: 246–7).

The dependent variables are the volume of employment and the national income measured in wage-units (*CW, VII*: 245). But as we saw earlier these are nearly the same thing. They both reflect the extent to which the available resources are employed. Since the capital equipment is given it follows that the more labour is employed and the higher national income (measured in wage-units) is the more intensively must capital equipment be employed, the limit being reached when output becomes inelastic.

Keynes's model is as comprehensive as it needs to be if it is to serve as a suitable setting in which to address a question relating to the economic system as a whole.[3] What he takes to be given must be taken as given if the question at issue is to be addressed in a manageable way. The question could not be isolated as the *quaesitum* in any other way. What is taken as given enables that question to be concentrated upon and prevents other issues from intruding upon the main issue. The given factors are consistent with one another so that the whole model is internally consistent. All the assumptions underlying what are regarded as given are highly plausible, as will become more clear later.

The independent variables emerge, or rather are discovered, in the process of theorizing. They are the variable factors which Keynes 'found' to be the ones that provide the method of addressing his question because (as explained in later chapters) it is the changes in these variables which determine the employment of the available resources. The range of possible determinants is narrowed down to these particular variables. The process of theorizing itself leads to their identification and to their segregation from the more permanent or constant factors which being taken to be given do not need, for the purposes of *The General Theory*, to be explained.

No more than the given factors do the independent variables involve any implausible assumptions. Even the device of the wage-unit is treated in such a way that it is close enough to reality to be plausible. At the same time it is logically derived within the context of the traditional theory that Keynes took to be valid and so provides a satisfactory way of making the model both quantitatively exact in principle and consistent.

It may be concluded that Keynes's model, is plausible, comprehensive and self-consistent. and that it meets the criteria which Keynes himself set for what he regarded as a good model.

THE MARKET

As we have seen, one of the factors taken to be given in the model is 'the degree of competition'. It seems clear that by this Keynes means that he is taking it for granted that the markets implied in his analysis are the ordinary workaday markets with which business is familiar. Consequently, he is not assuming that markets are 'perfect'.

Moreover, throughout *The General Theory* Keynes deals time and time again with the uncertainty in which all business is always conducted and with the consequent inescapable fact that decisions are based on expectations. As we have already mentioned and as we explain more fully later, Keynes analyzes the behaviour of the firm in terms of expectation. He thereby rules out the possibility that the entrepreneur can take price to be given. It follows that the demand curves 'facing' firms cannot be assumed to be horizontal as perfect competition would imply. Keynes also explicitly refers to the fact that

> the entrepreneur . . . has to form the best expectations he can as to what the consumers will be prepared to pay when he is ready to supply them . . . after the elapse of what may be a lengthy period (*CW, VII*: 46, *footnote omitted*).

Keynes elaborates on the foregoing in pointing out that a manufacturer has to form an expectation of the *price* he can expect to get (*CW, VII*: 46). It seems clear then that Keynes assumes that individual firms 'face' downward sloping demand curves and that these, in turn, are (as we show below) to be interpreted in expectational rather than in actual or intentional terms.

THE FIRM

Keynes does not restrict his analysis to any particular type or size of firm. The analysis is general enough to encompass all firms found in the everyday world of business. The firms compete with one another in order to 'attract to their own output as large a share as possible of current expenditure' (*CW, XXIX*: 90) and to obtain maximum quasi-rents (*CW, XIII:* 426), that is, to maximize profit (as discussed in Chapter 3).

Since the supply-side is concerned with the available resources, the capital equipment with which the firm operates has to be assumed to be given. The analytical issue relates to the scale on which that given equipment is operated. The equipment in question is that which the firm is assumed to have when it forms the expectations upon which its production decisions are made. These are the decisions which determine the scale on which its equipment is operated. The assumption that the capital equipment is given does not preclude, as we have seen, the possibility that the firm purchases inputs from other firms during the production process. If the inputs are not in the physical possession of the firm itself it must, of course, be assumed that it has the means of buying them when the relevant expectations are formed. Thus 'given' has to be interpreted as meaning that the firm has all the capital equipment it needs to implement its production decisions at the time the expectations upon which such decisions are made or else that it has the means of acquiring it from other firms. The extent to which the capital equipment is used, other things being equal, depends on the amount of labour the firm employs.

As Keynes's central question concerns the employment of the available resources, his analysis of the firm has to concentrate on the extent to which it employs labour. The factors that determine the employment of labour also automatically determine the employment of resources other than labour. Hence, as we saw above, the dependent variables are the volume of employment and the national income measured in wage-units. That being so, the analysis of the firm and ultimately the analysis of the supply-side as a whole is primarily and explicitly concerned with the employment of labour. The cost conditions of the firm, important though they are, are implicit and in the background. Keynes takes the standard treatment of cost, as it was in his time, for granted apart from his observations on user cost.

Accordingly, there are no restrictions in the analysis as to the (implicit) cost conditions of the firm. The supply-side, being concerned with the employment of labour and the consequent scale on which the capital equipment is being used, relates to the behaviour of the firm's (implicit) costs in the short run only. Even though Keynes always assumes diminishing returns in the case of the variable factors, because more efficient units of a factor are employed before less efficient units, there is no reason on logical grounds to rule out the possibility that average cost is falling in the short run. In the case of firms having high overhead costs, a firm may be operating under conditions of falling average cost.

Entrepreneurs do not need to know for what purpose the output they produce is bought. The analyst knows that output is used either for consumption purposes or for investment purposes. But it is necessary only to assume that the entrepreneur forms expectations as to the proceeds that will accrue to the firm. There is no need, for analytical purposes, to make any assumptions either as to knowledge or even expectations in regard to the purposes for which buyers buy current output. The sub-division of 'the proceeds which entrepreneurs expect to receive from the employment of N men', that is, D in Keynes's notation, into D_1, the amount which the community is expected to spend on consumption, and D_2, the amount which it is expected to devote to investment, is made from the point of view of the theorist rather than that of the entrepreneur (*CW, VII*: 29).

EXPECTATIONS

All decisions are based on expectations as to what the future will be. In business the entrepreneur has to forecast, as best he can, what his costs are likely to be at various rates of output and what buyers are likely to pay for the various possible quantities of output he might offer for sale. Thus expectations provide the behavioural foundation for the analysis of the supply-side of Keynes's theory of employment.

Short-term expectations, as we have mentioned already, are concerned with the price which the seller can get for his output when it is ready for sale and with the costs which will be incurred in producing it. Thus the decision to start a process of production is based upon this type of expectation. The firm's short-term expectations determine its 'daily' output. Hence the extent to which firms employ resources depends on these expectations. The results which it realizes in terms of production and sales may cause subsequent expectations to be modified. It is always 'the *current* expectations of *prospective* costs and sale-proceeds' (*CW, VII*: 47) which underlie the firm's decisions.

Short-term expectations are subject to continuous revision. But, as Keynes says,

in practice the process of revision . . . is a gradual and continuous one, carried on largely in the light of realised results; so that expected and realised results run into and overlap one another in their influence. For, although output and employment are determined by the producer's short-term expectations and not by past results, the most recent results usually play a predominant part in determining what these expectations are. It would be too complicated to work out the expectations *de novo* whenever a productive process was being started; and it would, moreover be a waste of time since a large part of the circumstances usually continue substantially unchanged from one day to the next. Accordingly it is

sensible for producers to base their expectations on the assumption
that the most recently realised results will continue, except in so far
as there are definite reasons for expecting a change...and producers' forecasts are more often gradually modified in the light of
results than in anticipation of prospective changes (*CW, VII*: 50–1).

By grounding his version of the theory of the firm on the expectations formed by the entrepreneurs, Keynes grounds it on fact rather
than on assumption. The theory he develops on that grounding is
close to reality and quite general. By taking expectation as his starting
point he is enabled, indeed compelled, to see demand from two
perspectives – from that of the seller and from that of the buyer.
That in turn leads to the need to analyze the firm's costs in a manner
which is consistent with the way in which the firm's perception of
demand is analyzed. What emerges are the three concepts – the
aggregate demand function, the aggregate supply function and effective demand. These three concepts are the essential elements of Keynes's theory of supply. They are purely analytical devices and are not
meant to be descriptive.

THE AGGREGATE SUPPLY FUNCTION

The supply price is the price at which a firm is willing to sell a unit of
its output. The 'aggregate supply price' is the price per unit multiplied
by the number of units offered for sale at the supply price. Thus it is
the amount the firm would need to realize from the sale of an output.
In other words it is the 'proceeds' which would need to accrue to the
firm from selling its output at the appropriate supply price per unit.
As the firm is assumed to seek to maximize its profit, its supply price
and its aggregate supply price are such as to lead to what it regards as
the maximum profit it could attain given its *expected* costs. Keynes
defines the aggregate supply price of the output of a given amount of
employment as 'the expectation of proceeds which will just make it
worth the while of the entrepreneur to give that employment' (*CW,
VII*: 24). By 'just make it worth the while' he is referring to expected
marginal proceeds in relation to expected marginal costs.

For the reasons given above, namely that resources are employed
by firms, Keynes concentrates on the amount of labour that would
have to be employed to produce any given level of output rather than
on the output as such. When measured in terms of labour units he

denotes the amount of employment as N. He designates the aggregate supply price of the output from employing N labour units as Z. He expresses the relationship between Z and N as $Z = \phi(N)$ and calls it the *aggregate supply function*. Thus the aggregate supply function is the relationship between the proceeds, as explained above, and the number of labour units that would be expected to be required to produce the output that when sold at its supply price per unit would result in these proceeds. This relationship, therefore, is the locus of all the potential maximum profit scales of employment since it relates each possible level of employment to its corresponding aggregate supply price. On the basis of the assumptions made regarding profit maximization the aggregate supply price is the profit maximizing level of proceeds.

Given expected costs, a firm's aggregate supply function can be derived by supposing that it can imagine a set of notional demand curves to be 'facing' it. The marginal revenue curves associated with each of these demand curves can be obtained. Assuming that the demand curves are elastic the marginal revenue will be positive. Corresponding to the point at which expected marginal cost is equal to the marginal revenue associated with each of the notional demand curves there will be a price at which profit would be expected to be maximized. These prices are the supply-prices. For each supply-price and corresponding level of output there would be an amount of proceeds and a number of labour- units. The locus of the points relating them is then the firm's aggregate supply function.[4]

As more labour is required to produce more output, given organisation and technology and given that total cost and profit must be expected to increase as output increases, a curve depicting the aggregate supply function on a two-dimensional diagram showing labour-units on the horizontal axis and proceeds on the vertical axis slopes upwards to the right.[5]

User cost is not deducted in the case of the individual firm because, as Keynes points out, to do so would deprive 'our analysis of all reality...since it [would divorce] the "supply price" of an article from any ordinary sense of its "price"...' (*CW, VII*: 67).

Keynes sums up the relationship between his version of the theory of the firm and the standard theory in pointing out that the set of definitions he uses

> has the advantage that we can equate the marginal proceeds (or income) to the marginal factor cost; and thus arrive at the

same sort of propositions relating marginal proceeds thus defined to marginal factor costs as have been stated by those economists who, by ignoring user cost or assuming it to be zero, have equated supply price to marginal factor cost (*CW, VII*: 55, *footnotes omitted*).

THE AGGREGATE DEMAND FUNCTION

Given that firms operate on the basis of expectations, it seems reasonable to assume as we have done before that a firm may be envisaged as being faced with several notional demand curves. That seems to be what Keynes has in mind when he observes that

An entrepreneur, who has to reach a practical decision as to his scale of production, does not, of course, entertain a single undoubting expectation of what the sale-proceeds of a given output will be, but several hypothetical expectations held with the varying degrees of probability and definiteness. By his expectation of proceeds [is meant], therefore, that expectation of proceeds which, if it were held with certainty, would lead to the same behaviour as does the bundle of vague and more various possibilities which actually makes up his state of expectation when he reaches his decision (*CW, VII*: 24, fn.3).

Keynes refers to the proceeds as '*D*', as we have said. Since his analysis runs in terms of employment, *D* is defined as 'the proceeds which entrepreneurs expect to receive from the employment of *N* men' (*CW, VII:* 25). He writes the relationship between *D* and *N* as $D = f(N)$ and denotes it the *aggregate demand function*. This function then is the hypothetical relationship between the proceeds expected and the number of labour units implied in the production of the quantity of output that would be expected to yield the amount in question.

It is clear that the aggregate demand function is derived directly from what is deemed to be the most probable of the 'notional' demand curves. The most probable of these demand curves may be described as the *expected* demand curve. Similarly, the total revenue expected on the basis of the expected demand curve may be described as the expected total revenue. Thus the aggregate demand function is the relationships between the expected total revenue or proceeds and the number of labour-units required to produce the various quantities of output that would yield the various amounts of proceeds in question. The shape of the aggregate demand function is the same as that of the standard total revenue function.

When the demand curve 'facing' the firm is regarded as representing the entrepreneur's expectations it has to be seen as the factor, given the firm's expected costs, which determines the output it produces and the employment it gives. For that reason, as we have already seen, the expected demand curve has to be distinguished from demand as seen from the buyer's perspective. It is reasonable, therefore, to regard the expected demand curve as being one of the factors underlying the decision to supply. Accordingly, it must be interpreted as a supply-side concept. For the same reason the aggregate demand function, being derived from the expected demand curve, is also to be seen as a supply-side concept.

As the aggregate demand function differs conceptually from expenditure looked at from the buyers' perspective, the amounts that buyers might wish to spend at any given level of employment might or might not be equal to the proceeds expected by the firm at that level of employment. That is to say the expenditure associated with any given level of employment might or might not coincide with the point on the aggregate demand function corresponding to that level of employment. As with the aggregate supply function user cost is not deducted from the aggregate demand function in the case of the individual firm.

In view of the assumptions underlying the standard theory of the firm the distinction between the proceeds which the entrepreneur expects to receive and the outlays which his customers would actually make does not arise. For that reason the demand curve facing the firm from which, in conjunction with the firm's cost conditions, the profit-maximizing rate of output is derived, can quite legitimately be regarded as representing the market demand and can be seen from an outlay perspective as well as from a receipts perspective.

In Keynes's firm the proceeds expected from the sale of output are seen as governing the decision to produce output and offer it for sale. At that stage of the analysis the outlays of the customers do not yet come in for consideration as a matter of logical necessity. In the standard theory of the firm the outlays depend on the decisions of buyers but for Keynes the expected proceeds depend on the entrepreneur's guess or estimate of what the prospective buyers will spend in the future. The expected proceeds are to be seen as being only in the mind of the entrepreneurs and neither paid by nor even in the minds of the buyers.

EFFECTIVE DEMAND

The concept of the aggregate supply function and the concept of the aggregate demand function lead to a third concept, namely, that of effective demand. Keynes states that

> if for a given value of N the expected proceeds are greater than the aggregate supply price, i.e. if D is greater than Z, there will be an incentive to entrepreneurs to increase employment beyond N and, if necessary, to raise costs by competing with one another for the factors of production, up to the value of N for which Z has become equal to D. Thus the volume of employment is given by the point of intersection between the aggregate demand function and the aggregate supply function; for it is at this point that the entrepreneurs' expectation of profits will be maximized. The value of D at the point of the aggregate demand function, where it is intersected by the aggregate supply function, will be called *the effective demand* (*CW, VII*: 25).

The point of effective demand implies that the aggregate supply function and the aggregate demand function intersect if there is an expected determinate maximum profit level of output derivable from the underlying cost function in conjunction with the underlying expected demand function of the firm. That will occur if the aggregate supply price and the expected proceeds coincide for some particular level of output. As Keynes put it

> the effective demand is the point on the aggregate demand function which becomes effective because, taken in conjunction with the conditions of supply, it corresponds to the level of employment which maximizes the entrepreneur's expectation of profit (CW, *VII*: 55).

Since each point on the aggregate supply function is a potential maximum profit point, the firm will pick the highest point it thinks it can reach. That point indicates what the firm regards as the highest attainable level of profit. It is the point at which proceeds are expected to be equal to the aggregate supply price. In other words, the firm's production and employment are determined by the maximum amount of profit it can hope to achieve and that amount is indicated by the highest point on the aggregate supply function at which it expects to be able to operate. This point is given by the highest level of proceeds it can expect to receive that is, the point of effective demand.

If at any given level of employment the expected proceeds were to be greater than the aggregate supply-price the firm would not be expecting to maximize its profit. It would be operating on a scale such that the distance between its expected total revenue curve and its total cost curve would not be at its greatest. In other words, it would be operating on a scale such that the slopes of the two curves would be different. The point at which the aggregate demand function and the aggregate supply function intersect corresponds to the scale of output at which the slopes of the two curves would be the same, that is, the scale at which expected marginal cost would be equal to expected marginal revenue. It follows that as the point of intersection is approached the slope of the aggregate demand function must be less than that of the *aggregate supply function.*[6]

If the argument which seeks to justify the interpretation of the aggregate demand function as a supply-side concept is valid, it follows that effective demand must also be regarded as a supply-side concept. That this may seem paradoxical is due merely to the use of somewhat misleading terminology on Keynes's part. The use of the term 'expected proceeds' in the definition of the aggregate demand function helps to mitigate, to some extent at least, the awkwardness in interpreting a concept denoted by the word 'demand' as a supply-side one.

The point on the aggregate demand function which becomes 'effective' by reason of its being intersected by the aggregate supply function may be said to become so because the entrepreneur decides on the scale of utilization of resources indicated by the point of intersection and so the quantity of output is effectively determined. For that reason the entrepreneur's demand for labour and other inputs is also effectively determined. Thus what the entrepreneur *expects* the level of demand to be is effectively the level of output he decides to produce, given his expected costs, and equally effectively it is what determines the extent to which he employs resources.

AGGREGATION

Having established what determines the volume of output to be
produced and the amount of employment to be given by each individual firm the next logical step in the analysis is to go from the
individual firm to the economic system as a whole, given that the
question Keynes is addressing concerns the economic system as a
whole. Hence some method has to be found whereby the outputs
produced and the numbers employed by the individual firms can be
analyzed at the level of the economic system as a whole. In other
words a way of dealing with supply as a whole has to be devised.

It is obvious that the outputs of the individual firms cannot be
aggregated since they are heterogeneous. The only logical way of
conceptualizing output as a whole is, as we pointed out in Chapter
3, as an array or complex of goods and services. There is no other way
of conceptualizing total output in physical terms.

By making labour units, as he defines them, homogeneous Keynes
can add them without any ambiguity or logical difficulty. In principle,
what is being added for the purpose of analyzing the supply-side of
Keynes's theory of employment is the number of labour units which
entrepreneurs expect to hire during the period in which they expect to
produce a particular array of goods and services.

Units of money, being homogeneous, can also be added without
ambiguity. Again, of course, the aggregate relates to expected
amounts. These amounts are the proceeds which would be expected
to maximize the profit to be realized from the production of the
various possible arrays of goods and services that could be produced
by the employment of the appropriate number of labour units.

The (total) aggregate supply function ($Z = \phi(N)$) and the (total)
aggregate demand function ($D = f(N)$) can, therefore, be derived in a
precise logical way for the economy as a whole from the aggregate
supply functions and the aggregate demand functions of the individual firms. Obviously, total proceeds and total employment can be
expressed as single numerical magnitudes in a way that total output in
physical terms cannot.

Keynes writes the aggregate supply function (net of user cost) as
$Z_r = \phi_r(N_r)$. He points out that if

the relation between employment and output is such that an
employment N_r results in an output O_r, where, $O_r = \Psi_r(N_r)$ it
follows that

$$p = \frac{Z_r + U_r(N_r)}{O_r} = \frac{\phi_r(N_r) + U_r(N_r)}{\Psi_r(N_r)}$$

is the ordinary supply curve, where $U_r(N_r)$ is the (expected) user cost corresponding to a level of employment N_r (*CW, VII*: 44–5).

He then goes on to point out that in the case of a homogeneous commodity, $O_r = \Psi(N_r)$ has a definite meaning so that 'we can evaluate $Z_r = \phi_r(N_r)$ in the ordinary way' and that

we can aggregate the N_r's in a way in which we cannot aggregate the O_r's since ΣO_r is not a numerical quantity (*CW, VII*: 45).

It is possible, or rather probable, that the production *plans* of the different firms would be, to a greater or lesser extent, incompatible. There is no inherent reason why, for example, the quantities of a given factor of production that the firms would want to employ would be no greater than the quantity of that factor available for hire or purchase. This, however, does not present a problem as far as aggregation is concerned because of the fact that the analysis is conducted in terms of *expected* amounts only. Attempts actually to employ more than the amount of a factor available would not be possible but it is perfectly possible to add amounts that are merely expected irrespective of the availability of actual amounts. Moreover, since Keynes, as we have seen, links expected proceeds with labour units rather than with output as such the matter of seeking to add the outputs does not even arise.

Just as effective demand represents the firm's decision to supply so effective demand at the level of the economy as a whole represents the decisions of firms as a whole to supply. Accordingly, the supply side in the case of the economy as a whole may be defined as the array of goods and services expected to be produced during any period by the amount of employment in conjunction with the given capital equipment that would correspond to the point where the (total) aggregate demand function and the (total) aggregate supply function relating to the economy as a whole intersect.

User cost is assumed to be deducted at the level of the economy as a whole whereas it is not, as we have stressed, in the case of the individual firm. When it is deducted the supply-side at the level of the economy as a whole may also be seen as the value of the constituents of output available for consumption and for investment which is expected to be equal to the total income (including profit) expected to be generated by the production of that output.

The proceeds expected at the effective demand level of employment depend on the prices at which each firm expects to sell its output and on the quantity it expects to sell at these prices. Hence at the level of the economy as a whole a constellation of expected prices is implicit.

PRELIMINARY VIEW OF EQUILIBRIUM

In the case of the individual firm equilibrium is reached when expenditure on the firm's output would be equal to the effective demand level of proceeds. These amounts, as noted above, include user cost. That implies that in *profit-equilibrium* the expenditure at the level of employment the firm decides on would be equal to the factor incomes generated in producing the output decided upon *plus* the profit anticipated *plus* the user cost arising in the production of the output that is, to the effective demand level of proceeds. To the extent that the amount on the demand side would be less than the amount corresponding to the effective demand level of proceeds, the firm would either make less than the profit anticipated or else would make a loss. To the extent that the amount on the demand side exceeded the effective demand level of proceeds the firm would make a profit greater than that which it expected. That means that it would be, so to speak, operating on the assumption that the hypothetical demand curve facing it was lower than the 'real' demand curve. In other words, its expected demand curve was not the 'right' one so that it took the point of effective demand on its aggregate supply function to be lower than it ought to have taken it to be. Consequently, what it thought to be its maximum profit point was erroneous. Other things being equal, therefore, the firm would tend to expand employment and output in the hope of getting nearer to its 'true' demand curve.

The firm would be in equilibrium if it made the profit it expected. Realization of the expected profit is thus the necessary and sufficient condition for the equilibrium of the firm. Indeed, in an analytical context, the realization of the expected profit may be regarded as the definition of the condition in which the firm is in equilibrium. The concept of *profit-equilibrium* (and its corollary, profit-disequilibrium) is, therefore, the crucial element in Keynes's theory of the employment of available resources in the economy as a whole. It corresponds to the condition of profit maximization which, it will be recalled, is the condition for the equilibrium of the firm in the standard theory of the firm.

In the case of the economic system as a whole, again in an analytical context, the overall equilibrium would be reached when the expenditure at the effective demand level of employment would be equal to the (total) effective demand level of proceeds. In this case user cost is deducted both from the supply-side and from the demand-side (that is from proceeds and outlays) so that neither the expenditure to which the effective demand level of proceeds is equal nor that level of proceeds itself includes user cost.

It follows that when the economic system as a whole is in equilibrium the outlay incurred on the output produced in any period is equal to the total factor incomes generated in the production of that output plus the total profit expected when it was decided to produce the output in question. That is to say that the economy is in equilibrium when the total proceeds are equal to the effective demand level of proceeds at the level of employment which the firms decided to give.

For reasons which are explained in the next chapter the sums spent for consumption purposes come out of the income generated in the course of producing the output on which they are spent for that purpose. For equilibrium to arise expenditure for investment purposes must be equal to the difference between the sum spent for consumption purposes and the effective demand level of proceeds. Again, as in the case of the individual firm, when that is so, the total profit expected by all the firms taken together will have been reached. The equilibrium of the economy as a whole can, therefore, be defined as profit-equilibrium at that level.

CONCLUSION

By basing his version of the theory of the firm on expectation Keynes 'found' one aspect of the part that expectation ought to play in economic theorizing. A theory of the firm which hinges on expectation inevitably leads to the distinction between what the entrepreneur expects costs and receipts to be, on the one hand, and what buyers would actually spend on the other. Thus the seller's perception of demand and what buyers would spend are no longer conflated. Consequently, the theory of the firm becomes a theory of supply only. By explicitly couching that theory in terms of the extent to which resources are used it becomes a theory of employment also. As such it is expressed in homogeneous units of quantity. Hence it can be extended in a precise logical way to encompass the economic system as a whole. Therefore, it is a theory of the supply of output as a whole and a theory of the demand for labour as well as a theory of the extent to which capital equipment is used.

5 The Demand-Side I: Consumption

Keynes formulated the theory of the supply of output as a whole in terms of employment. The next step is to discover what governs the demand for output as a whole. As we saw in the previous chapter, he based his theory of the supply of output as a whole on the received theory of the firm. There was no received theory on the demand-side on which he could base a corresponding theory of the demand for output as a whole. Consequently, he had to develop a completely new theory for that purpose. He did so by reference to the demand for output for consumption purposes and to the demand for output for investment purposes. By reckoning consumption and investment in wage-units the employment implied on the demand-side is taken into account. Thereby, the demand for output as a whole is put on the same footing as its supply and the two sides can be analyzed with a view to the discovery of the conditions in which they would be in equilibrium.

THE PURPOSE OF PRODUCTION

Keynes's analysis of the demand for output as a whole is derived from the recognition that '[a]ll production is for the purpose of ultimately satisfying a consumer' (*CW, VII*: 46). He regards this as self-evident, observing that '[c]onsumption – to repeat the obvious – is the sole end and object of all economic activity' (*CW, VII*: 104). That implies that all income generated in the course of producing output is destined ultimately to satisfy the desire for consumption. However, income considered as a stream over time cannot be totally and continuously used for immediate consumption purposes. Unless people are to exist on a purely hand-to-mouth basis they must make provision for consumption in the future in addition to consumption in the present. That can be done only out of current income and production. Hence, the whole of a current output/income cannot be consumed immediately. Part of it has to be set aside so as to provide the basis for production and consumption in the future. Thus an output/income is used both for the purpose of current

or immediate consumption and for the purpose of making provision
for consumption in the future. The latter is investment.

Accordingly, the demand for current output is attributable to consumption and to investment. In other words, total or aggregate
demand, is the sum of the demand for current output for consumption
purposes and for investment purposes. Ultimately, therefore, aggregate demand depends entirely on consumption. Or, as Keynes puts it,
'Aggregate demand can be derived only from present consumption or
from present provision for future consumption' (*CW, VII*: 104).

In the monetary economy people can make provision for consumption in the future by financial rather than by physical means in the
expectation that their financial provision will give them command
over goods for consumption purposes in the future. Keynes notes
that people 'will reserve' part of their income 'in *some* form of command over future consumption' (*CW, VII*: 166). He points out, moreover, that we 'cannot, as a community, provide for future
consumption by financial expedients but only by current physical
output' (*CW, VII*: 104). He adds that

> In so far as our social and business organisation separates financial
> provision for the future from physical provision for the future ...
> efforts to secure the former do not necessarily carry the latter with
> them ... (*CW, VII*: 104).

It is through the profit-seeking activities of entrepreneurs that
physical provision for consumption in the future for the community
as a whole is effected. The making of financial provision for
consumption in the future is not synonymous with the investment
which constitutes the physical provision and which is, as we have
seen, part of the aggregate demand for current output. Thus the
financial provision which is made for consumption in the future by
refraining from present consumption is not a constituent of
the demand for output whereas the physical provision for future
consumption is.

It is expenditure for immediate consumption purposes only that
is directly financed by income. Other types of expenditure, whether
on a current output or not, are not directly financed out of income.
That part of an income which is not used in the first instance
to finance consumption is to be seen as an addition to personal
wealth. In that way it constitutes the making of financial provision
for consumption in the future and so does not involve demand

for current output. For analytical purpose, expenditure even for consumption purposes, other than direct expenditure out of an income on the output the production of which generates the income, must be treated as coming out of wealth. That is to say, it must be treated as coming directly out of wealth and, therefore, only indirectly out of income. Thus on the basis of Keynes's definitions it is only the expenditure for consumption purposes on the output associated with the income out of which the expenditure is made which is directly financed by that income. It follows that any sum devoted to the making of physical provision for consumption in the future out of a current output, though constituting demand for that output, comes, conceptually at least, from wealth because any such sum does not, by definition, involve the use of an income for immediate consumption. Accordingly, it may be concluded that expenditure for consumption purposes on a current output comes from the income generated by that output and from that income only. Hence Keynes's treatment of the relationship between consumption and income concentrates on the expenditure on consumption out of the income associated with the particular output on which the expenditure is incurred.

Since Keynes's purpose, as we have seen, is to formulate a theory of the demand for output as a whole in terms of employment he measures consumption in terms of wage-units. He has to do the same in respect of income. Income expressed in terms of wage-units does, however, carry with it the implication that there is a unique relationship between income and employment. Keynes is conscious of the possibility that such might not be the case. He points out that the way in which a given amount of total employment is distributed over the various industries might affect income. In general, nevertheless, he thinks it is a good approximation to regard income measured in wage-units as uniquely determined by a given amount of total employment (*CW, VII*: 90; see also Chapter 9, below).

Although consumption-expenditure in terms of wage-units is related to income in terms of wage-units in Keynes's analysis there is no implication that consumption-expenditure constitutes demand for labour. The same holds true for investment. Demand for labour comes from the entrepreneurs. Thus Keynes's analysis does not amount to a final demand theory of employment. He makes it abundantly clear that the entrepreneur has to have the means to hire labour *before* he starts a process of production.[7]

THE GAP

As an income is not entirely used directly to purchase the output associated with it there is, so to speak, a direct and an indirect demand for output. Expenditure for consumption purposes constitutes the immediate direct demand since it comes directly out of income, while expenditure for investment purposes constitutes the indirect demand because it does not come directly out of income but rather from savings – current and past. These savings are the origin of personal wealth.

In the monetary-entrepreneur economy, as we shall see in Chapter 7, money serves as an asset in addition to its being a medium of exchange. It can be added to personal wealth as an alternative to its being used directly out of income to buy output for consumption purposes. There is, as we mentioned, a 'gap', as Keynes calls it (*CW, VII*: 30), between income and what is directly spent out of it. It is the non-use of income for direct expenditure on output, on the one hand, and the degree to which personal wealth is added to rather than used to buy output or drawn on to finance investment, on the other, which opens up the possibility that there could be a difference between aggregate demand and effective demand and so to the possibility of persistent profit disequilibrium in the economy as a whole.

The possibility of persistent profit-disequilibrium as a consequence of the gap between income and consumption can perhaps be most easily seen by contrasting the monetary-entrepreneur economy with the imaginary construction of the real exchange economy. In the latter money does not serve as an asset. It is a medium of exchange only. Hence all output is immediately sold (if not retained by the producer for his own use) because, by definition, no part of income is withdrawn from immediate use. It is all spent as it is received. Thus there is no gap between income and expenditure on output. Expenditure on the making of physical provision for the future is as direct and immediate as is consumption expenditure. As a result the 'proceeds' entrepreneurs receive are what they expect to receive. That implies that outlay on expenditure is always such as to enable the entrepreneurs to earn the profit they envisaged when making their decisions to produce.

Individual entrepreneurs could, of course, make losses or greater profits than they expected because the pattern of output was not properly adjusted to the pattern of demand. Such losses and profit would only be transitory. There would always be a tendency for output to be adjusted to demand through the expansion of some types of production and the contraction of others. The existence of the gap then is a characteristic feature of the monetary-entrepreneur economy and is one of the reasons why the question as to the employment of the available resources arises. We consider this matter further in Chapter 8.

Particular individuals can spend more than their incomes on consumption in certain circumstances. Even the community as a whole could consume more than its income in some circumstances. But in the latter case, the excess of expenditure on consumption over income would not constitute demand for the output from which the income was generated. Rather it would constitute disinvestment because it would mean that goods produced in a previous period were consumed in the current period. Indeed during almost any given period, no matter how long, some of the goods consumed will have been produced prior to that period thereby giving rise to disinvestment. As Keynes puts it, 'Consumption is satisfied partly by objects produced currently and partly by objects produced previously, i.e. by disinvestment' (*CW, VII*: 105). To the extent that disinvestment of this kind arises it is taken into account in the calculation of investment and so does not appear in the aggregate demand for a current output. Aggregate demand, as we have seen, is the sum of consumption expenditure and investment expenditure.

Investment, though it is part of the demand for current output, cannot be linked directly to income by reason of the manner in which it is financed. Moreover, it is undertaken primarily because of the prospect of its being profitable. For that reason too it would not be plausible to attempt to relate the purchase of output for investment purposes to income for analytical purposes. The factors which govern consumption and investment are 'largely distinct' (*CW, VII*: 90). Hence they call for different analytical treatment. That is why the analysis of the demand for output as a whole falls into two parts unlike the analysis of the supply of output as a whole which is the subject of one unified treatment.

THE INCOME RELEVANT TO CONSUMPTION

We have already seen that total income is the sum of what is paid to the factors of production and entrepreneurial profit and that this income, or income 'proper', as Keynes designates it, is equal to the value of output. However, even if we disregard for the time being the fact that provision is made for consumption in the future by refraining from consumption in the present, the whole of income proper is not available as expenditure for consumption purposes. The reason is that entrepreneurs do not regard their profit as being disposable in its entirety for consumption purposes because of certain costs, over and above user cost, which they have to incur. Keynes refers to these costs, as we have seen, as the supplementary cost and says that its psychological effect on the entrepreneur 'when he is considering what he is free to spend and to save' is 'virtually the same as though it came off his gross profit' (*CW, VII*: 57). But in his capacity as a consumer the entrepreneur sees supplementary cost as if it were part of prime cost. Hence it must be deducted from his income or profit so as to arrive at his net income. Net income is the income on the basis of which he decides what to spend for consumption purposes.

Although windfall gains and losses are not to be taken into account in reckoning net income they may, nevertheless, influence consumption but they do not do so 'on the same scale' as supplementary cost. Changes in the latter influence the decisions of the entrepreneur as consumer '*in just the same way* as changes in his gross profit' (*CW, VII*: 58) whereas changes in the former do not.

It is clear then that net income is not 'perfectly clear-cut' since it is 'based on an equivocal criterion' (*CW, VII*: 60). It is important, nevertheless, because it is the magnitude of income which is relevant to 'decisions concerning consumption' (*CW, VII*: 60). As net income is less than income proper and as net income is what is available for consumption and saving it follows that, even if there were no saving, consumption would be less than income proper. Thus the significance of net income lies in its influence on aggregate demand. In that way it plays a rôle in determining whether any particular level of output is a profit-equilibrium one or not.

INCOME AND CONSUMPTION

A person's ability to consume depends on his means. For the community as a whole its income is synonomous with its means. Unless the relationship between consumption-expenditure and income is regular and consistent there would be no possibility of employing the income-consumption relationship in a causal sense. If the relationship between them were erratic or random it would not be possible to ground a theory on it. The main reason then for investigating the relationship between income and consumption is to ascertain its nature and thereby to establish whether or not it is sufficiently regular to provide material for the formulation of the machinery of thought which, as we have seen, Keynes understands the theory of economics to be.

He argues that the relationship between the two is in fact consistent and regular in two senses. One is that given the determinants of consumption-expenditure at any given level of income there is likely to be a relatively stable level of consumption at each level of income because the determinants of consumption, other than income, are themselves relatively stable. The second is that there is also likely to be a consistent pattern in the relationship between levels of consumption and levels of income. The first is a prerequisite for the second. Keynes sets about the task of investigating the income-consumption relationship in a manner which well exemplifies his conception of what the process of theorizing is, as we outlined in Chapter 2. He identifies the various factors other than income which might affect consumption with a view to establishing whether or not they are of a 'semi-permanent or relatively constant' nature (*CW, XIV*: 296–7; see also Chapter 2, pages 23–4) . If they are, they can be put into the pound of *ceteris paribus* and income thereby can be established as the ultimate *causa causans* of consumption-expenditure. The nature of the relationship between income and expenditure can then be examined.

THE IDENTIFICATION OF CONSUMPTION-EXPENDITURE

Normally, goods cannot be classified as consumer goods or as investment goods by reference to any inherent characteristics of the goods themselves. Whether a particular good is one or the other depends on the intentions of its owner or possessor. We cannot see into the minds of people with a view to discerning what their intentions are with respect to their goods. That, however, does not prevent us from identifying the two sets of goods in a completely unambiguous way for analytical purposes. All we have to do is to distinguish between the consumer and the entrepreneur, or rather between individuals in their capacity as consumers and in their capacity as entrepreneurs. Since we can, in principle, identify what entrepreneurs sell to each other for business purposes it follows that total sales less this amount must be sales and, therefore, purchases for consumption purposes. We have seen that Keynes designates total sales as ΣA and transactions between entrepreneurs as ΣA_1. Hence the amount spent for consumption purposes is the amount $\Sigma(A - A_1)$.

Decisions to refrain from spending for consumption purposes are decisions to save. Saving is equal to $\Sigma(A_1 - U)$, since income is $\Sigma(A - U)$ and consumption is $\Sigma(A_1 - A)$. Net saving which is the 'excess of net income over consumption', is $\Sigma(A_1 - U - V)$ (*CW, VII*: 62). Thus as Keynes observes, saving is a 'mere residual' (*CW, VII*: 64). In that connection he urges that '[c]learness of mind...is best reached, perhaps, by thinking in terms of decisions to consume (or to refrain from consuming) rather than of decisions to save' (*CW, VII*: 64–5). The reason he takes that view is because decisions to consume or to refrain from consuming lie 'within the power of the individual' (*CW, VII*: 65). So too do decisions to invest or not to invest. But while

The amounts of aggregate income and of aggregate saving are the *results* of the free choices of individuals whether or not to consume and whether or not to invest...they are neither of them capable of assuming an independent value resulting from a separate set of decisions taken irrespective of the decisions concerning consumption and investment (*CW, VII*: 65).

Saving provides the means whereby the individual can make provision for consumption in the future. Peoples' preferences for consuming in the present rather than in the future is an aspect of their time-preferences. The implied trade-off between the use of an income for immediate consumption purposes and consumption purposes in the future means that time-preference cannot be absolute at least as far as the community as a whole is concerned. To postpone all consumption to the future is obviously impossible. To make no provision for the future would reduce even the richest community to poverty in a short time.

The income and consumption with which the general theory of employment is concerned relate to the community as a whole rather than to the individual, as they must, since the purpose of this part of the theory is to analyze aggregate demand. In this connection two points may be noted. The first is that 'the community as a whole' is a concept denoting any set of people and institutions involved in economic transactions with each other and engaged in the processes of production, consumption and investment. It can, therefore, be used indifferently to refer to a country as a whole, to part of a country, to several countries, and to the whole world. The second is that it is a comprehensive concept in the sense that it embraces all individuals and institutions, including government (*CW, VII:* 375). The income in question is that generated in the course of producing a particular output. Consequently, it is logically prior to and distinct from issues relating to internal re-distribution and transfers (whether brought about by individuals or by the government) of that income. Taxation and borrowing from the 'public' by the government are not determinants of the income from which expenditure is made for consumption purposes, though they may affect the amount of expenditure for immediate consumption purposes out of that income. Thus the income which is relevant to consumption is factor-income plus net profit and as such is the income which is generated by entrepreneurial activity. In so far as government comes into the picture as a generator of income it does so solely in its entrepreneurial capacity, that is to say, only if it performs the entrepreneurial functions.

TIME-PREFERENCE

Although consumption in relation to income is analyzed at the level of the community as a whole Keynes makes it clear that he considers consumption at that level to be the result, as of necessity it must be, of individual decisions to spend on consumption and to refrain from spending for that purpose. The extent to which a person chooses to consume in the present rather than in the future depends on his time-preference. Keynes sees time-preference as having two aspects. One relates to consumption and is what he terms the propensity to consume. The other is liquidity-preference which we consider in Chapter 7 (*CW, VII:* 166).

Keynes's task then is to identify whatever might influence people's propensity to consume but which at the same time would not be likely to cause it to change much. He considers that normally 'far-reaching social changes' and the slow effects of secular progress' can be ignored in this connection (*CW, VII:* 109). He takes it also that

> in so far as the distribution of wealth is determined by the more or less permanent social structure of the community, this also can be reckoned a factor, subject only to slow change and over a long period, which we can take as given in our present context (*CW, VII:* 110).

Apart from what he regards as given, Keynes finds that people's subjective preferences to consume or not to consume are influenced by two sets of factors. One set enables them to consume more or constrains them to consume less, given income. The other set impels them either to refrain from consuming or to consume. Keynes calls the former the objective factors and the latter the subjective factors. He warns, however, that 'the attempt to classify them runs the danger of false division' (*CW, VII*: 91).

The two sets of factors taken together constitute what Keynes refers to as 'the motives to spending' (*CW, VII*: 91). By spending, in this context, he is referring, of course, to spending for consumption purposes only. It does not include expenditure incurred in the purchase of an asset.

The motives to spending determine 'for each individual how much of his income he will consume and how much he will reserve' (*CW, VII*: 91). It follows that a person's propensity to consume will be stronger or weaker depending on the strength or weakness of these motives.

MOTIVES TO SPENDING

The strength or weakness of the propensity to consume is affected by changes in what Keynes regards as the principal objective factors which he identifies as the following

(1) A change in the wage-unit other than the kind of change allowed for 'by defining the propensity to consume in terms of income measured in terms of wage-units' (*CW, VII*: 91–2);
(2) A change in the difference between income and net income;
(3) Windfall changes in capital-values not allowed for in calculating net income;
(4) Changes in the rate of time-discounting, i.e. in the ratio of exchange between present goods and future goods;
(5) Changes in fiscal policy;
(6) Changes in expectations of the relation between the present and the future level of income (*CW, VII:* 91–5).

All these factors relate directly or indirectly to income. For that reason they are properly to be regarded as objective factors in contrast to the subjective or psychological factors which relate to certain aspects of human psychology and to certain social practices and institutions. They influence peoples' attitudes to their incomes because they are likely to be perceived as expanding or contracting the possibilities of spending out of a given income.

The psychological or subjective factors lead people to spend or to refrain from spending given what they perceive to be the means available to them. Keynes enumerates 'eight main motives or objects of a subjective character which lead individuals to refrain from spending out of their incomes' *(CW, VII:* 107).

(1) To build up a reserve against unforeseen contingencies;
(2) To provide for an anticipated future relation between the income and the needs of the individual or his family different from that which exists in the present, as, for example, in relation to old age, family education, or the maintenance of dependents;
(3) To enjoy interest and appreciation, i.e. because a larger real consumption at a later date is preferred to a smaller immediate consumption;
(4) To enjoy a gradually increasing expenditure, since it gratifies a common instinct to look forward to a gradually improving standard of life rather than the contrary, even though the capacity for enjoyment may be diminishing;
(5) To enjoy a sense of independence and the power to do things, though without a clear idea or definite intention of specific action;
(6) To secure a *masse de manoeuvre* to carry out speculative or business projects;
(7) To bequeath a fortune;
(8) To satisfy pure miserliness, i.e. unreasonable but insistent inhibitions against acts of expenditure as such (CW, VII: 107–8).

Keynes calls these 'the motives of Precaution, Foresight, Calculation, Improvement, Independence, Enterprise, Pride and Avarice *(CW, VII:* 108). He also lists corresponding motives which lead to actual consumption. These are 'Enjoyment, Shortsightedness, Generosity, Miscalculations, Ostentation and Extravagance' *(CW, VII:* 108).

In addition to the motives to refrain from spending there are the motives which lead governmental and other institutions as well as business organizations to save. Such motives are 'largely analogous to, but not identical with, these actuating individuals' *(CW, VII:* 108). The most important are

(1) The motive of enterprise – to secure resources to carry out further capital investment without incurring debt or raising further capital on the market;
(2) The motive of liquidity – to secure liquid resources to meet emergencies, difficulties and depressions;

(3) The motive of improvement – to secure a gradually increasing income, which, incidentally, will protect the management from criticism, since increasing income due to accumulation is seldom distinguished from increasing income due to efficiency;

(4) The motive of financial prudence and the anxiety to be 'on the right side' by making financial provision in excess of user and supplementary cost, so as to discharge debt and write off the cost of assets ahead of, rather than behind, the actual rate of wastage and obsolescence. The strength of this motive mainly depends on the quantity and character of the capital equipment and the rate of technical change (*CW*, *VII*: 108–9).

Corresponding to the 'motives which favour the withholding of a part of income from consumption' (*CW*, *VII*: 109) there are other motives which 'at times' lead to 'an excess of consumption over income' (*CW*, *VII*: 109) as, for example, negative saving 'to provide for family needs or old age' (*CW*, *VII*: 109). Keynes holds that '[u]nemployment relief financed by borrowing' (*CW*, *VII*: 109) should also be seen as negative saving. Whether or not these motives would result, at some particular time, in consumption being in excess of income at the level of the community as a whole, that is, in disinvestment, would depend on the circumstances prevailing for the time being but could not be the general case.

STABILITY OF THE RELATIONSHIP BETWEEN INCOME AND CONSUMPTION

Having seen how Keynes establishes that net income is the income relevant to decisions concerning expenditure for consumption purposes on a current output, how he identifies consumption in a way which is suitable for analytical purposes, how he shows that there is a gap between consumption and income and how, given income, he sees consumption as being determined by various subjective and objective motives, we are now in a position to consider the central theoretical issue with regard to consumption as a component of demand, namely, the nature of its relationship to income.

Ultimately the amount spent for consumption purposes on a particular current output cannot exceed the income associated with that output. The income associated with an output is always equal to the value of the output in question. Since net income (which is the income relevant to decisions regarding consumption) as we have seen, is less than income proper, expenditure for consumption purposes will be less than income proper. At the limit, expenditure on consumption could be zero. Thus the proportion between the amount of spending for consumption purposes and the income from which it comes lies between zero and something less than unity. Its possible range can be narrowed further when the phenomenon of time-preference is taken into account. Since time-preference is not absolute, part of the income of the community as a whole is, as we have seen, reserved for future purposes and part is used for present consumption purposes. Consequently, the proportion must be greater than zero. It must, therefore, be less than unity but greater than zero.

What has to be established in the first place is whether it is plausible to assume that the relationship between consumption and a given level of income within that range is likely to be stable or not. Keynes argues that

The subjective factors ... include those psychological characteristics of human nature and those social practices and institutions which, though not unalterable, are unlikely to undergo a material change over a short period of time except in abnormal or revolutionary circumstances (*CW, VII*: 91).

Nevertheless, from country to country and from epoch to epoch the psychological motives

will vary enormously according to the institutions and organisation of the economic society which we presume, according to habits formed by race, education, convention, religion and current morals, according to present hopes and past experience, according to the scale and technique of capital equipment, and according to the prevailing distribution of wealth and the established standards of life (*CW, VII*:109).

But in a particular country during a particular epoch the psychological motives are deeply ingrained in people and so are very slow to change. They are, therefore, the motives which tend to be the primary determinants of the propensity to consume. Consequently, it is the objective factors which generally bring about changes in it. Keynes assumes that 'the propensity to consume depends only on changes in the objective factors' (*CW, VII*: 91) but is satisfied that on the whole the objective factors too are rather constant. As he puts it

Windfall changes in capital-values will be capable of changing the propensity to consume, and substantial changes in the rate of interest and in fiscal policy may make some difference; but the other objective factors which might affect it, whilst they must not be overlooked, are not likely to be important in ordinary circumstances (*CW, VII*: 95–6).

On the basis of his examination of both the subjective and objective factors Keynes concludes that

short-period changes in consumption largely depend on changes in the rate at which income (measured in wage-units) is being earned and not on changes in the propensity to consume out of a given income (*CW, VII*: 110).

In other words, since the various factors (with some relatively unimportant exceptions), other than income, which determine consumption are likely to remain unchanged over long periods they will not result in different levels of consumption at a given level of income. Consequently, the only factor that can account for different levels of consumption in the ordinary way is income itself. That is to say, it can plausibly be taken that different levels of consumption imply different levels of income and that different levels of income imply different levels of consumption.

A consequence of the comparative absence of change in the objective and subjective factors which influence consumption-expenditure out of a given income is not merely that income is the active determinant of changes in consumption but also that the relationship between income and consumption is fairly stable by reason, in particular, of the operation of the subjective motives.

Accordingly, as Keynes says,

We are left...with the conclusion that in a given situation the propensity to consume may be considered a fairly stable function, provided that we have eliminated changes in the wage-unit in terms of money (*CW, VII*: 95).

That conclusion means that Keynes is satisfied that he has established that the various influences on consumption, other than income can on the whole be regarded as constant. Consequently, they are not likely to cause consumption to change erratically at any given income. Hence, consumption may be said to be causally dependent on, or functionally related to, income. The propensity to consume at the level of the community as a whole is the outcome of all the decisions of the members of the community to consume, given their incomes. Total consumption depends on the income of the community given all the various factors that determine the propensity to consume of the individuals who make up the community. At the level of the community also, consumption depends on income or is functionally related to income. Clearly, then, income has to be regarded as the *causa causaus* and the other factors which affect consumption can be put into the pound of *ceteris paribus.*

Since for the community as a whole consumption is the outcome of the various individual decisions to consume which themselves are the outcome of the various influences we have discussed the functional relationship between income and consumption is what Keynes refers to as a 'portmanteau function'. It carries within itself the effects of the multitude of causes, both constant and varying, of what a multitude of individuals decide to consume. In this connection Keynes says,

> The fact that, given the general economic situation, the expenditure on consumption in terms of the wage-unit depends in the main, on the volume of output and employment is the justification for summing up the other factors in the portmanteau function 'propensity to consume'. For whilst the other factors are capable of varying (and this must not be forgotten), the aggregate income measured in terms of the wage-unit is, as a rule, the principal variable upon which the consumption-constituent of the aggregate demand function will depend (*CW, VII*: 96).

The 'consumption-constituent of the aggregate demand function', it will be recalled, is the proceeds which entrepreneurs expect to receive from the sale of output for consumption purposes, that is, D_1. We argued that the distinction between D_1 and D_2 is a purely analytical one. It follows that the passage quoted above is a statement relating to the theorist's perspective.

THE PROPENSITY TO CONSUME

Keynes defines the propensity to consume for the community 'as the functional relationship χ between Y_w, a given level of income in terms of wage units, and C_w the expenditure on consumption out of that level of income' (*CW, VII*: 90). He expresses it as $C_w = \chi(Y_w)$, or as $C = W \cdot \chi(Y_w)$, in symbols (*CW, VII*: 90). This expression is an example of what, as we saw in Chapter 2, Keynes refers to as a schematic equation. A schematic equation is the result of a process of reasoning. It is a conclusion briefly and conveniently summarized in the shorthand of symbols. It is nothing in itself because it has no meaning apart from the reasoning which led to it. In this case the schematic equation sums up the reasoning by which the nature of the relationship between Y_w and C_w is established and says simply that consumption depends on income in a fairly regular way, other things being equal. Thus the role of the propensity to consume, and of the schematic equation in which it is expressed, in the general theory of employment considered as an apparatus of thought is to encapsulate the nature of the relationship between consumption and income in view of all the factors that underlie that relationship.

In using the theory of consumption as a method of reasoning one is led to take into account the constant and semi-permanent influences on consumption, as well as the other factors taken as given, all of which are in the pound of *ceteris paribus* and released one by one as the matter under investigation requires. For example, if questions arise as to why consumption remained unchanged over a period while income changed or why consumption changed while income remained unchanged the answer would be likely to emerge from an investigation of the motives underlying the propensity to consume. The objective motives to consume can be observed in principle. The subjective ones, obviously, cannot. Nevertheless, like the objective motives, the subjective motives too suggest areas of investigation with a view to the discovery of possible causes of change in them.

THE SHAPE OF THE PROPENSITY TO CONSUME

Building on what he says about the propensity to consume Keynes proceeds to ask: what is 'the normal shape of this function?' (*CW, VII*: 96). The possibility of lower levels of consumption as income increases can be ruled out as that implies that, in principle, there could be a level of income so high that there would be no consumption. The parallel possibility of higher levels of consumption as income decreases can be ruled out also as that would obviously be impossible. Another possibility that has to be ruled out is that consumption would be constant irrespective of the level of income. Still another possibility is that as income increases consumption increases relatively faster. That has to be ruled out too on the grounds that it implies that there would be a level of income so high that time preference would become absolute in that the whole of the income would be consumed.

There remains only one plausible possibility and that is that consumption increases as income increases either in the same proportion as income or to a relatively lesser extent. Keynes contends that it is the second variant of this possibility which holds. He argues that there is a

> fundamental psychological law, upon which we are entitled to depend with great confidence both *a priori* from our knowledge of human nature and from the detailed facts of experience, [which] is that men are disposed, as a rule and on the average, to increase their consumption as their income increases, but not by as much as the increase in their income (*CW, VII*: 96).

In other words, the higher income is, the higher also will consumption be, but the greater also will the gap be between consumption and income.

Keynes justifies this proposition on the grounds that over short periods of time as, for example, during the course of the trade cycle, habits are not likely to change very much so that people will tend as much as possible to adhere to their usual levels of consumption. Consequently, consumption will tend not to rise very much if income rises nor will it fall very much if income falls. 'Thus' as Keynes says 'a rising income will often be accompanied by increased saving, and a falling income by decreased saving, on a greater scale at first than subsequently' (*CW, VII*: 97).

Moreover, he argues that apart from 'short-period *changes* in the level of income' (*CW, VII*: 97) a higher absolute level of income will generally be associated with a larger gap between income and consumption because

> the satisfaction of the immediate primary needs of a man and his family is usually a stronger motive than the motives towards accumulation, which only acquire effective sway when a margin of comfort has been attained (*CW, VII*: 97).

For these two reasons Keynes contends that a greater proportion of income will tend to be saved as real income increases. But whether the proportion increases or not it may be taken as a fundamental psychological rule of any modern community that, when its real income is increased, it will not increase its consumption by an equal *absolute* amount, so that a greater absolute amount must be saved, unless a large and unusual change is occurring at the same time in other factors (*CW, VII*: 97).

It is clear that what concerns Keynes in regard to the 'shape' of the propensity to consume is the nature of the difference or gap between income and consumption. What he wants to do is to establish that as income increases the absolute size of the gap gets bigger. It is that implication of the shape, and that only, which is important in the theory of employment of which the theory of consumption is one of the main constitutents. Attempts to discover formulae linking consumption to income are misplaced as they miss the point that it is the gap which is really the issue in the use to which Keynes puts the shape of the propensity to consume. In the nature of things, in any case, there can be no such formulae.

Since, as income increases the gap between income and consumption gets bigger, the gap between each increment of income and each increment of consumption gets bigger too. In symbols, $(\Delta Y_w - \Delta C_w)$ gets bigger at each increment of income. At the margin Keynes expresses the relationship between changes in consumption and changes in income as dC_w/dY_w. Obviously, the expression is positive and less than unity. Keynes defines this quantity as the marginal propensity to consume.

Because $\Delta Y_w = \Delta C_w + \Delta I_w$ an increment of investment is implicit in an increment of income. Thus the marginal propensity to consume tells us how 'the next increment of output will have to be divided between consumption and investment' (*CW, VII*: 115). That means that the division between consumption and investment implicit in an increment of output, under conditions of equilibrium, is given by the marginal propensity to consume.

The marginal propensity to consume is the foundation upon which the theory of the multiplier is based. It is, therefore, one of the essential elements in the general theory of employment. Without it the question as to the determination of the available resources could not be addressed in the way Keynes addresses it.

CONCLUDING REMARKS

By way of conclusion three further points may be mentioned briefly. First, Keynes uses the term *average* propensity to consume in the context of a comparison of the implications of the marginal propensity to consume in a 'poor country' and in a 'wealthy country' (*CW*, *VII*: 125–7). As we shall see (Chapter 8) the 'average propensity to consume' is concerned with the general disposition to use income for consumption purposes in communities of different levels of wealth. It refers to the average or typical disposition to consume in communities differing from each other in regard to wealth and income. The result of differences in the disposition to consume is that the ratios of the total amount of expenditure on consumption to total income (*C/Y*) will differ in the different communities because the proportions are themselves the result of the different strengths of the determining subjective and objective factors which affect the readiness of people to spend on consumption from the different levels of income in the various communities.

Second, by measuring consumption expenditure and income in terms of wage-units Keynes is, in effect, defining the scale of utilization of a given capital equipment implied in particular amounts of expenditure for consumption purposes out of the corresponding income.

Third, while changes in relative prices affect the allocation of expenditure over the individual goods and services consumed they do not affect the propensity to consume since that is an aspect of time-preference. Hence they do not affect the total amount spent on consumption out of a given income. Accordingly, it is not necessary to take relative prices into account in considering the demand for consumption goods as a whole either by an individual or at the level of the community.

6 The Demand-Side II: Investment

Investment is the second source of demand for current output. For the most part, Keynes's predecessors and contemporaries did not see any need to explain what determines the demand for goods for investment purposes as a whole. They took it that, savings, whether in physical terms or in monetary terms, were invested and that the rate of interest provided the mechanism which ensured that investment and savings would be equal to each other. Keynes's insight that the question as to what determines the employment of the available resources had to be addressed, his model of the monetary-entrepreneur economy and his conception of the phenomenon of interest ruled out the possibility that the rate of interest would do any such thing. Accordingly, he had to work out a theory of the demand for output for investment purposes. He did so in a way that complemented his theory of the demand for output for consumption purposes.

DEFINITION OF INVESTMENT

Keynes defines investment as 'the current addition to the value of the capital equipment which has resulted from the productive activity of [a] period' (*CW, VII*: 62). Capital equipment as we have seen includes fixed capital, working capital, and liquid capital (*CW, VII*: 52, also 75). More precisely, and in terms of his own notation, investment is '... the increment in the *value* of the entrepreneur's equipment beyond the net value which he has inherited from the previous period' (*CW, VII*: 66, *emphasis added*). It may be expressed as $[G-(G'-B')]$. As we have already seen G is 'the actual value' of an entrepreneur's capital equipment at the end of a period; G' is the value the capital equipment 'might have had at the end of the period' if the entrepreneur 'had refrained from using it and had spent the optimum sum B' on its maintenance and improvement' (*CW, VII*: 66). The term 'period' in this connection denotes *any* period of time during which production takes place. It is not to be understood as referring to a particular standard or fixed length of time.

Alternatively investment can be expressed as $\Sigma(A_1 - U)$, ΣA_1 being the total value of transactions between entrepreneurs during the relevant period (*CW, VII*: 62–3). ΣU is the aggregate user cost of the sales, (ΣA), during the period. If supplementary costs, (ΣV), as well as user cost, (ΣU), are deducted from the aggregate value of transactions between entrepreneurs, (ΣA_1), *net* investment is obtained (*CW, VII*: 63).

Since $Y = \Sigma(A - U)$ and since $\Sigma U = \Sigma[A_1 + (G' - B') - G]$, it follows that $Y = \Sigma(A - A_1) + \Sigma[G - (G' - B')]$. That means simply that expenditure for consumption purposes, $\Sigma(A - A_1)$, *plus* the amount devoted to investment, $\Sigma[G - (G' - B')]$, are equal to income, and, therefore, to the value of output and to total expenditure less user cost in both cases.

Many of the activities which constitute investment as far as individuals are concerned cannot be regarded as investment in the context of Keynes's analysis because they do not constitute demand for current output. For, as Keynes says '[i]n popular usage it is common to mean by [investment] the purchase of an asset, old or new, by an individual or a corporation' (*CW, VII*: 74–5). Occasionally, as he goes on to note

the term might be restricted to the purchase of an asset on the Stock Exchange. But we speak just as readily of investing, for example, in a house, or in a machine, or in a stock of finished or unfinished goods; and, broadly speaking, new investment, as distinguished from reinvestment, means the purchase of a capital asset of any kind out of income (*CW, VII*: 75, also 61–2, 226, 387, fn.1).

Accordingly, expenditure on newly produced output for investment purposes only is what is relevant for analytical purposes. As Keynes says '[i]f we reckon the sale of an investment as being negative investment, i.e. disinvestment... exchanges of old investments necessarily cancel out' (*CW, VII*: 75). While it is necessary 'to adjust for the creation and discharge of debts (including changes in the quantity of credit or money)' this 'complication... cancels out when we are dealing with *aggregate investment*' because for 'the community as a whole the increase or decrease of the aggregate creditor position is always exactly equal to the increase or decrease of the aggregate debtor position' (*CW, VII*: 75, *emphasis added*).

Keynes holds that his terminology corresponds to ordinary usage

assuming that income in the popular sense corresponds to my net income, aggregate investment in the popular sense coincides with my definition of net investment, namely the net addition to all kinds of capital equipment, after allowing for those changes in the value of the old capital equipment which are taken into account in reckoning net income (*CW, VII*: 75).

As we have already observed, Keynes's definition of investment does not involve distinctions based on the physical characteristics of commodities. The distinction between consumption and investment arises from the purpose for which commodities are acquired, that is, it is based on the intentions of individual decision-makers.

THE INDUCEMENT TO INVEST

By contrast to the way in which Keynes sees consumption, he sees investment as being *induced*. Consumption is a 'habitual propensity' (*CW, VII*: 373) or disposition which is ultimately limited by income. But in a monetary, as distinct from a non-monetary economy, consumption in the future is provided for both in financial and in physical terms. The former is a corollary of the propensity or disposition to consume; the latter, however, is not. In a monetary economy physical provision will be made for future consumption only if there is sufficient inducement to do so. The inducement is the prospect of a profitable return on the necessary outlays rather than a desire to provide a store of physical goods which would be available for future consumption. Thus, for example, what entrepreneurs as investors do is that they pursue their individual profits rather than that they consciously make physical provision for future consumption.

Keynes's analytical treatment of investment as compared with his treatment of consumption reflects the fact that investment, being undertaken on the basis of subjective expectations, is not, so to speak, to be taken for granted or regarded as something which is, or becomes, merely habitual. Consumption, for its part, is treated, as we have seen, as a habitual disposition of the community as a whole within the limits of its income. But the treatment of consumption and investment is similar in that its purpose is to show what limits the amounts *spent* on consumption and devoted to investment at the level of the community as a whole.

The central thrust of Keynes's reasoning is related to what induces the individual investor, as a purchaser of a physical capital asset, to undertake a particular amount of investment, that is, to buy newly-produced output as capital equipment for the purpose of making physical provision for producing output in the future (or to produce output for his own use for that purpose). In acquiring capital equipment for investment purposes the entrepreneur does so because of the contribution he expects it to make to the profitability of the enterprise in the future, that is, because of its 'prospective yield' (*CW, VII*: 135, *emphasis omitted*). Thus, in the case of commodities to be used as capital equipment, Keynes begins by noting that

> When a man buys an investment or capital-asset, he purchases the right to the series of prospective returns, which he expects to obtain from selling its output, after deducting the *running expenses* of obtaining that output, during the life of the asset (*CW, VII*: 135, *emphasis added*).

The entrepreneur must incur certain outlays in order to acquire capital equipment for investment purposes. He must pay a price for the commodity, if it is being purchased from another entrepreneur, or incur the costs of directly employed factors and of other inputs, if it is being produced by the entrepreneur himself (*CW, VII*: 53, also 67–9). He must also either possess, or have access to, the necessary financial means to incur the relevant outlays. The investment decision of the entrepreneur involves the making of a comparison between the prospective or expected yield from using the capital equipment and the cost of acquiring it. Therefore, the essence of the investment decision lies in a comparison between the expected yield and the outlays required to acquire the capital equipment.

The prospective yield from the acquisition of output for capital equipment purposes is made up of the expected series of net returns from the use of the equipment *plus* the expected 'last return' or proceeds from selling it off. It 'wholly depends on the expectation of future effective demand in relation to future conditions of supply' (*CW, VII*: 212). Given Keynes's definition of effective demand (*CW, VII*: 55; Chapter 4 above) what that means is that prospective yield depends on the points on the future aggregate demand functions which are expected to become effective because taken in conjunction with the expected future conditions of supply or aggregate supply functions they are expected to correspond 'to the level of employment which maximises the entrepreneur's expectation of profit' (*CW, VII*: 55) Keynes follows through the *logic* of what the entrepreneur does in deciding to make outlays to acquire capital equipment for investment purposes as the foundation for that part of his analysis which deals with investment.[8]

In following through this logic, he takes account of the prices of the individual commodities purchased as capital assets. This contrasts with the way in which he treats the current consumption aspect of the demand-side of his analysis where, as we have argued, the need to consider the prices of individual commodities does not arise. Prices, of course, are implicitly taken into account by means of the aggregate demand function and the aggregate supply function as far as the *sellers* of the goods destined for consumption are concerned. But as the analysis of consumption as a component of demand is necessarily based on the relationship between consumption and income, there is no need to be concerned with the process by which the consumer evaluates the worth of individual commodities for consumption purposes by reference to the individual prices of these commodities. Nor is there any need to take account of the prices of commodities in dealing with the use of income by people as consumers in order to make provision for consumption in the future since such provision is made in financial terms and, again, the matter of individual goods and their prices do not arise.

By contrast, in dealing with entrepreneurs' expenditure for investment purposes the prices of individual commodities have to be taken into account explicitly because, in seeking to explain what determines investment-demand as a whole, the matter at issue *is* the purchase of individual goods for investment purposes in the expectation of a yield in the future. Consequently the problem for Keynes is to establish how much it is worth devoting to expenditure on commodities for investment purposes and, correspondingly, to establish what amount of finance it is worth acquiring in order to purchase (or produce) such commodities. The decision as to whether it is worth buying a capital asset or not involves a comparison between the series of net returns expected from the asset and the price or cost of obtaining it. Hence, in the case of expenditure for investment purposes Keynes has to formulate the analysis in such a way that the relationship between the prices and yields of individual commodities is explained.

THE SUPPLY PRICE OF CAPITAL GOODS

As Keynes sees it, the entrepreneur-investor, in considering the purchase of newly produced output for investment purposes, is to be distinguished from the investor as fund-manager whose task is to use a given amount of funds in one way rather than another, for example, as between *holding* money, real capital assets or debts (*CW, VII*: 81, 212). The investor as fund-manager is dealing with the question as to the best way in which to hold wealth. That question is analytically quite distinct from the question as to the amount to be spent on newly produced goods for investment purposes. Keynes regards the entrepreneur-investor as the purchaser of newly produced output for capital equipment purposes rather than as the manager of a financial portfolio. The question with which the entrepreneur as investor is confronted relates to the amount it would be profitable to spend on exploiting an investment opportunity which he perceives in his line of business as a producer. That is the entrepreneurial basis for Keynes's theory of investment.

Since Keynes's purpose is to develop a system of analysis relating to the determination of the employment of the available resources in the production of a current output the analysis, as far as the demand for commodities for investment purposes is concerned, centres on the question: will it be worth the entrepreneur-investor's while to pay a price such as will make it profitable for the producer to produce the particular asset the purchase of which is being contemplated? If not, the asset will not be produced and, other things being equal, fewer resources will be employed than would be the case if it were worth the entrepreneur-investor's while to pay the price in question.

The price in question is the supply price of capital assets. Keynes defines it as 'the price which would just induce a manufacturer newly to produce an additional unit of such assets' *(CW, VII*: 135). Accordingly, it is the price corresponding to the point at which expected marginal cost is equal to expected marginal revenue and so is the price at which the *producer* of the asset would expect to maximize profit.

In dealing with investment it is the supply price as such rather than the aggregate supply price which is relevant. As we have already remarked, it is the prices of individual goods which have to be taken into account in analyzing the demand for capital goods. The supply price is a component both of the aggregate supply price and of the aggregate supply function, as has been shown in Chapter 4. As the aggregate supply price is the supply price multiplied by the number of units on offer supply prices are implied in all points on the aggregate supply function. Each of these points denotes a potential profit maximizing level of output and employment. It follows that each of them represents a level of proceeds the expectation of which would 'just make it worth the while of the entrepreneurs' (*CW, VII*: 24) to employ the labour required, in conjunction with the given capital equipment, to produce the level of output the sale of which (at the supply price) would be expected to yield that level of proceeds. Because each of these points denotes a potential profit maximizing level of output they imply equality between the potential expected marginal costs and potential expected marginal revenues.

In using the supply price in the case of goods destined for investment, Keynes is not introducing a new method of analysis as compared with his analysis of the supply-side which we have discussed in Chapter 4. All he is doing is emphasizing a particular aspect of the general analysis of the supply-side so as to make explicit what is left implicit in that analysis. The purpose of making it explicit is simply to provide the means by which individual prices can be taken into account in the analysis of the *demand* for goods intended (by the buyers) for investment purposes. In the general treatment of the supply-side it is implied that all goods are sold at their supply prices (in equilibrium) since the aggregate supply function is derived from the supply price. Firms which sell goods destined for investment are not to be thought of as acting in any way that is different from the way in which firms in general act. Whether the good a firm produces is to be used for consumption or for investment, the firm's decision as to the scale of its operations is based, in Keynes's analysis, on what is perceived to be the demand for that good in conjunction with the anticipated conditions of supply (that is effective demand). Indeed, as we have argued, the firm does not even have to be assumed to know for what purpose its product will be used.

Keynes stresses that the price to be used in the analysis of the demand for investment goods is the supply price rather than the market price. 'Over against the prospective yield of an investment', he says, 'we have the *supply price* of the capital asset...not the market-price' (*CW, VII*: 135). Obviously goods are actually bought at their market prices. The supply price is the point on the expected demand or average revenue curve at which profit is expected to be maximized. The market price is the price per unit at which all units are sold. It is, therefore, an average price. If assets are sold at their supply price the firm that produces them is in profit-equilibrium because the proceeds it receives are the proceeds corresponding to the point of effective demand. By comparing prospective yield with supply price, Keynes is, as usual, dealing with the matter at issue from the analyst's perspective. In this case while he is following through the *logic* of what the entrepreneur does, he does so not from the entrepreneur's point of view but from that of the economist.

THE MARGINAL EFFICIENCY OF CAPITAL

In order to calculate how much it is going to be worthwhile to spend on the purchase of additional capital equipment for investment purposes the entrepreneur as investor has to make an estimate of the likely return which the capital equipment will yield and compare it with the rate of interest at which the necessary funds can be borrowed. For analytical purposes this rate stands for the whole complex of rates (*CW, VII*: 137, fn.1). Even if the entrepreneur-investor has funds of his own he has to be seen as lending them to himself on terms comparable to those on which the money could be borrowed from others (compare *CW, VII*: 151, fns.1 and 2).

In order to establish how much it would be profitable for an entrepreneur to spend on a newly produced output for investment purposes the rate of discount which would make the prospective yield from an additional unit of the asset in question, over its lifetime, equal to the supply price of the additional unit is compared to the rate of interest. If the rate of discount exceeds the rate of interest at which funds are available for this use it would be profitable for the entrepreneur to spend more on capital assets of this type. This rate of discount is what Keynes terms the 'marginal efficiency of capital' which, more precisely, he defines

> as being equal to that rate of discount which would make the present value of the series of annuities given by the returns expected from the capital-asset during its life just equal to its supply price (*CW, VII*: 135).

Obviously a higher rate of discount would make the prospective yield less than the supply price whereas a lower rate of discount would make it greater than the supply price.

The marginal efficiency of capital is an expectation and, therefore, subjective. It does not depend 'on the historical result of what an investment has yielded on its original cost if we look back on its record after its life is over' (*CW, VII*: 136), but rather on 'the rate of return expected to be obtainable on money if it were invested on a *newly* produced asset' (*CW, VII*: 136). Hence, different entrepreneurs are likely to estimate the marginal efficiency of a given type of capital asset differently. This leads to the idea of 'the marginal efficiencies of particular types of capital-assets' (*CW, VII*: 135). The entrepreneur in considering the purchase of an additional unit from among the different types of capital equipment, costing different amounts per unit in the case of each type of capital equipment, calculates the expected yield per pound of expenditure on each extra unit of equipment and, being a profit-maximizer, selects the number of units which he expects will give the highest yield per pound at the margin.[9] The rates of return thus calculated are, for the purchasing entrepreneur (or producer for own use), the 'rates of return' on the supply prices and, hence, are equivalent to the rates of discount which make the prospective yields equal to the supply prices of each type of capital asset, that is, to the marginal efficiencies of the various types of capital assets. Since there are different entrepreneurs who will differ in their perception of prospective yields and who also may face different supply prices in respect of a particular type of capital asset there will be a set of these marginal efficiencies for each entrepreneur and these sets may be different in respect of the ranking of the marginal efficiencies of whatever types of capital assets the entrepreneurs may have in common.

Keynes postulates that the marginal efficiency of any particular type of capital-asset would be lower the greater the investment in that type of capital-asset. He bases this assumption on two observations: first, that the prospective yield may be expected to be less the greater the supply of that type of capital-asset; and, second, that the supply price would be higher, the greater the 'pressure on the facilities for producing that type of capital' (*CW, VII*: 136).

As pointed out in Chapter 4, profit-maximizing entrepreneurs operating with a given capital equipment are assumed to be subject to decreasing returns (also *CW, VII*: 17–8). In justifying these postulates he sees 'the second of these factors [as] being usually the more important... in the short run, but the longer the period in view the more does the first factor take its place' (*CW, VII*: 136). Hence, for each entrepreneur in respect of each type of asset, there will be an inverse relationship between the amounts that would have to be spent on the various types of capital equipment and the corresponding expected rates of return on the money-outlay necessary to cover the supply price of additional units of these types of capital equipment.

For each type of capital-asset a schedule can be built up which shows the total amount of expenditure (or cost incurred), by all the relevant entrepreneurs, for investment purposes on that type of capital-asset corresponding to various marginal efficiencies. Since entrepreneurs are taken to be profit maximizers this schedule will be a schedule of amounts of investment expenditure corresponding to the greatest of the marginal efficiencies in respect of each entrepreneur. For the reasons given above, the relationship between these total amounts of expenditure will be such that the higher the total amount of expenditure the lower will be the (greatest) marginal efficiency of that type of capital-asset.

Given Keynes's argument that the marginal efficiency of capital would be lower the greater the investment in any particular type of capital-asset, it follows that, for each type of capital-asset, this schedule shows 'by how much investment in it will have to increase within the period, in order that its marginal efficiency should fall to any given figure' (*CW, VII*: 136). As usual this statement has to be interpreted in a hypothetical rather than a descriptive sense.

Once we have schedules in respect of each type of capital-asset they can all, in principle, be aggregated even though capital-assets are heterogeneous in physical terms. That can be done because the capital-assets are expressed in terms of money units of expenditure and of percentages (the marginal efficiencies). This aggregation provides a schedule relating the rate of aggregate investment to the greatest of the marginal efficiencies of the particular types of capital-assets. The greatest of the marginal efficiencies of the particular types of capital-asset for each rate of investment is called the 'marginal efficiency of capital in general' (*CW, VII*: 136). The schedule is called the 'investment demand-schedule' or the 'schedule of the marginal efficiency of capital' (*CW, VII*: 136).

LIMIT TO EXPENDITURE FOR INVESTMENT PURPOSES

The investment demand-schedule provides the means by which Keynes can answer the question as to what the amount of expenditure on an output for investment purposes will be. In the case of expenditure for consumption purposes, the ultimate limit, as we have seen, is set by income whereas in the case of expenditure for investment purposes there is no similar limit. An overall limit in physical terms is, of course, set by the amount of resources available in the economic system. The question which then arises for Keynes is: what limits expenditure for investment purposes to some particular amount rather than another out of the various possible amounts of expenditure which would be worthwhile on the basis of the supply prices of capital-assets in relation to given prospective yields from these assets?

The criterion for assessing the worthwhileness of any investment is the cost of borrowing the amount of money required to cover the supply price of the capital-asset, that is, the rate of interest. What the investor has to be satisfied about, as we have seen already, is not only whether the yield from investing in a particular type of capital-asset is better than that from another type of capital-asset but also whether any such investment is worthwhile compared with the cost of borrowing money. By comparing the rate of return expected on an amount of money 'if it were invested in a *newly* produced asset' (*CW, VII*: 136) with the rate of interest the investor can know whether the intended investment is worthwhile or not.

As Keynes says

> it is obvious that the actual rate of current investment will be pushed to the point where there is no longer any class of capital-asset of which the marginal efficiency exceeds the current rate of interest. In other words, the rate of investment will be pushed to the point on the investment demand-schedule where the marginal efficiency of capital in general is equal to the market rate of interest (*CW, VII*: 136–7, *footnote omitted*).

If expenditure for investment purposes were to be pushed to the point where the marginal efficiency of capital in general was less than the rate at which funds could be obtained losses would be expected, whereas if the amount of investment were such that the marginal efficiency of capital in general was to be greater than the rate at which funds could be obtained it would be expected that possible gains would have been foregone.

Thus the limit to expenditure for investment purposes would be reached when the rate of discount or marginal efficiency of capital (that is, the rate of return on an amount of money corresponding to the supply price of an asset) and the rate of interest are equal. Hence, the rate of interest serves to limit the amount that it would be profitable to spend on the acquisition of newly produced output for investment purposes. In other words, the expenditure for investment purposes that will be perceived to be worthwhile is the aggregate of the supply prices of the individual commodities bought by entrepreneurs for investment purposes. As Keynes puts it, 'the inducement to invest depends partly on the investment demand-schedule and partly on the rate of interest' (*CW, VII*: 137). This raises two questions. The first is: what governs the prospective yield that underlies the investment demand-schedule? The second is: what governs the rate of interest on borrowed funds? Both of these questions relate to the nature of the economic system. Since the latter is a monetary phenomenon it relates to those aspects of the system involving the nature and use of money. The former relates to those aspects of the economic system concerned with the characteristics of the factors and of the processes which induce investment and is considered next.

LONG-TERM EXPECTATIONS

Keynes's answer to the question as to what governs the prospective yield, underlying the investment demand-schedule, is grounded on considerations which though of a 'different level of abstraction from most of [his] book' (*CW, VII*: 149) are, nevertheless, fundamental to his analysis. The considerations involved relate to the 'actual observation of markets and business psychology' (*CW, VII*: 149) in connection with what he terms the 'state of confidence' (*CW, VII*: 148, *emphasis omitted*). While the details may vary with time and place, the type of phenomena which are the subject of these considerations must be thought of as an integral part of a theory of investment. The chapter on the state of long-term expectation (*CW, VII*: Chapter 12), with its discussion of the 'psychological expectation of future yield from capital-assets' (*CW, VII*: 247), provides the underpinnings of his theory of investment in the same way as his discussion of the 'psychological propensity to consume' (*CW, VII*: 247) provided the underpinnings of his theory of consumption.

All the firm's decisions, whether they relate to the scale on which it will use its capital equipment or to the making of additions to its capital equipment, are analyzed in expectational terms. Decisions relating to the scale of operation are supply decisions while decisions relating to investment are demand decisions. Thus the firm plays two rôles in the general theory of employment. The distinction between short-term and long-term expectations reflects these two rôles. Hence, it is a functional distinction. It has nothing to do with the passage of time in the sense that it does not connote that decisions based on short-term expectations necessarily relate to a shorter period of time than do decisions based on long-term expectations.

Keynes points out that

The considerations upon which expectations of prospective yields are based are partly existing facts which we can assume to be known more or less for certain, and partly future events which can only be forecasted with more or less confidence (*CW, VII*: 147).

Among the former considerations mentioned by Keynes are

the existing stock of various types of capital-assets and of capital-assets in general and the strength of the existing consumers' demand for goods which require for their efficient production a relatively larger assistance from capital (*CW, VII*: 147).

In the latter type of consideration Keynes includes

future changes in the type and quantity of the stock of capital-assets and in the tastes of the consumer, the strength of effective demand from time to time during the life of the investment under consideration, and the changes in the wage-unit in terms of money which may occur during its life (*CW, VII*: 147).

Thus so far as the marginal efficiency of capital is concerned the wage-unit represents an aspect of the prospective running costs which entrepreneurs must consider (*CW, VII*: 141).

Of their very nature expectations relate to matters which are, to a greater or lesser extent, uncertain. It may be noted that Keynes distinguishes 'uncertain' from 'improbable' (*CW, VII*: 148, fn.1). So far as the *formation* of expectations is concerned, as Keynes points out, it is not reasonable 'to attach great weight to matters which are very uncertain', rather

It is reasonable, therefore, to be guided to a considerable degree by the facts about which we feel somewhat confident, even though they may be less decisively relevant to the issue than other facts about which our knowledge is vague and scanty (*CW, VII*: 148).

Accordingly, in Keynes's view, the existing facts

enter, in a sense disproportionately, into the formation of our long-term expectations; our usual practice being to take the existing situation and to project it into the future, modified only to the extent that we have more or less definite reasons for expecting a change (*CW, VII*: 148).

As he points out:

> The *state of long-term expectation*, upon which our decisions are based, does not solely depend, therefore, on the most probable forecast we can make. It also depends on the *confidence* with which we make this forecast-on how highly we rate the likelihood of our best forecast turning out quite wrong. If we expect large changes but are very uncertain as to what precise form these changes will take, then our confidence will be weak (*CW, VII*: 148, *first emphasis added*).

Furthermore, he draws attention to the fact that 'The *state of confidence*, as *they* term it, is a matter to which practical men always pay the closest and most anxious attention' (*CW, VII*: 148, *second emphasis added*), and he goes on to say that economists, in contrast, 'have not analysed it carefully and have been content, as a rule, to discuss it in general terms' (*CW, VII*: 148–9). The relevance of the state of confidence to economic analysis arises because of its 'important influence on the schedule of the marginal efficiency of capital' (*CW, VII*: 149).

The state of confidence is itself a determinant of the marginal efficiency of capital. As Keynes says,

> There are *not two separate factors* affecting the rate of investment, namely, the schedule of the marginal efficiency of capital *and* that state of confidence. The state of confidence is relevant because it is one of the major factors determining the former, which is the same thing as the investment demand-schedule (*CW, VII*: 149, *emphasis added*).

The extent to which business opportunities are perceived depends in part on the state of confidence. Keynes's discussion of the state of confidence is based, as we have noted already, on 'actual observation of markets and business psychology' because there is 'not much to be said about the state of confidence *a priori*' (*CW, VII*: 149). Also, '[f]or convenience of exposition', he excludes from his considerations the effects of changes in the rate of interest on the values of investments. These effects, he suggests, can be 'easily superimposed on the effect of changes in the state of confidence' (*CW, VII*: 149).

THE PRECARIOUSNESS OF KNOWLEDGE

In practice little or nothing can be known about the future yields on investments. As Keynes puts it

> The outstanding fact is the extreme precariousness of the basis of knowledge on which our estimates of prospective yield have to be made. Our knowledge of the factors which will govern the yield of an investment some years hence is usually very slight and often negligible. If we speak frankly, we have to admit that our basis of knowledge for estimating the yield ten years hence of a railway, a copper mine, a textile factory, the goodwill of a patent medicine, an Atlantic liner, a building in the City of London amounts to little and sometimes to nothing; or even five years hence. In fact, those who seriously attempt to make any such estimate are often so much in the minority that their behaviour does not govern the market (*CW, VII:* 149–50).

Despite this extreme precariousness of knowledge, investment *is*, of course, undertaken. According to Keynes investments are made because certain people are disposed to take chances and because they achieve satisfaction from constructive action apart altogether from profit. Otherwise

> If human nature felt no temptation to take a chance, no satisfaction (profit apart) in constructing a factory, a railway, a mine or a farm, there might not be much investment merely as a result of cold calculation (*CW, VII:* 150).

Keynes holds that, '[i]n former times...investment depended on a sufficient supply of individuals of sanguine temperament and constructive impulses who embarked on business as a way of life' (*CW, VII*: 150). For them the

> affair was partly a lottery, though with the ultimate result largely governed by whether the abilities and character of the managers were above or below the average. Some would fail and some would succeed. But even after the event no one would know whether the average results in terms of the sums invested had exceeded, equalled or fallen short of the prevailing rate of interest; though, if we exclude the exploitation of natural resources and monopolies, it is

probable that the actual average results of investments, even during periods of progress and prosperity, have disappointed the *hopes* which prompted them (*CW, VII*: 150, *emphasis added*).

In business, as Keynes sees it, people 'play a mixed game of skill and chance, the average results of which to the players are not known by those who take a hand' (*CW, VII*: 150). The varying fortunes of a business will alter the value of the investment and will be taken into account at appropriate intervals by the entrepreneur. However, '[i]n the absence of security markets, there is no object in *frequently* attempting to revalue an investment to which we are *committed*' (*CW, VII*: 151, *emphasis added*). Investment would not be affected to any great extent by occasional and essentially private revaluations. However, the 'separation between ownership and management' and the 'development of organised investment markets' adds a new dimension to the process of investment (*CW, VII*: 150). The essence of this new dimension is that

> the Stock Exchange revalues many investments every day and the revaluations give a *frequent* opportunity to the individual (though not to the community as a whole) to revise his commitments (*CW, VII*, 151; *emphasis added*).

While the 'daily *revaluations* . . . are primarily made to facilitate transfers of *old investments* between one individual and another', they 'inevitably exert a decisive influence on the rate of *current* investment' (*CW, VII*: 151, *emphasis added*). There are two reasons for that. One is that 'there is no sense in building up a new enterprise at a cost greater than that at which a similar existing enterprise can be purchased' (*CW, VII*: 151). (The same consideration is applicable to, for example, the purchase of a second-hand as distinct from a new machine.) The other is that 'there is an inducement to spend on a new project what may seem an extravagant sum, if it can be floated off on the Stock Exchange at an immediate profit' (*CW, VII*: 151, *footnote omitted*). Consequently

> certain classes of investment are governed by the average expectation of those who deal on the Stock Exchange as revealed in the price of shares, rather than by the *genuine expectations of the professional entrepreneur* (*CW, VII*: 151, *footnote omitted, emphasis added*).

Hence, as Keynes sees it, sometimes investment is facilitated and sometimes the instability of the system is increased as a result of the existence of the Stock Exchange (*CW, VII*: 150–1).

Given that daily revaluations of *old* investments exert a 'decisive influence' on the amount spent on newly produced output for investment purposes, Keynes proceeds to consider how these 'highly significant daily, even hourly, revaluations of existing investments' are made in practice so as to provide a complete explanation of investment (*CW, VII*: 151).

Keynes asserts that the frequent revaluations of existing investments are carried out on the basis of what really amounts to a convention, the essence of which 'lies in assuming that the existing state of affairs will continue indefinitely, except in so far as we have specific reasons to expect a change' (*CW, VII*: 152). That does not mean that we 'really believe that the existing state of affairs' will continue indefinitely. As 'extensive experience' shows, the 'actual results of an investment over a long term of years very seldom agree with the initial expectation' (*CW, VII*: 152). The convention cannot be rationalized in terms of 'errors in either direction' being 'equally probable' to a person 'in a state of ignorance' because, '[i]n point of fact, all sorts of considerations enter into the market valuation which are in no way relevant to the prospective yield' (*CW, VII*: 152). Furthermore, as Keynes recognizes, 'it is not surprising that a convention, in an absolute view of things so arbitrary, should have its weak points' so that, in addition to the precariousness of the basis of knowledge which gives rise to the convention, the convention itself is also precarious (*CW, VII*: 153). Keynes points to this precariousness as creating 'no small part of our contemporary problem of securing sufficient investment' (*CW, VII*: 153).

Even though the convention is precarious, Keynes maintains that it 'will be compatible with a considerable measure of continuity and stability in our affairs, *so long as we can rely on the maintenance of the convention*' (*CW, VII*: 152). This is so because it is in the nature of 'organised investment markets' that '[i]nvestments which are 'fixed' for the community are...made 'liquid' for the individual' (*CW, VII*: 152–3). The nature of the organized investment markets combined with a reliance on the maintenance of the convention allows that

an investor can legitimately encourage himself with the idea that the only risk he runs is that of a genuine change in the news *over the near future*, as to *the likelihood of which he can attempt to form his own judgment*, and which is unlikely to be very large (*CW, VII*: 152–3, *second emphasis added*).

So, although 'he has not any notion what his investment will be worth ten years hence', the investment is 'reasonably 'safe' for the individual investor over short periods, and hence over a succession of short periods however many' (*CW, VII*: 153). Being able to rely on 'there being no breakdown in the convention' he has, therefore, 'an opportunity to revise his judgment and change his investment, before there has been time for much to happen' (*CW, VII*: 153).

Keynes lists five factors which accentuate the precariousness of this convention. These are, in brief, that

(1) 'the element of real knowledge in the valuation of investments by those who own them or contemplate purchasing them has seriously declined' as a consequence of increasing separation of ownership and management' (*CW, VII*: 153);

(2) 'fluctuations in the profits of existing investments, which are obviously of an ephemeral and non-significant character, tend to have an altogether excessive, and even an absurd, influence on the market' (*CW, VII*: 153–4);

(3) '[a] conventional valuation which is established as the outcome of the mass psychology of a large number of ignorant individuals is liable to change violently as the result of a sudden fluctuation of opinion due to factors which do not really make much difference to the prospective yield; since there will be no strong roots of conviction to hold it steady' (*CW, VII*: 154);

(4) the distinction between 'speculation' as the 'activity of forecasting the psychology of the market' and 'enterprise' as 'the activity of forecasting the prospective yield of assets over their whole life' (*CW, VII*: 158) implies that the 'professional investor and speculator' is 'largely concerned, not with making superior long-term forecasts of the probable yield of an investment over its whole life, but with foreseeing changes in the conventional basis of valuation a short time ahead of the general public', and that they are, therefore 'concerned, not with what an investment is really worth to a man who buys it "for keeps", but with what the market will value it at, under the influence of mass psychology, three months or a year hence' (*CW, VII*: 154–5);

(5) the 'state of credit', that is, 'the confidence of the lending institutions towards those who seek to borrow from them' must also be

reckoned with, since the speculative investor himself normally has not 'unlimited command over money at the market rate of interest' (*CW, VII*: 158).

Moreover, 'apart from the instability due to speculation,' Keynes holds that there is also the 'instability due to *the characteristic of human nature* that a large proportion of our positive activities depend on spontaneous optimism rather than on a mathematical expectation, whether moral or hedonistic or economic' (*CW, VII*: 161, *emphasis added*). That is because

> human decisions affecting the future, whether personal or political or economic, cannot depend on strict mathematical expectation, since the basis for making such calculations does not exist

and because

> it is our innate urge to activity which makes the wheels go round, our rational selves choosing between the alternatives as best we are able, calculating where we can, but often falling back for our motive on whim or sentiment or chance (*CW, VII*: 162–3).

Hence

> In estimating the prospects of investment, we must have regard . . . to the nerves and hysteria and even the digestions and reactions to the weather of those upon whose spontaneous activity it largely depends (*CW, VII*: 162).

And as far as enterprise is concerned, as Keynes puts it,

> It is safe to say that enterprise which depends on *hopes* stretching into the future benefits the community as a whole. But individual initiative will only be adequate when reasonable calculation is supplemented and supported by animal spirits, so that the thought of ultimate loss which often overtakes pioneers, as experience undoubtedly tells us and them, is put aside as a healthy man puts aside the expectation of death (*CW, VII*: 162, *emphasis added*).

This implies

not only that slumps and depressions are exaggerated in degree, but
that economic prosperity is excessively dependent on a political and
social atmosphere which is congenial to the *average* business man
(*CW, VII*: 162, *emphasis added*).

Thus

if the animal spirits are dimmed and the spontaneous optimism
falters, leaving us to depend on nothing but a mathematical expectation, enterprise will fade and die – though fears of loss may have a
basis no more reasonable than hopes of profit had before (*CW, VII*:
162).

Of course,

We should not conclude from this that everything depends on
waves of irrational psychology. On the contrary, the state of long-
term expectation is often steady, and, even when it is not, the other
factors exert their compensating effects (*CW, VII*: 162).

FACTORS WHICH MITIGATE THE EFFECTS OF IGNORANCE

Unless there were organized capital markets, through which an individual's commitment to an investment could easily be liquidated (*CW,
VII*: 160), people would tend to concentrate on short-term investments, where the 'effects of our ignorance of the future' (*CW, VII*:
163) would be less than in the case of long-term investments. In
addition to the existence of organized investment markets there are
'certain important factors which somewhat mitigate *in practice* the
effects of our *ignorance* of the future' (*CV, VII*: 163, *emphasis added*).
Keynes enumerates four such factors.

The first is that there are many individual investments which,
because of 'the operation of compound interest combined with the
likelihood of obsolescence with the passage of time', are 'dominated
by the returns of the comparatively near future' (*CW, VII*: 163). Thus,
for example, in the case of a piece of machinery, the physical life of
which might be long, its commercial life might be regarded by the
entrepreneur as short because of the possibility that it could be

quickly made obsolescent. That possibility would require the entrepreneur to regard its commercial yield as accruing over a comparatively short period. Besides, although a machine could turn out to be a
long-term investment, the nearer prospective yields have a greater
impact than the more remote prospective yields in calculating the
marginal efficiency of capital because, at any given rate of interest
or discount, the present value of a given sum is smaller the more
remote the sum.

The second factor which may mitigate the effects of our ignorance
of the future on our willingness to make long-term investments is that,
in the case of 'the most important class of very long-term investments', namely buildings, the risk to the investor contemplating the
prospective commercial yield 'can be frequently transferred . . . to the
occupier, or at least shared between them, by means of long-term
contracts, the risk being outweighed in the mind of the occupier by
the advantages of continuity and security of tenure' (*CW, VII*: 163).

The third mitigating factor is the 'important class of long-term
investments' namely public utilities, which provide the investors with
a satisfactory and more or less certain commercial return on their
investment because 'a substantial proportion of the prospective yield
is practically guaranteed by monopoly privileges coupled with the
right to charge such rates as will provide a certain stipulated margin'
(*CW, VII*: 163).

Keynes points to 'a growing class of investments' as the fourth
factor which mitigates the effects of our ignorance of the future.
These are investments where, in addition to the commercial yield
aspect, there are presumed to be social advantages which carry weight
in the investment decision, although they do not enter into the calculation of prospective yield. Such investments are

> entered upon by, or at the risk of, public authorities, which are
> frankly influenced in making the investment by a *general presump-
> tion* of there being prospective social advantages from the invest-
> ment, whatever its commercial yield may prove to be within a wide
> range (*CW, VII*: 163, *emphasis added*).

For example, in the case of public authority housing, where the
commercial yield may be low, considerations of social advantage
may induce the public authorities to undertake an investment of this
type. That implies that the public authorities as investors or guaran-
tors may not seek 'to be satisfied that the mathematical expectation of

the yield is at least equal to the current rate of interest' (*CW, VII*: 163). Nevertheless, the interest cost to the public authorities of funds used to finance investment of this type 'may still play a decisive part in determining the scale of investment operations which it can *afford*' (*CW, VII*: 164, *emphasis added*). Keynes makes the same point on a number of occasions in discussing public investment as a means of securing economic stability (*CW, XXI*: 133–7; also 386, 388, 394–5).

INVESTMENT BY PUBLIC AUTHORITIES

It is clear from the foregoing that so far as his analysis is concerned Keynes is considering investment as a whole, whether it is carried out by the private investor or by a public authority. In other words, he sees the state or the government as being an integral part of the community, just as he did when he was dealing with consumption.

It is also important to remember that the context in which the investment rôle of the public authorities is envisaged relates to the gap between income and consumption. The expenditure that fills that gap in Keynes's analysis is expenditure on newly produced output for investment purposes, that is, expenditure undertaken with a view to, and on the basis of, an expected yield. In other words, when he discusses investment by the public authorities he does so in terms of 'commercial yield' (*CW, VII*: 163) and of the 'scale of investment operations which [they] can *afford*' (*CW, VII*: 164, *emphasis added*). He is not discussing the type of 'investment' which in effect is tantamount to financing consumption expenditure. The effect of expenditure of that type by the public authorities operates through the propensity to consume by altering the distribution of income. This must be seen as a fundamental conceptual distinction for the purpose of the analysis. Investment is the purchase of a newly produced capital-asset for its yield *(CW, VII*: 135). It is not a matter of financing activities *purporting* to be investment but which, in reality, are disguised forms of income redistribution.

Thus in the context of investment the public authorities are assumed to operate on the basis of the estimation of the prospective yield, the confidence with which expectations are held, and the willingness to take into account 'the general social advantage' (*CW, VII*: 164). Consequently, expenditure for investment purposes by the public authorities cannot be seen as anything other than the purchase of newly produced output undertaken with a view to a yield in the future. The part played by the 'general presumption of there being prospective social advantages' (*CW, VII*: 163) is analogous to the part played in creating confidence by the 'satisfaction . . . in constructing a factory' (*CW, VII*: 150) in the case of investment by private individuals. Hence, whatever its 'commercial yield *may prove to be* within a wide range' (*CW, VII*: 163, *emphasis added*) as compared with what was expected when making the investment decision, the presumption of general advantage would have given the confidence to justify the undertaking of the investment despite the uncertainty associated with its prospective yield (*CW, VII*: 163). Just as in the case of private individuals who might not undertake 'investment merely as a result of cold calculation' (*CW, VII*: 150), there might not be much investment by public authorities if they had 'to be *satisfied* that the mathematical expectation of the yield is at least equal to the current rate of interest' (*CW, VII*: 163, *emphasis added*). In the case of the former, the precariousness of knowledge about the future, which limits 'cold calculation', is overcome by the fact that human nature is tempted 'to take a chance' and derives satisfaction from constructing factories and so on (*CW, VII*: 150). In the case of the latter, the precariousness of knowledge about the future, which deprives us of the basis for making 'strict mathematical expectation' (*CW, VII*: 163) is overcome by the general presumption of prospective social advantage. Keynes complements this line of reasoning in his comment that

> The capital requirements of home industry and manufacture cannot possibly absorb more than a fraction of what this country, with its present social structure and distribution of wealth, chooses to save in years of general prosperity.... Building and transport and public utilities, which can use large amounts of capital, lie half way between private and public control. They need, therefore, the combined stimulus of public policy and a low rate of interest (*CW, XXI*: 394).

In other words, the public authorities, directly or indirectly, by directly undertaking or by underwriting certain types of investments extend the range of investment activity and thereby may enable a state of profit-equilibrium to prevail in the economy as a whole at high levels of income.

The foregoing implies that Keynes envisages, in so far as the argument of *The General Theory* is concerned, that debt-financed expenditure for investment purposes by the public authorities would be self-liquidating. In other words, he implies that the expenditure would constitute an investment which would be expected to generate the means of repaying the debt incurred for the purpose of financing the expenditure rather than that it would lead to an accumulation of debt which would be the counterpart of expenditure for consumption purposes. Keynes says, as we have already observed in this connection, 'the rate [of interest] which the public authority has to pay may still play a decisive part in determining the scale of investment operations which it can afford' (*CW, VII*: 163–4).

CONCLUSION

As regards investment as a whole, Keynes concludes that

> [A]fter giving full weight to the importance of the influence of short-period changes in the stage of long-term expectation as distinct from changes in the rate of interest, we are still entitled to return to the latter as exercising, at any rate, in normal circumstances, a great, though not a decisive, influence on the rate of investment (*CW, VII*: 164).

Consequently, as far as the formal statement of the general theory of employment is concerned, given a particular investment demand-schedule, the rate of interest limits the amount of expenditure for investment purposes which entrepreneurs would see as being profitable. That is to say, given the various underlying factors, the state of long-term expectations, the state of confidence and the level of entrepreneurial activity, it is the prospective yield which is the inducement to spend for investment purposes while the rate of interest limits the amount invested. Profit-equilibrium requires that the relationship between the marginal efficiency of capital in general and the rate of interest is such that the amount of expenditure for investment purposes corresponds to the gap between income, on the one hand, and expenditure for consumption purposes, on the other, at the particular scale of utilization of the given capital equipment determined by effective demand. Thus, the theory of the rate of interest plays a central rôle in the theory of profit-equilibrium.

7 The Rate of Interest

The traditional theory of interest, as Keynes understood it (*CW*, *VII*: Chapter 14, with Appendix; also *CW*, *XIV*: 101–4), was an essential part of a body of economic theory which he regarded as dealing with the 'real-exchange economy' (*CW*, *XIII*: 409). The task which he sought to undertake, therefore, was to develop an explanation of the phenomenon of interest in the monetary economic system. In doing so he saw himself as filling one of the three major gaps, as he described them, in traditional economic theory (*CW*, *VII*: 31). His theory of the determination of the rate of interest and his explanation of the rôle of the rate of interest in the economic system completes his analysis of the 'system's determinants' on the demand-side. The other two determinants, it will be recalled, are the propensity to consume and the schedule of the marginal efficiency of capital (*CW*, *VII*: 183–4).

DEFINITIONS OF THE RATE OF INTEREST AND MONEY

Having shown that '[t]he schedule of the marginal efficiency of capital may be said to govern the terms on which loanable funds are demanded for the purpose of new investment; whilst the rate of interest governs the terms on which funds are being currently supplied' (*CW*, *VII*: 165), Keynes goes on to say that '[t]o complete our theory, therefore, we need to know what determines the rate of interest' (*CW*, *VII*: 165).

His investigation of the theory of interest is based on the recognition that interest on money is 'precisely what the books on arithmetic say it means; that is to say, it is simply the premium obtainable on current cash over deferred cash, so that it measures the marginal preference (for the community as a whole) for holding cash in hand over cash for deferred delivery' (*CW*, *XIV*: 101).[10] It is

> nothing more than the percentage excess of a sum of money *contracted* for forward delivery, e.g. a year hence, over what we may call the 'spot' or cash price of the sum thus contracted for forward delivery (*CW*, *VII*: 222; *emphasis added*).

Both of these definitions imply that the incurring of a debt is what gives rise to the phenomenon of interest on money. Hence the rate of interest may be seen as the return from holding a debt. For that reason Keynes regards the term the 'price of debts' as being equivalent to the term 'the rate of interest' (*CW, VII*: 173). The equivalence between the two ways of looking at the same phenomenon may be seen from the following example. If £100 can be obtained now in exchange for £110 a year hence, the rate of interest is 10 per cent. But if £102 could be obtained now in exchange for £110 a year hence, the 'price' paid by the buyer of the debt would have risen (that is, from £100 to £102) while the rate of interest to the person obtaining the money (the 'seller' of the debt) would have fallen from 10 per cent. to 7.8 per cent. (approximately).

Keynes's definition of money is based on a pragmatic distinction between money and debts ' at whatever point is most convenient for handling a particular problem' (*CW, VII*: 167, fn.1). As an example, he notes that

we can treat as *money* any command over general purchasing power which the owner has not parted with for a period in excess of three months, and as *debt* what cannot be recovered for a longer period than this; or we can substitute for 'three months' one month or three days or three hours or any other period; or we can exclude from *money* whatever is not legal tender on the spot (*CW, VII*: 167, fn.1).

As in *A Treatise on Money* (1930), he assumes 'that money is co-extensive with bank deposits' (*CW, VII*: 167, fn.1). What constitutes money in an absolute sense is an intractable problem in practice and any definition is ultimately arbitrary. However, having made the judgement as to what is to be regarded as money, the important thing for analytical purposes is to hold consistently to the same definition.[11]

THE PURCHASE AND SALE OF DEBTS

When a loan is made a debt is incurred. The process by which the debt is incurred, as the example given above suggests, may be regarded as one of purchase and sale. Each such purchase and sale involves the acquisition of money by the seller (borrower) and the acquisition of the right to a return in the form of interest by the buyer (lender). In addition to the making of new loans, that is, the incurring of new debts, old loans or old debts are also bought and sold. In all cases the prospective buyers of the debts have money. In Keynes's analysis the rate of interest is determined by the interaction of the purchasers and the sellers of debts, both new and old.

Decisions have to be made as to whether debts will be bought or not. These decisions depend on peoples' preferences for holding ready money over money for deferred delivery, that is, on liquidity-preference. Liquidity-preference, therefore, determines the *form* in which a person 'will hold the command over future consumptions which he has reserved, whether out of his current income or from previous savings' (*CW, VII*: 166). For that reason Keynes regards liquidity-preference as the second aspect of time-preference, the first, as will be recalled, being the propensity to consume.

Thus there is a supply-side and a demand-side in the analysis of the determination of the rate of interest. It must be stressed that what is in question here is the supply of and the demand for debts as such.

There are three main elements in Keynes's analysis of the determination of the rate of interest, namely, (i) the phenomenon of liquidity-preference, (ii) debts, and (iii) money. In his analysis, the quantity of money is held constant while the influence of liquidity-preference is explained, and liquidity-preference is held constant while the influence of the quantity of money is explained. The holding of the one constant while the other is explained is an example of the use of *ceteris paribus* in the process of theorizing. In practice, of course, both liquidity-preference and the quantity of money are likely to change at the same time. However, in *The General Theory* Keynes is concerned not with practice but with theory.

Changes in the quantity of money imply corresponding changes in the total amount of debts. The way in which changes in the quantity of money occur is explained below.

LIQUIDITY-PREFERENCE

Given that the price of debts and the rate of interest are two ways of looking at the same phenomenon, the explanation of the determination of the rate of interest may be sought in the explanation of the determination of the price of debts. Like all prices, the price of debts is determined by supply and demand. Debts being bought with money and sold for money, it follows that the demand for and the supply of debts is the converse of the supply of and the demand for money. Debts are the means of acquiring money just as money is the means of acquiring debts. In this context, as we saw above, the quantity of money is assumed to be given. Hence the 'supply of money' in this context is simply the amount of money which those who hold money are prepared to offer for debts. The holding of money and the holding of debts are alternative ways of holding wealth. As we saw in Chapter 1, the holding of wealth in the form of money is the defining characteristic of the monetary, as distinct from the real exchange, economy.

Why people hold wealth in the form of debts is obvious. They get, or hope to get, a return on the debt in the form of interest. But money, however held, yields no interest. That being so, the question arises as to why people do in fact hold money. Keynes's answer to that question reveals what he considers to be the essential function of the rate of interest on money and leads to the explanation of the determination of the rate of interest. He identifies two reasons for holding money. They are based on 'the ancient distinction between the use of money for the transaction of current business and its use as a store of wealth' (*CW, VII*: 168).

The first reason is merely for the purpose of transacting current business. Money held for that purpose provides an obvious convenience both to individuals and to firms. The second reason for holding money is that it provides a way of holding personal wealth. The use of money as a 'store of wealth' (*CW, VII*: 168) in contrast to the holding of money for the purpose of transacting current business requires examination.[12] Since the holding of money does not apparently offer what the owner of wealth 'really desires', namely a *'prospective yield'* (*CW, VII*: 212), the question has to be addressed as to why people should wish to hold part of their wealth in the form of a money balance rather than in forms which yield a return. The solution to this problem lies, in the first instance, in the nature of the return on assets. That, in turn, is the basis of the demand for any particular asset including money as a means of holding wealth.

The demand for money, like the demand for any asset, whether a physical asset or not, must arise from the return which the asset is expected to give to its owner. The return from an asset arises, according to Keynes, from one or more of the 'three attributes which different types of assets possess in different degrees' (*CW, VII*: 225).

The first attribute is that

> Some assets produce a yield or output q, measured in terms of themselves, by *assisting* some process of production or supplying services to a consumer (*CW, VII*: 225, *emphasis added*).

This attribute is the basis of Keynes's view that 'It is much preferable to speak of capital as having a yield over the course of its life in excess of its original cost, than as being *productive*' (*CW, VII*: 213). By yield Keynes means that an asset 'during its life [furnishes] services having an aggregate *value* greater than its initial supply price' (*CW, VII*: 213, *emphasis added*).

The second attribute is that

> [m]ost assets, except money, suffer some wastage or involve some cost through the mere passage of time (apart from any change in their relative value), irrespective of their being used to produce a yield; i.e. they involve a carrying cost c measured in terms of themselves (*CW, VII*: 225).

The carrying cost is distinct from the running cost (that is, prime cost or the sum of user and factor costs) associated with the use of a capital-asset to produce an output. The latter is allowed for in the estimation of the yield (q) on an asset (*CW, VII*: 135). The carrying cost is concerned solely with the *holding* of a capital-asset rather than with its *use* in assisting some process of production or in supplying services to a consumer. For Keynes's purpose in *The General Theory*, it does not matter where the line is drawn 'between the costs which we deduct before calculating q and those which we include in c, since ...we shall be exclusively concerned with q-c' (*CW, VII*: 226).

The third attribute of an asset is that

> the *power of disposal* over an asset during a period may offer a potential convenience or security, which is not equal for assets of different kinds, though the assets themselves are of equal initial value (*CW, VII*: 226, *emphasis added*).

Although this 'power of disposal' leaves 'nothing to show ... at the end of the period in the shape of output [in the sense of q above]; yet it is something for which people are ready to pay something' (*CW, VII*: 226). Keynes calls

[t]he amount (measured in terms of itself) which [people] are willing to pay for the potential convenience or security given by this power of disposal (exclusive of yield or carrying cost attaching to the asset), . . . its liquidity-premium l (*CW, VII*: 226).

The potential convenience or security is purely psychological and is not a physical or objective characteristic of an asset. It will apply to any asset in different and varying degrees. It can change over time. As Keynes notes, for example, 'in certain historic environments the possession of land has been characterised by a high liquidity-premium in the *minds of owners* of wealth' (*CW, VII*: 241, *emphasis added*). Thus a liquidity-premium is 'a payment, not for the expectation of increased tangible income at the end of the period, but for an increased sense of comfort and confidence during the period' (*CW, XXIX*: 294). People are prepared to 'pay' for this benefit in the sense of foregoing the return they might obtain by parting with the power of immediate disposal. By selling land, for example, the rent obtainable from letting it is foregone.

It follows from the three attributes, possessed in different degrees by all assets, that

the total return expected from the ownership of an asset over a period is equal to its yield *minus* its carrying cost *plus* its liquidity-premium, i.e. to $q - c + l$ (*CW, VII*: 226).

This analysis reveals that while money does not offer any yield (q) and has only a negligible carrying cost (c), it offers a return in the form of a liquidity-premium 'in the minds of owners of wealth' (*CW, VII*: 241, fn.1). As Keynes further notes, while liquidity is an attribute of money, money and liquidity are not to be taken as synonymous since money can lose this attribute in certain circumstances (*CW, VII*: 241, fn.1). Keynes takes it that the essential characteristic of money is that 'its *yield* is *nil*, and its carrying cost negligible, but its liquidity-premium substantial (*CW, VII*: 226, *first emphasis added*). Accordingly, it may be concluded that

it is an essential difference between money and all (or most) other assets that in the case of money its liquidity-premium much exceeds its carrying cost, whereas in the case of other assets their carrying cost much exceeds their liquidity-premium (*CW, VII*: 226–7).

The rate of return that the holding of wealth in the form of money, as measured in terms of itself by its liquidity-premium, l, yields arises from the importance a person attaches to the holding of money, that is, to immediate command over general purchasing power. It is a purely psychological phenomenon, as we mentioned, since the holding of wealth in the form of money does not yield a monetary return. Thus, in effect, the desire for money as such, as a means of holding wealth, is a desire for the psychological benefits that the holding of wealth in the form of a money balance is perceived to offer a person. These benefits are measured by the liquidity-premium the person attaches to the holding of money.

The recognition that wealth held in the form of money (or what may be regarded as the equivalent of money) could yield a potential return of a non-monetary nature, measured by the liquidity-premium attached to money by the individual holder, provides the rationale for the holding of wealth in the form of money instead of in the form of debts or capital-assets. However, as we are concerned at this point only with explaining how the rate of interest is determined, attention must be confined to money and debts as alternative ways of holding wealth.

The analysis of the nature of the return on an asset points to the second reason given by Keynes for holding money as a store of wealth. As an asset, money possesses the advantage of being immediately disposable or usable, that is of being liquid. This advantage is valued by people, and it is measured, as we have seen, by the amount of the liquidity-premium (l) which they attach to money. In contrast debts, although yielding a monetary return in the form of an interest payment, have the disadvantage that their future value is uncertain. That is to say, the future of the rate of interest is uncertain. Keynes sees this as the necessary condition for the existence of liquidity-preference (*CW, VII*: 168). As he puts it, the answer to the question

> given that the rate of interest is never negative, why should anyone prefer to hold his wealth in a form which yields little or no interest to holding it in a form which yields interest...? (*CW, VII*: 168),

is the 'existence of *uncertainty* as to the future of the rate of interest'. This he regards as a

> necessary condition failing which the existence of a liquidity-preference for money as a means of holding wealth [as distinct

from holding it for transactions purposes] *could not* exist (*CW, VII*: 168, *emphasis added*).

Keynes contrasts the situation which would hold if it were assumed that the future was certain with what holds under the conditions of uncertainty which actually prevail, in order to establish how the existence of *uncertainty* as to the future of the rate of interest, or price of debts, gives rise to the existence of the phenomenon of liquidity-preference. In this connection it must be borne in mind that by the rate of interest he means 'the complex of rates of interest for [debts of] varying maturities which will rule at future dates' (*CW, VII*: 168).[13]

Keynes builds his argument on the fact that conditions of *certainty* would necessarily imply that all present rates of interest for debts of different maturities 'would be adjusted to the knowledge of the future rates' (*CW, VII*: 168) so that a particular determinate relationship would hold between all rates. In this situation the realization of a debt before it reached maturity would involve neither a gain nor a loss. However, when uncertainty as to future rates of interest prevails, people are faced with the fact that 'there is a risk of a *loss* being incurred in purchasing a long-term debt and subsequently turning it into cash, as compared with holding cash' (*CW, VII*: 169, *emphasis added*). The contrast between the implications of certainty and uncertainty is easily seen in terms of a simple numerical example based on the general illustration given by Keynes.

Assume that the annual rate of interest on debts maturing in five years is 3.4 per cent. and that the annual rate of interest on debts maturing in three years is 3 per cent. The present value of a £1.00 debt maturing in five years would then be £0.846 and the present value of a £1.00 debt maturing in three years would be £0.915. Under conditions of certainty the amount which the holder of the five year debt would get if he were to turn it into money after, let us say, three years can be calculated. The amount he would get would be such that it would come to £0.836 when the discount factor of 0.915 is applied to it. That amount is £0.925 (approximately). In order that the transaction would involve neither a capital gain nor a capital loss £0.925 would have to be the present value of a £1.00 debt with two years to go to maturity. That implies an annual rate of interest of 4 per cent. Thus, on the assumption made an annual rate of interest of 4 per cent. on debts of two years maturity three years hence can be inferred from the two present rates of interest. Under conditions of certainty all this would be known from the outset. But under conditions of uncertainty it would not. Hence, the holder of the five year debt would not know beforehand what he would get for it if he sold it before maturity. Accordingly, future rates of interest could not be inferred from present rates because there is no way of deducing what the rate of interest on an unknown sum would have to be in order that it would account to any given sum after any particular number of years.

As Keynes puts it in a general and more concise way

if $_1d_r$ is the value in the present year 1 of £1 deferred r years and it is known that $_nd_r$ will be the value in the year n of £1 deferred r years from that date, we have

$$_nd_r = \frac{_1d_{n+r}}{_1d_n}$$

whence it follows that the rate at which any debt can be turned into cash n years hence is given by two out of the complex of current rates of interest (*CW, VII*: 168–9).[14]

Accordingly it follows that under conditions of certainty in regard to the future of the rate of interest

If the current rate of interest is positive for debts of every maturity, it must always be more advantageous to purchase a debt than to hold cash as a *store of wealth* (*CW, VII*: 169, *emphasis added*).

In other words, since no loss could be incurred, there would be no need to hold money arising from the wish to ensure a particular capital value and there would not be any *logically necessary* grounds for the existence of liquidity-preference. Under conditions of certainty as to the future of the rate of interest it would be convenient to hold money 'for the transaction of current business' (*CW, VII*: 168). In these circumstances, money would function 'merely as a temporary convenience' (*CW, XXIX*: 77; also 67). While it would permit indirect exchange to take place, its existence would not mean that the economic system was a monetary one (*CW, XXIX*: 66–8; also 76–9; *XIV*: 115).

On the other hand, under conditions of uncertainty as to the future rates of interest on debts of different maturities 'we cannot safely infer that $_nd_r$ will prove to be equal to $_1d_{n+r}/_1d_n$ when the time comes' (*CW, VII*: 169).

Under conditions of uncertainty as to the future of the rate of interest it cannot be taken that the present rates of interest on debts of different maturities are adjusted to future rates in such a way that there will be neither a capital loss nor a capital gain on the realization of a debt before it reaches maturity. The possibility of a capital loss arising from the existence of uncertainty as to future rates of interest is, therefore, the logically 'necessary condition' for holding *wealth* in the form of money as distinct from the *convenience* of holding money for transactions purposes. Once this uncertainty is there, there has to be a liquidity-premium. Thus the existence of liquidity-preference is the outcome of uncertainty regarding future rates of interest.

In addition to this necessary reason for the existence of a liquidity-preference for money there is, according to Keynes 'a further ground for liquidity-preference' (*CW, VII*: 169). Under conditions of uncertainty, apart from the possibility of loss on the realization of debts before maturity as already discussed, there is also the possibility of a *gain*, by reason of the emergence of a regular or 'organised market for dealing in debts' (*CW, VII*: 169) which permits speculation (*CW, VII*: 158–9). The possibility of gain is a further ground for the existence of liquidity-preference because

> different people will estimate the prospects differently and anyone who differs from the predominant opinion as expressed in market quotations may have a good reason for keeping liquid resources in order to profit, if he is right, from its turning out in due course that the $_1d_r$'s were in a mistaken relationship to one another (*CW, VII*: 169, *footnote omitted*).

Consequently, as Keynes puts it, 'expectations as to the future of the rate of interest as fixed by mass psychology have their reactions on liquidity-preference' (*CW, VII*: 170), so that the individual

> who believes that future rates of interest will be above the rates assumed by the market, has a reason for keeping actual liquid cash, whilst the individual who differs from the market in the other direction will have a motive for borrowing money for short periods in order to purchase debts of longer term (*CW, VII*: 170, *footnote omitted*).

Keynes also notes that this implies that the market price of debts 'will be fixed at the point at which the sales of the 'bears' and the purchases of the 'bulls' are balanced' (*CW, VII*: 170). Thus the necessary condition for the existence of the phenomenon of liquidity-preference, namely, the possibility of loss, is reinforced by the possibility of gain arising from the existence of an organized market for debts. The basic reason for liquidity-preference is uncertainty as to the future of the rate of interest on money. That reason is strengthened by the existence of organized markets for debts.

Two points may be noted here. First, the fact that interest as such, apart from risk and administrative charges, is paid justifies Keynes's assertion that there are psychological advantages to be gained from holding money as otherwise no inducement would be necessary to get people to part with it. Second, since interest is the compensation for parting with the return from holding money, that is, for foregoing the perceived benefits of holding money, as measured by its liquidity-premium, it follows that a person will hold wealth in the form of money if the return from holding debts is regarded as an inadequate compensation for parting with money.

It is now convenient to draw together the main elements of Keynes's explanation of the determination of the rate of interest as developed up to this point. There is a supply-side which comprises individuals and institutions in their capacity as holders of money. For the purpose of the formal statement of the theory, the quantity of money is assumed to be constant. That implies that the banking system is taken to be neither a net creator nor destroyer of money. Thus, in effect, the supply-side is concerned with the rôle of people and institutions as holders of the existing quantity of money and with what motivates them to buy debts with it. The supply-side, therefore, relates to the means of acquiring debts. It is not concerned in this context with the supply or creation of new money.

On the demand-side, there are two reasons for wishing to acquire money, namely, to transact current business and to use it as a store of wealth. With a given amount of money in existence, the public's requirements for money for these two purposes must be met by that given quantity. It follows, therefore, that those who want a greater part of the given total amount of money than they already hold have to induce others, in their capacity as current holders of money, to part with it if the requirements of the former are to be satisfied. Given that the holding of money may yield a non-monetary return, measured by its liquidity-premium, it also follows that a person holding money has to be offered an inducement to part with it. This inducement must overcome the psychological advantages of holding money. The inducement is effected by means of a debt, the price of which must be such as will be sufficiently attractive to lead someone to buy the debt and, thereby part with money. In other words, the money rate of interest is the inducement which may lead people to part with money they currently possess. That is what lies behind the common sense definition of interest to which Keynes refers, as we have already seen (page 118 above). The amount of interest which a person who is parting with money is prepared to accept for parting with a particular amount reflects the sacrifice of parting with what are perceived to be the net advantages of holding that amount of money. As Keynes says

> ...the mere definition of the rate of interest tells us in so many words that the rate of interest is the *reward for parting with liquidity for a specified period*. For the rate of interest is, in itself, nothing more than the inverse proportion between a sum of money and what can be obtained for parting with control over the money in exchange for a debt for a stated period of time (*CW, VII*: 167, *emphasis added, footnote omitted*).

Thus, given that money is held for two reasons, to transact current business and to serve as a store of wealth, on the one hand and given the quantity of money in existence, on the other hand, it follows that the rate of interest or price of debts must be such as to leave those holding debts and those holding money satisfied. That means that the desire to hold money and the desire to hold debts are in balance. By implication, if this balance were to be different, by virtue of a shift in the willingness of people and institutions to hold debts as against money, the price of debts and so the rate of interest would also be different.

One particular point needs to be emphasized in regard to Keynes's explanation of the determination of the rate of interest. It is the purchase and sale of debts and the consequent transfer of money from the purchasers to the sellers which actually determines the price of debts, and therefore, the rate of interest. In other words, given the stock of money, it is the pressures arising from the desire to hold the given amount of money in existence in relation to the desire to hold debts which determines the inducement, that is the rate of interest, which has to be paid by those wanting more of the given quantity of money than they already possess to those who already hold the money in order to induce the latter to forego the advantages of holding that money themselves.

THE MOTIVES FOR HOLDING MONEY

In addition to the convenience that the holding of money affords for the purpose of engaging in transactions Keynes establishes, as we have seen, that money is held as a store of wealth for two reasons, namely, the fear of incurring a capital loss and the prospect of making a capital gain. Accordingly, three aspects or 'divisions' (*CW, VII*: 170) of liquidity-preference may be distinguished. Underlying these three divisions and corresponding to them are what Keynes terms the motives for holding money. These motives are the transactions-motive, the precautionary-motive and the speculative-motive (*CW, VII*: 170). He uses them as the framework within which the determination of the actual rate of interest can be explained in terms of their strength or otherwise, given the quantity of money in existence.

Keynes stresses that, 'Money held for each of the three purposes forms...a single pool, which the holder is under no necessity to segregate into three water-tight compartments' (*CW, VII*: 195). The purposes 'need not be sharply divided' in the mind of the holder and 'the same sum can be held primarily for one purpose and secondarily for another' so that

> we can – equally well, and, perhaps, better – consider the individual's aggregate demand for money in given circumstances as a single decision, though the composite result of a number of different motives (*CW, VII*: 195).

But even though there is only one pool of money, the three motives identified for analytical purposes must be examined separately so as to develop an understanding of their rôle in the economic process and, thereby, their place in the overall analytical scheme.

The transactions-motive is 'the need of cash for the current transaction of personal and business exchanges' (*CW, VII*: 170). One aspect of this motive is the income-motive. It originates from the need to hold money 'to bridge the interval between the receipt of income and its disbursement' (*CW, VII*: 195) and for which the

> strength...in inducing a decision to hold a given aggregate of cash will *chiefly* depend on the amount of income and the normal length

of the interval between its receipt and its disbursement (*CW, VII*: 195, *emphasis added*).

The other aspect of this motive is the business-motive which arises because

> cash is held to bridge the interval between the time of incurring business costs and that of the receipt of the sale- proceeds; cash held by dealers to bridge the interval between purchase and realisation being included under this heading (*CW, VII*: 195),

and for which '[t]he strength ... will *chiefly* depend on the value of current output (and hence on current income), and on the number of hands through which output passes' (*CW, VII*: 195–6, *emphasis added*).

The precautionary-motive is 'the desire for security as to the future cash equivalent of a certain proportion of total resources' (*CW, VII*: 170), so as

> To provide for contingencies requiring sudden expenditure and for unforeseen opportunities of advantageous purchases, and also to hold an asset of which the value is fixed in terms of money to meet a subsequent liability fixed in terms of money (*CW, VII*: 196).

Since 'there is no necessity to hold idle cash to bridge over intervals if it can be obtained without difficulty at the moment when it is actually required' (*CW, VII*: 196), the strength of both the transactions and precautionary motives will also

> *partly* depend on the cheapness and the reliability of methods of obtaining cash, when it is required, by some form of temporary borrowing, in particular by overdraft or its equivalent (*CW, VII*: 196, *emphasis added*).

Although 'likely to be a minor factor except where large changes in the cost of holding cash are in question' (*CW, VII*: 196), the strength of both of these motives will also depend on the relative cost of holding money. For example, the cost of holding money is increased, and the motive weakened, if 'the cash can only be retained by forgoing the purchase of a profitable asset', whereas the cost of holding money is decreased, and the motive strengthened, if 'deposit interest is earned or if bank charges are avoided by holding cash' (*CW, VII*: 196).

The speculative-motive is 'the object of securing profit from knowing better than the market what the future will bring forth' (*CW, VII*: 170). It is concerned with forecasting 'the rate of interest as given by changes in the prices of bonds and debts of various maturities' (*CW, VII*: 197) and is a feature of organized markets (*CW, VII*: 169). It is, essentially, tantamount to 'anticipating what average opinion expects the average opinion to be' (*CW, VII*: 156; also 159). Thus speculation is 'the activity of forecasting the psychology of the market' (*CW, VII*: 158). The liquidity-preference for money as a means of *holding wealth* due to the speculative-motive arises because

> the individual, who believes that future rates of interest will be above the rates assumed by the market, has a reason for keeping actual liquid cash, whilst the individual who differs from the market in the other direction will have a motive for borrowing money for short periods [i.e. setting short-term debts] in order to purchase debts of longer term instead (*CW, VII*: 170, *footnote omitted*).

By its nature, the speculative-motive is highly influenced by changes in the 'news' or in the 'atmosphere' (*CW, VII*: 155). As a result the market is 'subject to waves of optimistic and pessimistic sentiment, which are unreasoning and yet in a sense legitimate where no solid basis exists for a reasonable calculation' (*CW, VII*: 154). Thus, the strength of the speculative-motive is highly changeable and inevitably the subject of great uncertainty. It depends on how each person thinks changes in the news will affect other people's expectations (*CW, VII*: 198) as well as on the confidence with which forecasts are made (*CW, VII*: 148). Ultimately then it depends on expectations 'as to the future of the rate of interest as fixed by mass psychology' (*CW, VII*: 170).

These considerations lead to the conclusion that the rate of interest will be higher or lower depending on the strength or weakness, on balance, of the motives underlying liquidity-preferences, given the quantity of money.

THE RELATIONSHIP BETWEEN THE RATE OF INTEREST AND THE QUANTITY OF MONEY

The final stage in the formulation of Keynes's explanation of the determination of the rate of interest involves an examination of the specific relationship between the rate of interest and the amount of money in the economic system. This requires consideration of the logical implications of different possible amounts of money, on the assumption that the state of liquidity-preference remains unchanged. In other words, possible variations in the strength of the particular motives relating to each of the three particular reasons for holding money are set aside for the time being while differences in the quantity of money are considered in relation to the rate of interest.

The rationale for the approach Keynes follows in order to establish the relationship between various hypothetical amounts of money and the rate of interest is founded on the observation that it is of the very nature of a monetary economic system that, as we have already seen, money will be held not only to transact current business but also for precautionary and for speculative purposes. He points out that

In *normal circumstances* the amount of money required to satisfy the transactions-motive and the precautionary-motive is mainly a resultant of the general activity of the economic system and of the level of money-income (*CW, VII*: 196, *emphasis added*),

and that

the demand for money to satisfy [these] motives is generally irresponsive to any influence except the actual occurrence of a change in the general economic activity and the level of incomes (*CW, VII*: 197).

It follows that, within limits, there is no *direct* connection between the amount of money that would be held to satisfy the transactions-motive and the precautionary-motive on the one hand and the rate of interest as such on the other (also *CW, VII*: 168; also 196–7). By contrast, the amount of money that would be held to satisfy the speculative motive is, by its very nature, directly related to the rate of interest since that motive is concerned with the decision whether to hold wealth in the form of money or debts.

Building on these considerations, Keynes prepares the ground for his analysis by treating the holding of money as if there were two distinct amounts of money held for satisfying the three divisions of liquidity-preference, namely, for (i) the transactions-motive and the precautionary-motive taken together and (ii) the speculative-motive. While he accepts that 'the amount of cash which an individual decides to hold to satisfy the transactions-motive and the precautionary-motive is not entirely independent of what he is holding to satisfy the speculative-motive' (*CW, VII*: 199), he takes it to be 'a safe first approximation to regard the amounts of these two sets of cash-holdings as being largely independent of one another' (*CW, VII*: 199). He designates the amount of money that would be held to satisfy the transactions and precautionary motives taken together, as M_1 and the amount that would be held to satisfy the speculative-motive as M_2. Corresponding to these 'two compartments of cash' (*CW VII*: 199) there is a relationship between the rate of interest and the quantity of money which people wish to hold for these two purposes and which Keynes designates as the liquidity functions L_1 and L_2. The liquidity function corresponding to M_1 is L_1. It 'mainly depends on the level of income'. L_2 is the liquidity function corresponding to M_2. It 'mainly depends on the relation between the current rate of interest and the state of expectation' (*CW, VII*: 199). On this basis he sets out the framework within which to develop the analysis further as follows

$$M = M_1 + M_2 = L_1(Y) + L_2(r)$$

M is the amount of money in existence all of which has to be held. M_1 and M_2 are the notional sub-divisions of this amount. The liquidity function corresponding to an amount of income (Y) is L_1. It determines the amount M_1. The liquidity function of a particular rate of interest (r) is L_2. It determines M_2 (*CW, VII*: 199–200).

In using that schematism it is important to keep in mind that the amounts of money M_1 and M_2 are only conceptual distinctions relating to the motives of persons for holding money. The purpose of the schematism is to provide a summary framework within which Keynes conducts his detailed analysis of what determines the relationship between different possible amounts of money and the rate of interest.

THE QUANTITY OF MONEY AND THE RATE OF INTEREST

The logical starting point for the analysis of the relationship between different possible quantities of money and the rate of interest is the way in which differences in the quantity of money arise.

The amount of money in the economic system is the result of the activities of the banking system. Prior to *The General Theory*, Keynes had dealt comprehensively with monetary matters, including the technical process by which money is created and destroyed, in several books (1913, 1923, 1930) articles and memoranda. As we have seen, he saw the development from *A Treatise on Money* (1930) to *The General Theory* as a 'natural evolution in a line of thought [which he had] been pursuing for several years' (*CW, VII: xxii*), so that the *Treatise* must be seen as complementary to *The General Theory* in matters relating to the banking system. For that reason it was not necessary for Keynes to go over the same ground again so that, as he says, 'technical monetary detail falls into the background' in *The General Theory* (*CW, VII:* xxii).

For the purpose of the analysis in *The General Theory* the essence of the process by which the amount of money in the economic system comes into being is through a banking system in which commercial banks operate, subject to a central bank or monetary authority, as 'dealers in money and debts and not in assets or consumables' (*CW, VII*: 205; also 174, 200, 205–6, 247). The monetary authority itself is not 'as a rule, an equally willing dealer in debts of all maturities' (*CW, VII*: 206). As dealers in debts, the activities of the banks in purchasing debts (which includes the making of loans), create the deposits which constitute the money in the economic system. Thus, having defined money as co-extensive with bank deposits (*CW, VII*: 167, fn. 1), the willingness or otherwise of the banking system to purchase debts gives it the power to determine the amount of money in existence. The banks, as business enterprises, endeavour to maximize profit. Hence it is plausible to assume, for analytical purposes, that they are dealing in debts to the limit given by the requirements set down by the monetary authority and by their own expectations of profit. Consequently, other things being equal, the purchase of a new debt can be made only if another debt is correspondingly reduced.

That is the essence of the money-creation process (or supply-side) as Keynes describes it in *The General Theory*. Additional money comes into existence when the banking system as a whole is a net purchaser of debt. Thus, in this context, he can 'sometimes regard' the 'quantity of money as determined by the action of the central bank' as one of the 'ultimate independent variables' in the economic system although 'capable of being subjected to further analysis' (*CW, VII*: 246–7). The creation of money cannot, in general, be related specifically to the rate of interest because the amount created is, essentially, the result of a quasi-political decision by the monetary authority. The public must hold the amount of money actually in existence but the 'quantity of money is not determined by the public' (*CW, VII*: 174). For purposes of analysis a clear distinction must, therefore, be kept on the one hand between the fact that while there is an inverse relationship between the quantity of money and the rate of interest, this relationship is not in the nature of a supply schedule, and on the other, the fact that the monetary authority may try to influence the rate of interest by changing the quantity of money, by open market operations or by relaxing the conditions of credit because it considers the rate of interest inappropriate.

Since the process by which money is created by the banking system is one in which debts are purchased from the public and from the government by the banks, it follows that all the money in existence must be taken to be the counterpart of debt and that it was acquired, in the first instance, by the sale of debt to the banking system. It also follows that with a given quantity of money, the government and the public can acquire money by selling debt to the non-banking public, that is, to other members of the public in their capacity as holders of money.

Given the process by which additional quantities of money are created it follows that a greater amount of money is brought into existence 'by a relaxation of the conditions of credit by the banking system, so as to induce someone to sell the banks a debt or a bond in exchange for the new cash' (*CW, VII*: 200). That inducement takes the form of a higher price for a debt or bond. Consequently, a lower rate of interest is the concomitant of the greater quantity of money, other things being equal.[15]

The task of isolating the relationship between the rate of interest and different possible quantities of money held by the public is complicated by the fact that the rate of interest and income are also related. Hence, in order to establish the relationship between the rate of interest and different possible quantities of money the effect of the rate of interest on income and by implication, therefore, on the holding of money for transactions purposes, has to be taken into account. Obviously, to do otherwise, would be tantamount to the assumption that the level of income could be taken to be constant at different rates of interest. Such an assumption would be inconsistent with Keynes's argument.

Other things (capital equipment, the propensity to consume, the marginal efficiency of capital and the state of liquidity-preference) being unchanged, the rate of interest and the level of income are related to each other. The level of income itself depends on the amount of investment that entrepreneurs consider it would be profitable to undertake. Given the marginal efficiency of capital that amount depends on the rate of interest. Thus, a higher level of income would mean, other things unchanged, that more money would be required to satisfy the transactions and precautionary motives.

But given the nature of the monetary economy, a portion of any additional amount of money would go towards the purchase of debts, thereby lowering the yield on these debts. Since 'every fall in the rate of interest may increase the quantity of cash which *certain* individuals will wish to hold because their views as to the future of the rate of interest differ from the market views' (*CW, VII*: 172, *emphasis added*), it follows that more money will also be held to satisfy the speculative-motive. Thus, the augmented amount of money would be used to satisfy the two broad divisions of liquidity-preference.

This brief description of the processes which would be set in motion by an increase in the amount of money provides the justification for Keynes's analytical argument that the equilibrium levels both of income (Y) and of the whole complex of rates of interest (r) would have to be such that the amount of money held to satisfy the transactions and precautionary motives (M_1) and the amount of money held to satisfy the speculative-motive (M_2), would be the total amount of money in existence (M). As he puts it

> The division of the increment of cash between M_1 and M_2 in the new position of equilibrium will depend on the responses of investment to a reduction in the rate of interest and of income to an increase in investment. Since Y partly depends on r, it follows that a given change in M has to cause a sufficient change in r for the resultant changes in $M1$ and $M2$ respectively to add up to the given change in M (*CW, VII*: 201, *footnote omitted*).

Keynes's conclusion that 'a change in M can be *assumed* to operate by changing r, and [that] a change in r will lead to a new equilibrium partly by changing M_2 and partly by changing Y and therefore M_1 (*CW, VII*: 200–1, *emphasis added*) is based on a combination of empirical observation and intuition as to what the *outcome* of a change in the quantity of money is likely to be. But since he is developing a *theory* of interest he must go beyond this in order to derive a logical basis for this outcome. That is to say he must establish the conditions which would logically produce this outcome taking the notional (and, therefore, unobservable) division of M into M_1 and M_2 with their corresponding liquidity functions, L_1 and L_2 into account. Moreover, he must establish whether or not such conditions could be taken to be plausible in relation to the 'facts of experience'. That means that he must establish the nature of the relationships between r and M_1 and between r and M_2. In other words, he must establish what determines the 'shapes' of L_1 and L_2 (*CW, VII*: 200). Besides, for the analysis to be carried further, it is necessary for him to establish not only that L_1 and L_2 have determinate shapes but also that they have shapes which are consistent with each other. Otherwise the relationship between the quantity of money held and the rate of interest would be arbitrary. Were that to be the case, it would not be possible to reach a logical conclusion as to the effect of differences in the quantity of money on the rate of interest.

THE SHAPES OF THE LIQUIDITY FUNCTIONS

In order to establish the shapes of the liquidity functions Keynes has to address two questions. The first is: how do we know that more money will be used for transactions (and precautionary) purposes if there is an increase in Y? The second is: how do we know that there will be an increase in the price of debts?

If more money is to be absorbed in the satisfaction of the transactions-motive the income velocity-of-money would have to be such that it would not change in a manner that would counterbalance the change in the quantity of money. It is necessary, therefore, that the velocity of that part of the quantity of money held to satisfy the transactions-motive (M_1) be constant in relation to income. Otherwise a change in the quantity of money could be compensated, as far as transactions are concerned, by a contrary change in the income-velocity of money. Keynes points out that there is no reason to suppose that the income-velocity of money is constant under all circumstances. But unless it can be established that it is plausible to assume that velocity is more or less constant the logical argument could not be pursued any further. He justifies his taking it to be constant on the grounds that 'its value will depend on the character of banking and industrial organisation, on social habits, on the distribution of income between different classes and on the effective cost of holding idle cash' so that 'if we have a short period of time in view and can safely assume no material change in any of these factors, we can treat [the income-velocity of money] as nearly enough constant' (*CW, VII*: 201).

Thus, assuming that the income-velocity of money is constant, the shape of the relationship between the quantity of money held and the rate of interest will be such that the lower the rate of interest the greater will be the amount of money held to satisfy the transactions-motive. In other words, as Keynes puts it, 'it is *likely, cet. par.,* that more money will be absorbed by liquidity-preferences due to the transactions-motive' (*CW, VII*: 171), since income and, therefore, the volume of transactions, will be higher the lower is the rate of interest. Accordingly,

> the amount of money which it is convenient to keep for transactions will be increased more or less *proportionately* to the increase in income; whilst, at the same time, the cost of the convenience of plenty of ready cash in terms of loss of interest will be diminished (*CW, VII*: 171–2, *emphasis added*).[16]

Thus there is a determinate relationship, albeit indirect, between the quantity of money held as M_1 to satisfy the transactions-motive and the rate of interest. However, given the velocity of money and its constancy, M_1 will not absorb the whole of an increase in the quantity of money. The balance, therefore, must be absorbed by M_2. Once the income-velocity-of-money is taken to be constant, it necessarily follows that the augmented quantity of money will be absorbed into M_1 and M_2, respectively, in the same proportions as before.

We have already seen that Keynes attributes the 'type of liquidity-preference L_2 which leads to the holding of cash M_2' to the existence of uncertainty as to the future of the rate of interest (*CW, VII*: 201). It follows 'that a given M_2 will not have a definite quantitative relation to a given rate of interest of r' because

> what matters is not the *absolute* level of r but the degree of its divergence from what is considered a fairly *safe* level of r, having regard to those calculations of probability which are being relied on (*CW, VII*: 201).

However, he suggests that, in any *given state of expectation*, a lower rate of interest will be associated with the holding of a greater amount of money to satisfy the speculative-motive for two reasons. The first is that, given the general view as to what is a 'safe' level of the rate of interest (or the price of securities), the wider the divergences of market rates of interest below what is considered to be the safe rates the higher will be the perceived risk of illiquidity (*CW, VII*: 202). Hence, people will be disposed to hold money rather than debts. Therefore, the lower the rate of interest, the greater is the quantity of money held by reason of the speculative-motive and, obviously this determinate shape of L_2 is consistent with the determinate shape established in the case of L_1. The second reason is that every fall in the rate of interest reduces the current earnings from illiquidity, which as Keynes says, 'are available as a sort of insurance premium to offset the risk of loss on capital account' (*CW, VII*: 202).[17] Thus the more the rate of interest is below what is considered to be the 'safe' level, the less the amount of the annual or running yield available to offset an expected capital loss arising from a fall in the price of the debt, consequent on an increase in the rate of interest towards the 'safe' rate of interest. For example, if the safe rate is considered to be 5 per cent. and if the current rate is 2 per cent. it would be expected that there would be a very large increase in the rate of interest and, consequently, a substantial capital loss for which the yield could not compensate. Thus, it would be preferable to hold money rather than to buy the debt.

For these two reasons, the lower the rate of interest compared with what is considered to be the safe rate, the more money will people wish to hold as compared with the situation in which the rate of interest is closer to the safe rate. Thus, for the reasons identified, it can be taken that L_1 and L_2 have comparable shapes, denoting in each case that there is an inverse relationship between the amount of money held and the rate of interest.

Keynes places particular emphasis on the rôle played by M_2 and the speculative-motive in transmitting the effect of differences in the quantity of money to the rate of interest. He illustrates the argument encapsulated in his schematic equation as to how the interplay between the two sets of motives brings about the relationship that holds between the quantity of money and the rate of interest by pointing out that

> if the liquidity-preferences due to the transactions-motive and the precautionary-motive are assumed to absorb a quantity of cash [M_1] which is not very sensitive to changes in the rate of interest as such and apart from its reactions on the level of income, so that the total quantity of money [M], less this quantity, is available for satisfying liquidity-preferences due to the speculative-motive, the rate of interest and the price of bonds have to be fixed at the level at which the desire on the part of certain individuals to hold cash (because at that level they feel 'bearish' of the future

of bonds) is exactly equal to the amount of cash available for the speculative-motive [M_2]. Thus each increase in the quantity of money must raise the price of bonds sufficiently to exceed the expectations of some 'bull' and so influence him to sell his bond for cash and join the 'bear' brigade. If, however, there is a negligible demand for cash from the speculative-motive except for a short transitional interval, an increase in the quantity of money will have to lower the rate of interest almost forthwith, in whatever degree is necessary to raise employment and the wage-unit sufficiently to cause the additional cash to be absorbed by the transactions-motive and the precautionary-motive (*CW, VII*: 171).

The existence of a definite relationship between the rate of interest and the quantity of money may now be seen to depend on the following:

(1) the desire of people to hold their wealth in the form of money;
(2) the nature of interest as the payment which has to be made to overcome this desire;
(3) the fact that all money has to be held;
(4) the fact that the actual rate of interest on money is the 'price' that balances the desire to hold wealth in the form of money with the amount available.

Keynes's argument, as we have outlined it, establishes the grounds for each of these four elements of his explanation of the determination of the rate of interest. The reason for the first is that although money is obviously held to satisfy the transactions and precautionary motives, as well as to satisfy the speculative-motive, it is the latter which is 'particularly important in transmitting the effects of a *change* in the quantity of money' (*CW, VII*: 196). That is the reason his method of analysis is ultimately centred on the holding of wealth either in the form of money or in the form of debts. The second reflects his view that the essential nature of interest is synonymous with the price of debts. In the case of the third, as Keynes put it, if his explanation is correct, then 'the quantity of money is the other factor, which, in conjunction with liquidity-preference, determines the actual rate of interest in given circumstances' (*CW, VII*: 167–8).

The fourth follows from Keynes's contention that the rate of interest is 'the "price" which equilibrates the desire to hold *wealth* in the form of cash' with the available quantity of cash (*CW, VII*: 167, *emphasis added*). From which he concludes that this implies that if the rate of interest were lower, i.e. if the reward for parting with cash were diminished, the aggregate amount of cash which the public would wish to hold would exceed the available supply, and that if the rate of interest were raised, there would be a surplus of cash which no one would be willing to hold (*CW, VII*: 167).

In other words, Keynes's definition of the rate of interest on money implies that there is a particular type of relationship between the quantity of money and the rate of interest. To understand this part of Keynes's argument it is necessary always to bear in mind that his statements are made in the context that money is only one of the ways in which people may seek to hold their wealth but, at the same time, that the amount of money which people must actually hold at any time *is* the total amount of money in existence in the economic system. Hence, given that all the money in existence has to be held, Keynes establishes that the relationship between any given amount of money in existence in the economic system and the rate of interest must be such that a rate of interest other than the rate of interest at which people are satisfied to hold all the money in existence cannot logically prevail.

Furthermore, again arising from the logical necessity that all the money in existence at any particular time must be held, it also follows that, given a particular amount of money, the stronger the desire for holding wealth in the form of money, the lower will be the preference for holding wealth in the form of debts; thus the lower will be the price of debts and the higher, therefore, will be the rate of interest. The converse will also hold. More generally, since wealth can be held in the form of physical assets, besides money and debts (*CW, VII*, 212; also 142, 81–2), the return at the margin from holding money, debts and physical assets, other things being equal, must be the same (*CW, VII*: 142, also 212–13). Given a particular amount of money, the rate of interest must be such as to balance the attempts to hold wealth in the form of money and the attempts to hold it in the form of debts. Or as Keynes himself says

the rate of interest is, in itself, nothing more than the inverse proportion between a sum of money and what can be obtained for parting with control over the money in exchange for a debt for a stated period of time (*CW, VII*: 167, *footnotes omitted*).

Keynes encapsulates his theoretical argument in symbolic form as $M = L(r)$ (*CW, VII*: 168), which is to be read as the schematic equation elucidating the general idea (Chapter 2 above) that the rate of interest (r) must be such as to balance or equilibrate the quantity of money in the economic system with the strength of the desire to hold *wealth* in the form of money. Consequently, the rate of interest is determined by the strength of liquidity-preference, in conjunction with the quantity of money. Liquidity-preference, therefore, has the inherent capacity (in Keynes's words it is 'a potentiality or functional tendency') to fix 'the quantity of money which the public will hold when the rate of interest is given' (*CW, VII*: 168). This, as he says, 'is where, and how, the quantity of money enters into the economic scheme' (*CW, VII*: 168).

CORRESPONDENCE BETWEEN THE QUANTITY OF MONEY AND THE RATE OF INTEREST

Keynes summarizes his explanation as to how the rate of interest is determined in the proposition that

> in any given state of expectation there is in the minds of the public a certain potentiality towards holding cash beyond what is required by the transactions-motive or the precautionary-motive, which will realise itself in actual cash-holdings in a degree which depends on the terms on which the monetary authority is willing to create cash (*CW, VII*: 205),

where the potentiality for holding money to satisfy the speculative-motive is 'summed up in the liquidity function L_2' (*CW, VII*: 205). He goes on to point out that 'corresponding to the quantity of money created by the monetary authority, there will, therefore, be *cet. par.* a determinate rate of interest or, more strictly, a determinate complex of rates of interest for debts of different maturities' (*CW, VII*: 205). He draws attention to the fact that the same thing, 'would be true of any other factor in the economic system taken separately' (*CW, VII*: 205). For example, there would be a correspondence between any given quantity of money and the prices of individual goods. However, so far as he is concerned, for these kinds of correspondences to be 'useful and significant' for the purposes of analysis, there must be 'some specially direct or purposive connection' (*CW, VII*: 205) between the quantity of money and the other factors. This clearly does not hold in the case of the prices of individual goods. Such correspondences, being neither purposive nor direct, could not be regarded as providing an adequate foundation for 'causal analysis' (*CW, VII:* 39).

The kind of a purposive connection to which Keynes alludes is an example of the fact that a theory, or apparatus of thought, could not be based on randomly connected phenomena, that is, on phenomena which are not related in a causal way to one another. But in the case of the correspondence between the quantity of money and the rate of interest, there is 'a special connection' of a direct and purposive nature arising 'from the fact that, broadly speaking, the banking system and the monetary authority are dealers in money and debts and not in assets or consumables' (*CW, VII:* 205). The 'extent to which the price of debts as fixed by the banking system is "effective" in the market (in the sense that it governs the actual market-price) varies in different systems', depending on the specific practices in different banking systems. These variations must be allowed for in applying the theory in any particular case (*CW, VII:* 206; also 205–8). In this connection also Keynes states that

> it is ... important to distinguish between the changes in the rate of interest which are due to *changes in the supply of money* available to satisfy the speculative-motive, without there having been any change in the liquidity function, and those which are primarily due to *changes in expectation* affecting the liquidity function itself (*CW, VII:* 197, *emphasis added*).

THE RATE OF INTEREST – A PSYCHOLOGICAL PHENOMENON

Keynes describes the rate of interest as 'a highly psychological phenomenon' (*CW, VII:* 202) because liquidity-preference is an aspect of time preference and because of the particularly volatile rôle the speculative-motive plays. The possibility that expectations may change and therefore, also the willingness of people to hold debts or money, recalls the reasons for the existence of liquidity-preference itself, namely, the existence of uncertainty as to the future of the rate of interest or price of debts. Thus, even with a given quantity of money the rate of interest may change if the balance of expectation within the community shifts. Keynes illustrates the force of this possibility by reference to the likelihood that a monetary policy intended to reduce the long-term rate of interest may fail due to the possibility that M_2 would increase more or less indefinitely once the rate of interest had fallen below a certain level. This would tend to happen if public opinion saw the policy as being experimental or liable to change in the near future. Conversely, the very same policy might be quite successful in a situation where the public views it as credible or, as Keynes puts it, 'reasonable and practicable and in the public interest, rooted in strong conviction, and promoted by an authority unlikely to be superseded' (*CW, VII*: 203). This aspect of the determination of the rate of interest is the basis for Keynes's further characterisation of the rate of interest as 'a highly conventional, rather than a highly psychological, phenomenon' since its 'actual value is largely governed by the prevailing view as to what its value is expected to be' (*CW, VII*: 203).

We have now reached the point where the theory of the determination of the rate of interest on money is completed and, thereby, also the theory of the employment of the available resources.

8 Profit-Equilibrium

A preliminary view of the magnitudes at which equilibrium would hold was given in Chapter 4. Now that all the elements of the theory of employment, including Keynes's resolution of the perplexities that confronted him, his method of dealing with the supply-side, his explanation of what determines consumption and investment on the demand-side as well as his explanation of the nature and function of the rate of interest are in place, it is possible to provide a comprehensive account of these magnitudes and of their interrelationships with one another. These interrelationships lead naturally to the concept of equilibrium that is inherent in the general theory of employment.

THE EQUILIBRIUM OF THE FIRM

As has been shown in Chapter 4 the firm is assumed to seek to maximize profit. With that end in view it is thought of as making its decisions in regard to the scale of its output and in regard to the employment of the resources required to produce the output decided upon in the light of the proceeds it expects to receive from the sale of the output. The firm has to operate on the basis of expectations because it does not know the future. That being so, the analysis has to allow for a demand for the firm's output which is conceptually quite distinct from the demand which the firm *expects*. It is distinct in that it is the result of decisions made by buyers – consumers, investors and firms – and not by the selling firm itself. Inter-firm transactions cancel out at the level of the economic system as a whole. That is why Keynes's treatment of the demand side is confined to an examination of the factors that determine the decisions of consumers and investors – the final buyers.

Normally, the firm can only estimate or guess as best it can what the decisions of buyers will be. Only if its estimate or guess as to what its customers would spend were to be the same as what the customers decided to spend would the firm receive by way of sales-proceeds what it expected to receive. In such a case the sales-proceeds would cover the factor incomes generated in the process of production and the user cost incurred and leave the profit which the firm sought to achieve.

Thus the proceeds would equal the total income (factor cost plus profit) the firm hoped to generate and in addition would cover user cost in full. For that reason the firm could be described as being in equilibrium. Moreover, since the profit aimed at would be obtained, the equilibrium could be designated as what Keynes calls 'profit equilibrium' (*CW, VII*: xxiii). This is the essence of the concept of equilibrium developed in *The General Theory*.

Profit equilibrium implies that all the costs incurred in the production of any current output by means of the application of labour to a firm's capital equipment are covered by the proceeds received from the sale of that output (including in sales any addition the firm might make to its capital equipment by 'purchasing' its own output) and that profit is maximized.

In view of the question Keynes is addressing, as explained in Chapter 4, he is primarily concerned with the resources which firms employ. The extent to which labour units are employed in conjunction with a firm's capital equipment indicates the degree to which the resources are employed. Accordingly, as shown in Chapter 4 also, it is necessary to relate the proceeds expected from the sale of the firm's output to the number of labour-units required to produce the output. The concept of effective demand relates to the employment of the number of labour-units which would be expected to yield the maximum profit.

Similarly, as shown in Chapters 5 and 6, the demand-side is expressed in terms of wage units, thereby allowing the number of labour units implied in purchases to be taken into account. This is done so that the supply-side and the demand-side would be comparable and so that, as a result, the possibility of an equilibrium between the two sides could be established. Such an equilibrium would hold if the effective demand level of employment were to be equal to the level of employment implied in the demand for the firm's output. Keynes refers to the latter as aggregate demand. Thus the conditions of profit equilibrium may be said to hold when employment (in the individual firm) is such that effective demand and aggregate demand are equal. As the value of the current output of a firm is equal to the income generated in the production of that output (Chapter 3), the equilibrium conditions may also be expressed in terms of the value of the output at which the profit component of the corresponding income is the level of profit expected at the effective demand level of employment.

For every state of expectation there is a corresponding level of effective demand. It follows that for every state of expectation there is a *potential* profit equilibrium. In practice if a firm were to make more profit than it expected it would tend to expand and thereby increase employment and generate more income. If it were to make less profit than it expected it would tend to contract its scale of operation thereby reducing employment and income or else it would tend to try to produce the same level of output at a lower cost either by reducing payments to the factors or by employing fewer factors. In both cases the income generated would be reduced unless the reduction in factor costs were to be counterbalanced by an increase in profit.

The non-attainment of the profit expected when the firm decides on a particular level of employment implies that it is mistaken as to what Keynes formalizes as the aggregate demand function. The foregoing analysis draws attention to the fact that firms are normally likely to be so mistaken and that, therefore, they are continuously seeking to correct their errors. It also indicates that the process of correcting them tends to be accompanied by changes in income and in employment. Keynes observes that

> Entrepreneurs have to endeavour to forecast demand. They do not, as a rule, make wildly wrong forecasts of the equilibrium position. But, as the matter is very complex, they do not get it just right; and they endeavour to approximate to the true position by a method of trial and error. Contracting where they find that they are overshooting their markets, expanding where the opposite occurs. It corresponds precisely to the higgling of the market by means of which buyers and sellers endeavour to discover the true equilibrium position of supply and demand (*CW, XIV*: 182).

He also remarks, as we already mentioned, that 'it is probable that the actual average results of investments, even during periods of progress and prosperity, have disappointed the hopes which prompted them' (*CW, VII*: 150).

These statements, superficially at least, seem to be contradictory. They are merely impressions as to what actually happens and so do not affect the logic of the theory the proper purpose of which is to help the observer or analyst to understand and explain about why firms in certain circumstances might have performed better or worse than expected. Above all it must be emphasized that the first quotation above does not imply that there is an equilibrium position that exists objectively and which could be 'found' if entrepreneurs were to search for it for a sufficiently long time. What Keynes is doing is contrasting the continuous process of trial and error by which firms try to attain their objective of making as much profit as they can and staying in business with the formulation of this process in a theoretical way and its conceptualization in terms of profit-equilibrium.

In this connection Keynes says in the notes that he prepared for his lectures in 1937 that he feels that if he were writing the book again he should begin by stating his theory 'on the assumption that short-period expectations were always fulfilled; and then have a subsequent chapter showing what difference it makes when short-period expectations are disappointed' (*CW, XIV*: 181). To do that would be to simplify the exposition as the hypothetical conditions of equilibrium would be revealed more directly. Nevertheless, the conceptual distinction between expected demand from the point of view of the seller and demand from the point of view of the buyer would remain.

THE EQUILIBRIUM OF THE ECONOMY AS A WHOLE

The individual firm is in equilibrium when profit is maximized. The conditions for profit maximization are that the effective demand level of employment in the firm is equal to the level of employment implied in the money demand for the firm's output and that therefore at that level of employment the money receipts are equal to the expected proceeds. For this to be so receipts must cover user cost.

Since amounts of money and numbers of labour units only are involved in the analysis of the firm they can be aggregated and the total supply side therefore can, in principle, be arrived at as shown in Chapter 4. Similarly, on the demand-side what is spent on consumption and what is devoted to investment are expressed in money terms and in wage-units thereby giving the number of labour-units implied so that all the individual demands can also be aggregated and a total demand-side obtained in respect of any period to which the expected amounts on the demand-side relate. This total also includes user cost since it is identical with the receipts received by firms in respect of their current output.

Thus the 'total' supply may be represented as the employment which would be required to produce output the value of which would cover total factor cost and total user cost and leave the maximum aggregate profit. The demand-side may be represented as the employment implied in expenditure for consumption plus expenditure

for investment plus the expenditure that covers user cost. If the
employment implied in the demand-side were to be such as to be
equal to the employment on the supply-side which would result in
maximum aggregate profit, the economy as a whole would be in
(profit) equilibrium. As user cost is the same on both sides it cancels
out. Hence equilibrium holds at the level of the economy as a whole if
the amounts spent on consumption and devoted to investment and the
employment implied therein were to be equal to factor cost plus
maximum (that is, the effective demand level of) profit and the
employment required to produce the output that would yield that
amount of value.

In symbols (denoting factor cost as F, user cost as U, profit as π,
consumption as C, investment as I, and income as Y) the magnitudes
on both sides may be expressed as follows:

	Supply-Side	Demand-Side
	$F + \pi + U =$	$C + I + U$
Therefore,		
	$F + \pi \quad =$	$C + I$
or	$Y \quad =$	$C + I$

Profit equilibrium holds when π is equal to the effective demand
profit, that is, expected maximum profit. All quantities are to be
understood as being in wage-units.

Since, as has already been shown (Chapter 5), C is less than Y, I
must be such as to make $C + I$ equal to the Y at which π would be at
its effective demand level if equilibrium at the level of the economy as
a whole is to hold.

If π were to be less than its effective demand level, the employment
implied in $C + I$ would be less than the employment at the effective
demand level and so would not be maintainable. If π were to be
greater than its effective demand level the employment implied in Y
would be greater than the effective demand level. That would imply
that some or all firms had underestimated demand in the sense that
the total of the aggregate demand functions would imply a lower
effective demand level of employment than could have been achieved.

The equilibrium position in the economy as a whole is the sum of all
the equilibrium positions of each firm. This must be so because it is
only at the level of the individual firm that the profit the prospect of

which would induce the firm to embark on a particular scale of production could be identified. Hence for analytical purposes total profit has to be the sum of these individual profits. It would serve no analytical purpose to try to devise an equilibrium statement which would allow for the balancing of below equilibrium profits by above equilibrium profits. Descriptively, of course, firms that make larger profits than expected tend to expand while those that make less tend to contract. This tendency, however, is what the analysis draws attention to. It is not itself part of the analysis.

One important difference between the formal statement of the conditions of equilibrium at the level of the firm and at the level of the economy as a whole may be noted. In the case of the firm the demand comes from buyers and it does not matter what the intentions of the buyers are, nor is it necessary to be concerned with whether the source of the demand is income or not. All that is necessary is that the employment implied in what the customers buy from the firm (including what the firm 'buys' from itself) be the same as the effective demand level of employment.

In the case of the economy as a whole, however, it is necessary to emphasize that the portion of the demand which is for consumption purposes comes from, or is financed by, the income generated by the output which is being demanded. This is necessary so as to make clear that the other portion of demand, that for investment purposes, has to be equal to the difference between the expected effective demand level of income (F + effective demand π) and what is spent for consumption purposes out of that income if (profit) equilibrium is to hold.

It may also be noted that while $C + I$ is always equal to Y the equality does not necessarily imply equilibrium. It is only if the profit component of income is the effective demand level that the equality between $C + I$ and Y also denotes equilibrium. The arithmetical equality between $C + I$ and Y is a definitional or accounting one. The equilibrium condition (profit is at its effective demand level) is an analytical requirement which is derived from the nature of the method of theorizing that Keynes employs.

For equilibrium to hold there are, of course, a number of prerequisites. Given the effective demand level of employment and the propensity to consume, the marginal efficiency of capital and the rate of interest must be such as to lead to the level of investment that when added to consumption will amount to a level of demand which will produce the effective demand level of profit. Furthermore, the quantity of money and the state of liquidity-preference must be such as will produce the rate of interest in question.

Effective demand determines employment. Indeed, effective demand is defined as the amount of employment which when combined with the given capital equipment will produce an output the proceeds expected from which would be expected to maximize profit. It is because that amount of employment would be expected to yield the maximum profit that it is the amount that would be decided upon. Only an effective demand level of employment could be a profit-equilibrium level of employment. But an effective demand level of employment is not necessarily also a profit-equilibrium one. As has been shown, for an effective demand to maximize profit, as distinct from merely being expected to do so, aggregate demand must be equal to effective demand.

As the supply-side is defined in terms of the intersection of the aggregate demand function and the aggregate supply function, in the case of each firm, effective demand is a unique combination of labour units and expected proceeds. The output which corresponds to the relevant number of labour units is also unique. In the economy as a whole, therefore, effective demand denotes a unique array of individual outputs produced by a definite total number of labour units and expected to yield a definite total sum of proceeds. In graphical terms effective demand would be denoted by a point. That means that the supply-side has to be conceptualized as a point defining the number of labour units at which the expected proceeds would maximize profit.

On the other hand aggregate demand, in the economy as a whole, can be conceptualized as a function or curve relating labour units to total expenditure for consumption and for investment purposes. It is only if this function passes through the effective demand point that profit-equilibrium holds.

In order to obtain the effective demand level of employment and expected proceeds for the economy as a whole it is necessary only to add the expected proceeds and number of labour units corresponding to the point of effective demand in each firm. It is not necessary to add all the individual aggregate demand functions and all the individual aggregate supply functions. Logically it seems best to analyze the supply side in the case of the individual firm in terms of the aggregate demand and aggregate supply functions and confine the conceptualization of the supply-side in the case of the economy as a whole to the point of effective demand. This may also be thought of as the aggregate supply price of output as a whole (the array of outputs) at the level of employment upon which entrepreneurs decide. Profit equilibrium holds when expenditure on the array of output in question is equal to its aggregate supply price.

Keynes sometimes refers explicitly to the equilibrium level of employment as when, for example, he points out that 'given the propensity to consume and the rate of new investment, there will be only one level of employment consistent with equilibrium; since any other level will lead to inequality between the aggregate supply price of output as a whole and its aggregate demand price' (*CW, VII*: 28). But sometimes he leaves equilibrium implicit in his discussions of effective demand as, for example, when he says that 'the effective demand, being the sum of the expected consumption and the expected investment, cannot change, if the propensity to consume, the schedule of the marginal efficiency of capital and the rate of interest are unchanged. If without any change in these factors, the entrepreneurs were to increase employment as a whole, their proceeds will necessarily fall short of their supply-price' (*CW, VII*: 261). It seems clear from the context that Keynes is here referring to the profit-equilibrium level of effective demand and employment.

THE MULTIPLIER

So far the supply-side and the demand-side pertaining to the economy as a whole and the conditions of equilibrium appropriate to them have been derived from the individual firm, the individual consumer and the individual investor. The analysis of the economy as a whole as a result, apart from the way in which user cost is treated, is the counterpart of the analysis of the individual firm, the individual consumer and the individual investor.

There is, however, an element in the analysis of the economy as a whole which has no counterpart at the individual level. That is the concept of the multiplier. Investment is erratic compared with consumption. Nevertheless, there is a determinate relationship between investment and income. The multiplier or 'the logical theory of the multiplier' (*CW, VII*: 122) is the way by which Keynes formulates this relationship. He does so in terms of its being a corollary to the propensity to consume.

The multiplier is the analytical device which is to be used as a framework for explaining in general terms 'how fluctuations in the amount of investment, which are a comparatively small proportion of the national income, are capable of generating fluctuations in aggregate employment and income so much greater in amplitude than themselves' (*CW, VII*: 122). It is the method of addressing questions relating to differences (or changes) in the employment of the available resources, given the capital equipment and the propensity to consume and is, therefore, an essential part of the general theory dealing with the employment of resources. Keynes refers to it as 'an integral part of our theory of employment, since it establishes a precise relationship, given the propensity to consume, between aggregate employment and income and the rate of investment' (*CW, VII*: 113).

The starting point for the derivation of the principle of the multiplier is the propensity to consume. Income determines consumption given the propensity to consume. Hence income is logically prior to consumption. Consequently, again given the propensity to consume, consumption cannot be seen as being able to change autonomously. But investment can be regarded as being able to change independently of income since it depends on the relation between the marginal efficiency of capital and the rate of interest. In (profit) equilibrium $Y_w = C_w + I_w$. It follows that $\Delta Y_w = \Delta C_w + \Delta I_w$, if equilibrium is to be maintained. The multiple by which income is greater (or increases) if investment is greater, or if there is an increment of investment, is $\Delta Y_w / \Delta I_w$. Keynes denotes this magnitude, the investment multiplier, as K.

Since $\quad\quad\quad \Delta C_w/\Delta Y_w + \Delta I_w/\Delta Y_w = 1$
it follows that $\quad \Delta C_w/\Delta Y_w + 1/\Delta Y_w/\Delta I_w = 1$.
That implies that $\quad \Delta C_w/\Delta Y_w = 1 - 1/K$.
At the margin $\quad\quad 1 - 1/K = dC_w/dY_w$.

It will be recalled from Chapter 5 that dC_w/dY_w is the marginal propensity to consume, which shows 'how the next increment of output will have to be divided between consumption and investment' (*CW, VII*: 115). Thus given the propensity to consume, if profit equilibrium is to hold, an increment of investment will be accompanied by an increment of output which is a determinate multiple of the increment of investment and by an increment of consumption which is the difference between the increment of output and the increment of investment. In other words, an increment of investment implies a determinate increment in income and in consumption given the propensity to consume if profit equilibrium is to hold.

A further implication of the logical theory of the multiplier is that an increment in investment must also be accompanied by a corresponding increment in saving since the difference between income and consumption is saving (Chapter 3). Keynes argues that an increment in investment cannot take place unless there is a corresponding increment in savings and that in the ordinary way the public will not increase its savings unless aggregate income is also increasing. The efforts of the public to consume a part of its increased income will 'stimulate output until the new level (and distribution) of incomes provides a margin of saving sufficient to correspond to the increased investment' (*CW, VII*: 117).

Investment is a constituent of demand. An increment in the demand for goods for investment purposes (that is, a higher rate of investment compared to a lower rate) must translate into an increment in effective demand and thereby into an increase in employment and output if it is to affect total employment and total income. It will do so in such a way that a new (profit) equilibrium level of employment and income will be attained only if the increase in the output of goods for investment purposes is accompanied by an appropriate increase in the output of goods for consumption purposes. Alternatively, it may be said that small differences in investment, other things being equal, imply determinate differences in saving, income and employment. That is,

> [the] law that increased employment for investment must necessarily stimulate the industries producing for consumption and thus lead to a total increase of employment which is a multiple of the primary employment (*CW, VII*: 118).

That reasoning, it must be stressed, is conducted on the assumption that only different (profit) equilibrium levels of income and employment are in question. It does not deal formally with the 'path' which the economic system would follow in going from one position of equilibrium to another. Neither does it deal with the implications of different levels of the stock of capital. It does, however, draw attention to the fact that there must be a process of change following an actual change in the rate of investment and that such a process takes time to work itself out.

Keynes elaborates on the law in a number of respects. He points out that it applies to a net increment in investment. By that he means that an increase in investment in one direction may be offset, to a greater or lesser extent by a reduction, in another. The multiplier effect is limited to the net increase. He says that if, for example, there were to be an increase in investment in public works it would be quite possible that investment elsewhere would be reduced so that the net increase in investment would be less than the increase in the investment on public works. In regard to the particular case of public works he mentions three factors which might be expected to have that effect.

The first is that the method of financing the investment and the extra money that would be required for transactions purposes consequent on the increase in the employment on the public works might lead to an increase in the rate of interest and as a result reduce other types of investment. The second is that the increased cost of capital goods resulting from the increase in the demand for them would reduce their marginal efficiency as far as the private investor was concerned. Private investment would, therefore, tend to decline unless there was a reduction in the rate of interest to match the decline in the marginal efficiency of capital rather than the rise which would have to be expected (*CW, VII*: 119–20). The third is that an increase in investment in public works might have an adverse effect on the state of confidence and so tend to increase liquidity-preference and/or diminish the marginal efficiency of capital. Other types of investment might be reduced as a result (*CW, VII*: 120).

Keynes also points out that some part of the effects of increased investment in one country will show up in increased employment in other countries. Hence if we consider only the effect on domestic employment as distinct from world employment, we must diminish the full figure of the multiplier (*CW, VII*: 120).

Bearing in mind, moreover, that the logical theory or law of the multiplier relates only to very small changes (or differences) in investment it follows that 'substantial changes' would lead to changes in the marginal propensity to consume 'as the position of the margin is gradually shifted' and so also to changes in the multiplier (*CW, VII*: 120).

Keynes mentions two other factors which are likely to affect the marginal propensity to consume and the multiplier. The first of these is that an increase in employment on a given capital equipment will tend to increase the entrepreneurs' proportion of total income by reason of the operation of the principle of diminishing returns. As the individual marginal propensity to consume of the entrepreneurs 'is probably less than the average for the community as a whole' (*CW, VII*: 121) the result of such an increase would be to reduce the size of the multiplier. The second is that unemployment is likely to involve negative saving because the unemployed may be living on their own savings and on those of their friends or on public relief which is 'partly financed out of loans' (*CW, VII*: 121). A reduction in unemployment would tend to 'diminish these particular acts of negative saving and reduce, therefore, the marginal propensity to consume more rapidly than would have occurred from an equal increase in the community's real income accruing in different circumstances' (*CW, VII*: 121). Thus, as Keynes puts it,

> the multiplier is likely to be greater for a small net increment of investment than for a large investment; so that, where substantial changes are in view, we must be guided by the average value of the multiplier based on the average marginal propensity to consume over the range in question (*CW, VII*: 121).

A further limitation on the size of the multiplier to which the logic of the theory draws attention is that a change in the production of goods for investment purposes may not be foreseen generally. If the change has been foreseen the production of goods for consumption purposes can be increased *pari passu* with the production of goods for investment purposes. Such an increase would tend to involve a rise in the prices of consumption goods but it would be no more 'than is consequential, in conditions of decreasing returns, on an increase in the quantity which is produced' (*CW, VII*: 122).

But the normal situation is one in which an increase in investment is not fully foreseen. In the extreme case the expansion of employment in the production of goods for investment purposes is not accompanied by an increase in the output of goods and services for consumption purposes. The result will be that the prices of consumption goods will tend to rise

> until a temporary equilibrium between demand and supply has been brought about partly by the high prices causing a postponement of consumption, partly by a redistribution of income in favour of the saving classes ... and partly by the higher prices causing a depletion of stocks (*CW, VII*: 123–4).

That implies that there is 'a temporary reduction of the marginal propensity to consume, i.e. of the multiplier itself' (*CW, VII*: 124). The depletion of stocks means that aggregate investment increases by less than the increased demand for goods for investment purposes which causes an increase in the output of such goods. But as time goes on production for consumption purposes is adjusted to the new demand in a way that may involve a temporary rise in the marginal propensity to consume and a temporary increase in aggregate investment due to the building up of stocks again.

The foregoing reservations and caveats do not affect the significance of the theory of the multiplier. It remains the general method of addressing questions concerning the relationship between different possible levels of investment and income subject to a given propensity to consume.

Mention may also be made of the implications of the average propensity to consume as distinct from the marginal propensity to consume. A high marginal propensity to consume involves 'a larger *proportionate* effect from a given change in investment' than does a low marginal propensity to consume but 'the *absolute* effect will, nevertheless, be small if the *average* propensity to consume is also high' (*CW, VII*: 125). A high average propensity to consume implies that income is low. The absolute increase in a small income will be less than the absolute increase in a large income following a given proportionate increment in investment though the former may represent a greater proportional increase in income than the latter. It is for that reason, according to Keynes, that even though the multiplier in a poor country is large

the effect on employment of fluctuations in investment will be much greater in a wealthy community, assuming that in the latter current investment represents a much larger proportion of current output (*CW, VII*: 126).

INVOLUNTARY UNEMPLOYMENT

It has now been established that (profit) equilibrium in the economy as a whole holds when effective demand and aggregate demand are such that the employment required by the former is equal to the employment implied by the latter. This level of employment, whilst it is consistent with the maximization of profit in the economy as a whole given the capital equipment and the expectations of producer-entrepreneurs, need not be full employment in the sense that the marginal disutility of work in relation to the real wage is the only factor that limits employment. The level of employment consistent with (profit) equilibrium 'cannot be *greater* than full employment, i.e. the real wage cannot be less than the marginal disutility of labour'

(*CW, VII*: 28). But there is no reason, according to Keynes's analysis, why it must be equal to full employment. The full employment level of (profit) equilibrium is what Keynes refers to as a 'special case' (*CW, VII*: 28) and it is realized only 'when the propensity to consume and the inducement to invest stand in a particular relationship to one another' (*CW, VII*: 28). That full employment is not presupposed is one of the reasons why his theory of employment is to be seen as a general one.

Setting 'frictional' and 'voluntary' unemployment (*CW, VII*: 6) aside, Keynes designates the difference between full employment and the profit equilibrium level of employment (if there is a difference) as 'involuntary unemployment'. Such unemployment would arise if the (profit) equilibrium level of effective demand were to be too small to provide employment for all those who would be willing to work for a real wage which would compensate them for the marginal disutility of the labour. If profit equilibrium were to hold, the deficiency in effective demand underlying involuntary unemployment would be attributable to a level of aggregate demand which would not be sufficient to allow for the absorption of the full employment level of output. If entrepreneurs were to produce such a level of output in these circumstances they would find that they could not sell it all profitably. Some of them, or perhaps, even all of them would, therefore, be induced to curtail output and employment.

Given the propensity to consume a deficiency in aggregate demand of that kind would be due to the level of investment. Within the framework provided by Keynes's analysis a level of investment in conjunction with the propensity to consume which would be insufficient to produce a level of aggregate demand equal to a full employment level of effective demand, would have to be seen as being attributable to the level of the schedule of the marginal efficiency of capital and/or to the level of the complex of the rates of interest. It may be noted that the marginal efficiency of capital is a sufficiently broad concept as to embrace not only the prospective returns from existing types of investments but also the ability to identify or discover new opportunities for investment.

Keynes's concept of involuntary unemployment relates to the relationship between the real wage and the marginal disutility of labour. He defines involuntary unemployment as arising

if, in the event of a small rise in the price of wage-goods relatively to the money-wage, both the aggregate supply of labour willing to work for the current money-wage and the aggregate demand for it [that is, the aggregate effective demand] at that wage would be greater than the existing volume of employment (*CW, VII*: 15, *emphasis omitted*).

Subsequently, in the article he published in *The Quarterly Journal of Economics* in 1937, he accepted that his treatment of involuntary unemployment was 'particularly open to criticism' (*CW, XIV*: 110). Nevertheless, it seems clear enough that the purpose of that definition is to convey that involuntary unemployment has nothing to do with the wage-rate as such. In principle, such unemployment could arise no matter how low the wage-rate is. Involuntary unemployment is rather an aspect of Keynes's concept of profit equilibrium and of the logical possibility that the profit equilibrium level of effective demand is not necessarily the level at which full employment, as Keynes defines it, is reached. (The next chapter discusses what Keynes means by full employment.) That being so, in so far as there is a logical way by which involuntary unemployment can be reduced or eliminated it lies in the possibility of increased investment and the consequent operation of the multiplier (*CW, VII*: 118).

Keynes sees money and the rate of interest on money as playing a special role in limiting effective demand and employment. He remarks that

the *rate of interest on money* plays a peculiar part in setting a limit to the level of employment, since it sets a standard to which the marginal efficiency of a capital-asset must attain if it is to be newly produced (*CW, VII*: 222).

He develops his argument in support of this contention in the context of the unemployment and falling prices which were characteristic of the depression phase of trade cycles before 1914.

The 'peculiar part' which the rate of interest plays can best be seen by contrast with the imaginary non-monetary economy. Keynes defines such an economy as one in which 'there is no asset for which the liquidity-premium is always in excess of the carrying costs' (*CW, VII*: 239). Anything could be taken as the numéraire in the non-monetary economy. The marginal efficiencies of all other assets would be measured in terms of the numéraire.

All assets have their own-rates of interest expressed as $q - c + l$ (as we saw in Chapter 7). The numéraire would have its own-rate of interest too. If an asset were to be newly produced its marginal efficiency would have to match the own-rate of interest of the numéraire. The production of all assets, including the commodity used as numéraire, could be expected to be expanded to the point where their marginal efficiencies were equal. The own-rate of interest of the numéraire could not become higher than the marginal efficiency of capital in general for long because resources would be diverted to its production, since such a higher rate would imply that its exchange value in terms of other assets would have risen. The expansion of its production and the possibility of substituting relatively cheaper commodities for it would tend to reduce its exchange value. The essential point that emerges from this line of reasoning is that the numéraire would behave like any other commodity. Production in the economy as a whole would tend to be expanded either until full employment was reached or until the own-rates of interest reached zero (that is, $q - c + l = 0$).

In the monetary economy money itself has neither a q nor a c. Its own-rate is entirely in terms of l. Entrepreneurs cannot change the quantity of money as they could change the quantity of the numéraire in the non-monetary economy. If prices are falling the demand for money will tend to increase thereby still further increasing the rate of interest and lowering investment and employment. Money is inelastic both as to production and to substitution. Hence if the rate of interest on money comes to exceed the marginal efficiency of assets their production ceases.[18]

SAY'S LAW

Given Keynes's theory of interest there is no mechanism by which the demand for new capital equipment is equated with the supply of savings. There is, therefore, no automatic way by which the gap between income and consumption is filled. Nor is there any inherent tendency for resources to be fully employed as a result.

Keynes was convinced that the 'classical' economists assumed Say's Law partly at least in view of the role they ascribed to the rate of interest. He observed, however, that neither his predecessors nor his contemporaries had explicitly established the law. They simply assumed, often implicitly, its validity as a corollary to their theory of interest.

This led Keynes to examine Say's Law with a view to identifying the assumptions required for its validity. As he saw it 'supply creates its own demand' must mean that the aggregate supply function and the aggregate demand function are the same at all levels of employment and output. Consequently, the level of effective demand is not unique in the sense that it does not correspond to any one level of employment. Instead, it holds for all levels of employment. If it is assumed that entrepreneurs want to make as much profit as possible and that the more output they produce and sell the more profit they will make it would follow that entrepreneurs would seek to employ as many resources as possible so as to produce as much output as possible. That would ensure that there would be full employment. Moreover, as the existing theory did not distinguish expected demand from demand from the buyers' perspective it implied that aggregate demand and effective demand were equal to each other. Hence full employment would necessarily be a profit-equilibrium level of employment. None of the assumptions required to support Say's Law is tenable in the light of Keynes's analysis. For Keynes, the aggregate demand function and the aggregate supply function have to be thought of as intersecting rather than as coinciding. Hence effective demand corresponds to a unique level of employment. Aggregate demand is not necessarily equal to effective demand as there is no way of ensuring that the incomes (including profit) generated on the production of an output will be spent on that output. Indeed it is not even possible to make the relationship between effective demand and income precise (*CW, XIV*: 179).

If Say's Law were valid the question Keynes sought to address would not arise. Keynes was convinced that the unemployment that was all too evident, particularly during the trade cycle, ruled out the possibility that Say's Law could be valid as an adequate description of what happens in practice. His analysis suggested the possibility of involuntary unemployment which is a category of unemployment inconsistent with Say's Law. His analysis also suggested that even if all individual firms were to be in profit equilibrium there would be no inherent reason why the employment given in these firms would add up to full employment of all the available labour and other resources seeking employment. In other words his analysis leads to the conclusion as mentioned above, that a full employment profit equilibrium is no more than a limiting case, the conditions for the existence of which can be identified in *The General Theory*.

9 Wages, Prices and Money

Keynes regarded the received treatment of money-wages and of the quantity of money as being particularly unsatisfactory. As he saw it, the presuppositions of the existing theory were irredeemably flawed as far as the effects of changes in money-wages and in the quantity of money were concerned. For that reason he elaborated on the general principles of his own analysis with a view to formulating an explanation of the part wages and the quantity of money play in determining the employment of the available resources which would be consistent with his own method of analysis.

THE RELATIONSHIP BETWEEN WAGES AND EMPLOYMENT

Keynes conducts his analysis of the relationship between wages and employment by tracing the effects of a reduction in money-wages on the propensity to consume, on the marginal efficiency of capital and on the rate of interest. He argues that a

> reduction in money-wages will have no lasting tendency to increase employment except by virtue of its repercussion either on the propensity to consume for the community as a whole, or on the schedule of marginal efficiencies of capital, or on the rate of interest (*CW, VII*: 262).

He contends, moreover, that '[t]here is no method of analysing the effect of a reduction in money-wages, except by following up its possible effects on these three factors' (*CW, VII*: 262).

The propensity to consume is likely to be affected by a reduction in money-wages because of the consequent redistribution of income. Since a reduction of money-wages will tend to result in lower prices there will be a certain amount of redistribution of real income from wage-earners to the suppliers of factors the remuneration of which has not been reduced. This, in Keynes's judgement, is likely to reduce the propensity to consume. There will also be a tendency for the real incomes of entrepreneurs to be reduced and for those of the rentiers to be increased because the money-incomes of the latter are fixed.

What the net effect on the propensity to consume of these changes would be is not certain since it would depend on the sizes of the incomes of the two groups and on the disposition of each of them to spend income on consumption.

Another way in which a reduction in money-wages is likely to influence the propensity to consume is through the terms of trade. Though the balance of trade is likely to be favourably affected, the effect on the terms of trade is likely to be unfavourable as a result of the reduction in money-prices. This will lead to a reduction in real incomes (except in the case of those who are newly employed by reason of the reduction on money- wages and the consequent increase in exports) and, therefore, to a tendency for consumption to be higher in relation to income.

In the case of an open economy a reduction in money-wages without a corresponding reduction abroad and also without an off-setting change in tariffs and quotas will tend to improve the balance of trade and so be 'favourable to investment' (*CW, VII*: 262). As 'the volume of foreign investment is necessarily determined by the size of the favourable balance of trade' (*CW, VII*: 335) and as home investment and foreign investment 'between them, make up aggregate investment' (*CW, VII*: 335) it follows that an increase in foreign investment means an increase in total investment. The result is the same, therefore, as if there was an increase in the marginal efficiency of capital.

A further possibility as far as the marginal efficiency of capital is concerned is that the reduction in money-wages may be expected to be followed by an increase in money-wages in the future. If so, it will have the effect of increasing the marginal efficiency of capital and so result in more investment. It may also increase the propensity to consume, but if the expectation is that any given reduction in money-wages will be followed by another reduction, the marginal efficiency of capital and the propensity to consume will both tend to decrease (*CW, VII*: 263).

A reduction in money-wages is perceived by the individual entrepreneur as being advantageous to himself. A general reduction in money-wages may be seen by each entrepreneur as if it applied only to himself and so may produce what Keynes calls 'an optimistic tone in the minds of entrepreneurs' (*CW, VII*: 264) and that may result in an increase in the marginal efficiency of capital and so to an increase in investment. But on the other hand the reduction in prices and the increase in the real burden of debt consequent on a reduction of money-wages may have a 'depressing influence on entrepreneurs'

(*CW, VII*: 264) which 'may partly offset any cheerful reactions from the reduction of wages' (*CW, VII*: 264). Keynes also notes that 'the effect of the lower price-level on the real burden of the national debt and hence on taxation is likely to prove very adverse to business confidence' (*CW, VII*: 264).

The reduction in money-wages may also have the effect of reducing the rate of interest through its impact on liquidity-preferences. A reduction in money-wages will tend to reduce not only prices but the total wages-bill and money incomes generally as well as wages. As a result the community's requirements for money for consumption purposes and for business purposes would be reduced. In other words, there would be a reduction in the schedule of liquidity-preference for the community as a whole. Other things being equal that would reduce the rate of interest and lead to greater investment. But if wages and prices are expected to rise again later 'the favourable reaction will be much less pronounced in the case of long-term loans than in that of short-term loans' (*CW, VII*: 263). Moreover, if

> ...the reduction in wages disturbs political confidence by causing popular discontent, the increase in liquidity-preference due to this cause may more than offset the release of cash from the active circulation (*CW, VII*: 264).

Thus the consequences of a reduction in money-wages are virtually impossible to foresee in practice. The effects of such a reduction are liable to be ambiguous, complicated and contradictory in the case of each of the three independent variables, propensity to consume, marginal efficiency of capital and liquidity-preference.

Keynes further considers in greater detail the likely effects of a reduction in money-wages on the marginal efficiency of capital and on the rate of interest, assuming a closed economy. In doing so he reveals both the complexity of the economic system and the versatility of the general principles of his analysis in handling it.

The situation in which a reduction in money-wages is likely to have the most favourable effects on the marginal efficiency of capital is one in which wages are believed to have fallen as low as it is possible for them to fall so that it has to be expected that they will increase in the future. On the other hand the most unfavourable situation is one 'in which money-wages are slowly sagging downwards and each reduction in wages serves to diminish confidence in the prospective maintenance of wages' (*CW, VII*: 265). Accordingly, as Keynes sees it, if effective demand is weakening, the best way to increase it would be by way of 'a sudden large reduction of money-wages' (*CW, VII*: 265) to such a low level that no-one would believe that they would remain at that level. However, Keynes rules that out as a practicable proposition on the grounds that it 'could only be accomplished by administrative decree and is scarcely practical politics under a system of free wage-bargaining' (*CW, VII*: 265).

Keynes draws attention to the similarity between the effects of changes in money-wages and changes in the quantity of money by pointing out that

if the quantity of money is virtually fixed, it is evident that its quantity in terms of wage-units can be indefinitely increased by a sufficient reduction in money-wages; and that its quantity in proportion to incomes generally can be largely increased, the limit to this increase depending on the proportion of wage-cost to marginal prime cost and on the response of other elements of marginal prime cost to the falling wage-unit (*CW, VII*: 266).

Thus, 'theoretically at least' (*CW, VII*: 266), it is possible to produce the same effect on the rate of interest as that brought about by a change in the quantity of money by means of a change in money-wages. From this Keynes draws the conclusion that

wage reductions, as a method of securing full employment, are also subject to the same limitations as the method of increasing the quantity of money. The same reasons... which limit the efficacy of increases in the quantity of money as a means of increasing investment to the optimum figure, apply *mutatis mutandis* to wage reductions (*CW, VII*: 266).

However, even though, analytically, wage flexibility and the possibility of changing the quantity of money are very much the same, as they are both ways 'of changing the quantity of money in terms of wages-units' (*CW, VII*: 267), there are also profound differences between them. The most important of these are the following

(1) There is no way by which wage reductions can be brought about in a uniform way for labour as a whole. On the other hand the authorities can readily bring about a change in the quantity of

money by means of open-market operations 'or analogous measures' (*CW, VII*: 268).

(2) The effects of changes in the quantity of money on wage-earners and on others whose incomes are more or less fixed in terms of money would be much the same if money wages also were to be 'comparatively inflexible' (*CW, VII*: 268). But if money-wages were to be reduced while other money incomes remained unchanged an element of arbitrariness would enter into the distribution of income which would be lacking in 'fairness' (*CW, VII*: 268).[19]

(3) The two methods of increasing the quantity of money in terms of wage-units have opposite effects as far as the burden of debt is concerned. The wage reduction method increases it while the quantity of money method lessens it. Keynes believes the latter to be the more preferable of the two.

(4) To try to bring about a lowering of the rate of interest by means of a reduction in money wages imposes 'a double drag on the marginal efficiency of capital and a double reason for putting off investment' (*CW, VII*: 269).

In this context Keynes, it must be remembered, is dealing with the complex of wages in general rather than with relative wages. Indeed he accepts that

There are advantages in some degree of flexibility in the wages of particular industries so as to expedite transfers from those which are relatively declining to those which are relatively expanding (*CW, VII*: 270).

But he contends that 'the money-wage level as a whole should be maintained as stable as possible, at any rate in the short period' (*CW, VII*: 270). While this is a normative statement about practical affairs (and it is by no means the only one in *The General Theory*) its importance lies in its theoretical setting. It serves to encapsulate the results of a long and closely reasoned theoretical argument. When examined more carefully it becomes obvious that it scarcely leaves the realm of theory in so far as there is no practical suggestion as to how the combination of 'some degree of flexibility in the wages of particular industries' with stability in the 'money-wage level as a whole' could be attained (*CW, VII*: 270). It is perhaps best to interpret this statement as part of Keynes's refutation of the doctrine which attributed unemployment to a lack of sufficient flexibility in money wages, in other words, to what was regarded as undue rigidity in the money-wage. Keynes not only refutes this doctrine on theoretical grounds, but also, in effect, asserts that in practice fairly rigid money-wages would be more likely to be conducive to general economic stability than would flexible money-wages. In that way his discussion of the practical and normative aspects of the stability or otherwise of the money-wage is part of the argument underlying the general principles of Keynes's method of analysis rather than an expression of opinion in regard to economic policy.

THE EFFECTS OF CHANGES IN THE QUANTITY OF MONEY

So far the quantity of money has been brought into the analysis in order to explain the determination of the rate of interest on money and in order to establish the shapes of the liquidity functions. As we have just seen changes in the quantity of money are in some respects the same as changes in the money wage rate from an analytical point of view as far as employment is concerned. In order to complete the elaboration of the general principles of his analysis Keynes examines the specific effects of the quantity of money, and of changes therein, on employment and therefore, also on output. Keynes's analysis suggests that the quantity of money, again like money-wages, may affect prices. Accordingly, it is necessary to disentangle the influence of the quantity of money on output from its influence on prices.

Since the level of employment is determined by the level of effective demand the analytical problem facing Keynes in investigating the impact of the quantity of money on employment is that of tracing the effects of differences in the quantity of money on expenditure in money terms and thereby on the conditions influencing effective demand. We have already remarked that Keynes sees the theory of what determines the employment of the available resources as being also a theory of output as a whole. He reminds us too that 'we require the complete theory of a monetary economy' if we are to deal with 'the problem of what determines output and employment as a whole' (*CW, VII*: 293). His investigation of the impact of the quantity of money on effective demand completes his theory of the monetary economy.

Keynes's method of addressing these particular issues involves the use of a concept which he designates the *employment function*. He uses it to show that under certain conditions employment and, therefore, output can reach a level, both in individual industries and in industry as a whole, at which they become inelastic. This then provides him with the means of distinguishing between the effects of changes in the quantity of money on output and on prices.

The employment function is the inverse of the aggregate supply function and is expressed in terms of the wage-unit. Accordingly, it is an aspect of Keynes's adaptation of the standard theory of the firm to which we have already alluded in Chapter 4. The aggregate supply function, as we have seen, relates the proceeds from the sale of an output, the expectation of which would induce the entrepreneur to produce that level of output, with the quantity of labour required to produce it. Thus it implies an expected amount of money and a particular quantity of labour. Its inverse, therefore, is the relationship between particular quantities of labour and expected amounts of money. The amounts of money have to be measured in terms of wage-units so that the amount of labour implied in the expected proceeds can be ascertained irrespective of any changes that might occur in the wage unit itself as a result of changes in the quantity of money. Since effective demand is the point on the aggregate demand function at which the aggregate supply function determines what the amount of employment will be, it follows that the employment function summarizes the relationship between an amount of effective demand measured in terms of the wage unit and an amount of employment which would produce an output the supply price of which would be equal to the amount of effective demand in question. In Keynes's own words, 'the object of the employment function' is

> to relate the amount of the effective demand, measured in terms of the wage-unit, directed to a given firm or industry or to industry as a whole with the amount of employment, the supply price of the output of which will compare to that amount of effective demand (*CW, VII*: 280).[20]

Thus as the aggregate supply function is symbolized as $Z = \phi(N)$, the aggregate demand function as $D = f(N)$, and as effective demand is the 'value of D at the point of the aggregate demand function, where it is intersected by the aggregate supply function' (*CW, VII*: 25), so Keynes symbolizes the employment function as $N_r = F_r(D_{wr})$ where D_{wr} is an amount of effective demand measured in wage-units 'directed' to a firm or industry, and N_r is the corresponding amount of employment. Furthermore, if it is assured that 'D_{wr} is a unique function of the total effective demand D_w', then the employment function may be symbolized as $N_r = F_r(D_w)$, meaning that '...N_r men will be employed in industry r when effective demand is D_w' (*CW, VII*: 280).

In principle, a change in the quantity of money might be expected to lead to a change in demand and ultimately to a change in supply. The problem of explaining how such a change in supply comes about is made altogether more tractable by the use of the concept of the employment function instead of the ordinary supply function as such. It does so because it enables the difficulties inherent in the use of supply functions in the context of the economic system as a whole to be overcome. Apart from the obvious fact that the notion of a single supply function relating to the economy as a whole is meaningless, the employment function has two advantages compared to supply functions relating to individual firms and industries. The first is that 'it expresses the relevant facts in terms of the units to which we have decided to restrict ourselves' (*CW, VII*: 281). The second is that 'it lends itself to the problems of industry and output *as a whole*, as distinct from the problems of a single industry or firm in a given environment, more easily than does the ordinary supply curve' (*CW, VII*: 281). There are a number of reasons for this.

The demand curve for any commodity is drawn on the assumption that everything else in the economic system can be set aside for the purpose of establishing the relationship between the quantity of the commodity bought and its price. In particular, the influence of income on the quantity bought is ignored in the sense that income is taken to be given. If income were assumed to be different from the level assumed for the purposes of the demand curve in question another demand curve would have to be drawn. In other words, each different level of income implies a different demand curve in respect of each commodity. Similarly, in the case of the supply curve for any particular commodity it is assumed that total output is given. Accordingly, different levels of total output imply different supply curves for any given commodity.

Keynes's analysis shows that different levels of aggregate employment imply different levels of output and income under conditions of profit-equilibrium, since they are associated with different levels of effective demand. As aggregate effective demand is simply the sum of the effective demands in each firm it implies aggregate employment. Different levels of aggregate employment imply not only different levels of employment in the various firms and industries but also different levels of output (the relevance of the latter will become apparent later). The effect of different levels of aggregate employment on the output of the various individual industries could be ascertained only by identifying what Keynes terms the 'response' of these industries to the various possible levels of aggregate employment. But this would involve the drawing of the supply and demand curves for each industry for each level of aggregate employment. And this in turn would involve the making of assumptions, as we shall see, as to the income associated with each level of employment because employment on the one hand and output and income on the other are not necessarily uniquely related. In Keynes's words

> When ... we are examining the response of individual industries to changes in *aggregate* employment, we are necessarily concerned, not with a single demand curve for each industry, in conjunction with a single supply curve, but with two families of such curves corresponding to different assumptions as to the aggregate employment (*CW, VII*: 281).

On the other hand with the employment function, Keynes argues that 'the task of arriving at a function for industry as a whole which will reflect changes [that is to say, differences] in employment as a whole is more practicable' (*CW, VII*: 281).

Keynes then proceeds to demonstrate how this can be done. He does so in the context of the elements in the economic system which he takes to be given and which are listed in Chapter 18 of *The General Theory* and also on the assumption that the propensity to consume is given. He further assumes that 'we are considering changes in employment in response to changes in the rate of investment' (*CW, VII*: 281). Other things remaining the same, changes in employment can come about only through changes in investment. There will be a particular level of aggregate employment corresponding to every level of effective demand in terms of wage-units. By reason of the logical theory of the multiplier and under conditions of profit-equilibrium, effective demand (D) will be divided in determinate proportions between D_1 and D_2. It is not of course necessary, as we have seen, to assume that the entrepreneurs know what these proportions are, but as entrepreneurs' decisions determine the generation of income, including profit, under conditions of profit-equilibrium, each given distribution of income implies a certain level of effective demand. Accordingly,

Keynes concludes that it is reasonable to assume also 'that corresponding to a given level of aggregate effective demand there is a unique distribution of it between different industries' (*CW, VII:* 282).

From this it is possible to deduce the amount of employment in each industry which corresponds to a given level of aggregate employment. In other words there is an amount of employment in each industry corresponding to any given level of aggregate effective demand (measured in terms of wage-units). This is the employment function expressed in the form, $N_r = F_r(D_w)$. Since this function is expressed in labour units (the $N's$) and in money (the wage-units) it is additive. So the sum of the employment functions for each industry at a given level of effective demand is equal to the employment function for industry as a whole at that level of effective demand, that is $F(D_w) = N = \Sigma N_r = \Sigma F_r(D_w)$ for the economy (*CW, VII:* 282).

Building on the employment function Keynes defines what he terms the *elasticity of employment* as the measure of 'the response of the number of labour-units employed in the industry to changes in the number of wage-units which are expected to be spent on purchasing its output' (*CW, VII:* 282). He expresses it symbolically as

$$e_{er} = \frac{dN_r}{dD_{wr}} * \frac{D_{wr}}{N_r}$$

Since the individual employment functions are additive it follows that there can be an elasticity of employment for industry as a whole. This is symbolized as

$$e_e = \frac{dN}{dD_w} * \frac{D_w}{N}$$

It is to be expected that different total levels of expenditure would be distributed in different proportions between the various industries. That is partly because the income elasticity of demand differs from one individual and one commodity to another individual and commodity and partly because relative prices change in response to different levels of expenditure (*CW, VII:* 286). That being so, Keynes concludes that

It follows from this that the assumption upon which we have worked hitherto, that changes in employment depend solely on changes in aggregate effective demand (in terms of wage-units), is no better than a first approximation, if we admit that there is more than one way in which an increase of income can be spent (*CW, VII*: 286).

He points out that the way in which aggregate demand is distributed between different commodities may affect not only the distribution of employment but also its total volume. For example if a higher level of aggregate demand, compared with a lower level, is for commodities with a high elasticity of employment, total employment will be greater than if the higher level of aggregate demand were for commodities with a low elasticity of employment. Similarly, even under conditions of a given aggregate demand there could be different levels of employment depending on the distribution of the demand between products having generally high or generally low elasticities of employment. In this connection it must be remembered that Keynes's argument implies profit-equilibrium so that effective demand is assumed to be the same, both as to total amount and as to its distribution, as aggregate demand.[21]

At the stage in the presentation of his analysis at which the inducement to invest and the determination of the rate of interest had first been explained, Keynes had warned that we should not be tempted to draw naive conclusions regarding the possibility that the level of activity in the economic system depends solely on the quantity of money in existence (*CW, VII*: 173; also above, pp. 135–6). The foregoing considerations now allow the question as to the effect of differences in the quantity of money on the economic system to be investigated in greater detail.

Other things being equal, the greater the quantity of money the lower will the rate of interest be and therefore, the higher the level of investment. With a given propensity to consume the higher the level of investment the greater must be the level of income. Under conditions of profit-equilibrium, the higher level of income, the higher must be the amount of effective demand. Or looked at from the perspective of the supply-side the higher the amount of proceeds expected from expenditure for investment and for consumption purposes the greater will be the amount of effective demand and therefore the greater, under conditions of profit-equilibrium, will be the level of income. If the *only* effect of a greater quantity as compared with a smaller quantity of money on effective demand were to be through the rate of interest its impact on the level of economic activity could be derived from the schedule of liquidity-preference, the schedule of marginal efficiencies, and the multiplier.

However, there is more to it than that. The schedule of liquidity-preference depends on the distribution of the quantity of money between 'the income and industrial circulations' (*CW, VII*: 298).[22] But that in turn depends on the amount of effective demand and on how at each level of the quantity of money the impact of effective demand on prices, wages, output and employment differs from its previous impact – always, of course, at profit-equilibrium levels of income and employment. The schedule of marginal efficiencies of capital at the various different levels of the quantity of money depends in part on expectations as to what the quantity of money and its effects will be in the future. The quantity of money will influence the multiplier since, for the reasons already given, different quantities of money will be associated with different levels of demand and, there-fore, with different levels of income which will be 'distributed between different classes of consumers' (*CW, VII*: 299). But at all possible levels of the quantity of money there will be a particular amount of effective demand consequent on all the various factors which deter-mine effective demand at each level of the quantity of money. That is to say, given the quantity of money, the amount of effective demand under conditions of profit-equilibrium must be compatible with that given quantity because, as Keynes puts it

There will be a determinate amount of increase in the quantity of effective demand which, after taking everything into account, will correspond to, and be in equilibrium with, the increase in the quantity of money (*CW, VII*: 299).

This is merely another way of looking at what is summarized as

$$M = M_1 + M_2 = L_1(Y) + L_2(r)$$

since, as already stressed, under conditions of profit-equilibrium the amount of effective demand is equal to income. A greater quantity of money as compared with a smaller quantity could be associated with a smaller quantity of effective demand. But according to Keynes this would be 'only in highly exceptional circumstances' (*CW, VII*: 299).

THE ELASTICITY OF SUPPLY

For the reasons already mentioned a greater quantity of money as compared with a smaller quantity will be associated with a higher level of employment, assuming capital equipment to be given, but the supply of commodities is likely to be less than perfectly elastic. There is a twofold reason for this. The wage-earners in any given category are not likely to be equally efficient though their wage is likely to be the same. Hence, the higher the level of employment associated with any given equipment the higher will be labour costs, unless it is assumed that the least efficient worker would be employed in preference to the more efficient at low levels of employment. Furthermore, if the capital equipment itself is not homogeneous, as is virtually certain to be the case, prime cost per unit of output will not be uniform. On the likely assumption that the more efficient capital equipment will be used before the less efficient, marginal prime cost will be greater the higher the level of employment. Consequently, the higher is the output from a given equipment the greater will its supply price be. It follows that 'increasing output will be associated with rising prices, apart from any change in the wage-unit' (*CW, VII*: 300).

At higher levels of employment compared with lower levels the production of some commodities will be relatively greater than that of others. That is because the supply of individual commodities may have become inelastic at certain levels of employment while the supply of others may be imperfectly or even perfectly elastic. As a result, at any particular level of employment below full employment the output of some commodities may be inelastic. Accordingly, inelasticity of output in some industries has to be seen as a possibility even though some resources are unemployed. In this type of situation

> as output increases, a series of 'bottle-necks' will be successively reached, where the supply of particular commodities ceases to be elastic and their prices have to rise to whatever level is necessary to divert demand into other directions (*CW, VII*: 300).

Keynes's analysis also draws attention to the possibility that 'the elasticity of supply partly depends on the elapse of time' (*CW, VII*: 300). If the assumption that the capital equipment is not given is dropped and replaced by the assumption that there is 'a sufficient interval for the quantity of equipment itself to change, the elasticities of supply will be decidedly greater eventually' (*CW, VII*: 300). In that case

> a moderate change in effective demand, coming on a situation where there is widespread unemployment, may spend itself very

little in raising prices and mainly in increasing employment; whilst a larger change, which, being unforeseen, causes some temporary 'bottle-necks' to be reached, will spend itself in raising prices, as distinct from employment, to a greater extent at first than subsequently (*CW, VII*: 300–1).

There are two other reasons, both arising on the supply-side, for a tendency for prices to rise as the quantity of money expands. The first is that the wage-unit will tend to rise before full employment is reached. This tendency arises

[S]ince each group of workers will gain, *cet. par.*, by a rise in its own wages, there is naturally for all groups a pressure in this direction, which entrepreneurs will be more ready to meet when they are doing better business (*CW, VII*: 301).

In other words, given a greater quantity of money rather than a smaller quantity the wage-unit will tend to be higher rather than lower. Accordingly, assuming profit-equilibrium at both the greater and lesser quantities of money, a part of the greater effective demand in money terms, when the quantity of money is greater, will be accounted for by the higher level of the wage-unit, rather than by such a higher level of employment as would be reached if the wage-unit were to be what it would be if the quantity of money were lower. From this Keynes concludes that

in addition to the final critical point of full employment at which money-wages have to rise, in response to an increasing effective demand in terms of money, fully in proportion to the rise in the prices of wage-goods, we have a succession of earlier semi-critical points at which an increasing effective demand tends to raise money-wages though not fully in proportion to the rise in the price of wage-goods; and similarly in the case of a decreasing effective demand (*CW, VII*: 301).

It may be noted that the necessity for money-wages to rise fully in proportion to the rise in the price of wage-goods under conditions of full employment is required by the definition of effective demand itself. If, with an increase in the quantity of money at full employment, the wage-unit were to fall the real wage would become less than the marginal disutility of labour so that employment would fall. That would be tantamount to a fall in effective demand though full employment as such would still prevail except that it would be at a lower level than before.

The second reason for the tendency of prices to fall as the quantity of money expands is that at different levels of the quantity of money the composition of marginal cost is likely to be different too because

> the rates of remuneration of different factors in terms of money will show varying degrees of rigidity and they may also have different elasticities of supply in response to changes in the money-rewards offered (*CW, VII*: 302).

Keynes believes that the relationships between marginal user cost, in particular, and the wage-unit is likely to differ considerably at different levels of activity. That is because

> marginal user cost may increase sharply when employment begins to improve, if (as will probably be the case) the increasing effective demand brings a rapid change in the prevailing expectation as to the date when the replacement of equipment will be necessary (*CW, VII*: 302).

Thus, as Keynes sees it, an expansion in the quantity of money beginning in a state of unemployment leads to an expansion in output, though the extent of the expansion may vary from industry to industry, and to a gradual, though not necessarily uniform, rise in prices. This will last so long as there are efficient resources of all types still unemployed. But if the expansion continues until the 'bottle-neck' stage begins to be reached 'there is likely to be a sharp rise in the prices of certain commodities' (*CW, VII*: 300).

Keynes's more extended analysis, therefore, points to the conclusion that differences in the quantity of money in the economic system are accompanied by differences in the level of employment on the one hand and by different patterns of output and of *relative* prices on the other.

It also points to the conclusion that a reduction in effective demand below the level at which full employment would prevail will diminish both employment and prices, whereas an increase in effective demand beyond the minimum level required to produce full employment will affect prices only. Keynes attributes this 'apparent asymmetry' to the fact that, whilst labour is always in a position to refuse to work on a scale involving a real wage which is less than the marginal disutility of that amount of employment, it is not in a position to insist on being offered work on a scale involving a real wage which is not greater than the marginal disutility of that amount of employment (*CW, VII*: 291, also 303–4).

THE THEORY OF MONEY AND PRICES

An implication of Keynes's method of reasoning, which Keynes himself regarded as a very important implication, is that 'the price level as a whole' is determined by the conditions of supply and demand in relation to individual commodities (*CW, VII*: *xxxiv–xxxv*). The quantity of money, and changes therein, enter into the matter only in so far as it affects the conditions of supply and the conditions of demand at the level of the individual commodity.
    To begin with Keynes points out that

In a single industry its particular price-level depends partly on the rate of remuneration of the factors of production which enter into its marginal cost, and partly on the scale of output (*CW, VII*: 294).

That is simply another way of saying that the price of individual goods are determined by supply and demand. But Keynes goes on to argue that

There is no reason to modify this conclusion when we pass to industry as a whole. The general price-level depends partly on the rate of remuneration of the factors of production which enter into marginal cost and partly on the scale of output as a whole, i.e. (taking equipment and technique as given) on the volume of employment (*CW, VII*: 294).

Since the concept of a general price-level has already been ruled out for the purposes of a 'causal analysis' (*CW, VII*: 39) it must be presumed that the term 'general price-level' in this passage refers to the level of the array or complex of individual prices in the economic system as a whole rather than to anything in the nature of an index of average prices. Thus what Keynes is arguing is merely that all prices are determined by supply and demand in the sense that all prices in terms of money are determined by costs of production and by demand both of which in a monetary economy are necessarily expressed in terms of money values. He admits that when industry as a whole is being considered the costs of production in any particular industry are not wholly independent of the output of the other industries. However, he contends that at the level of industry as a whole, as compared with a single industry,

> the more significant change, of which we have to take account, is the effect of changes in *demand* both on costs and on volume. It is on the side of demand that we have to introduce quite new ideas when we are dealing with demand as a whole and no longer with the demand for a single product taken in isolation, with demand as a whole assumed to be unchanged (*CW, VII*: 294–5).

The 'theory of prices' (*CW, VII*: 296), or as Keynes also calls it the 'theory of money and prices' (*CW, VII*: 292), is concerned with

> the analysis of the relation between changes in the quantity of money and changes in the price-level with a view to determining the elasticity of prices in response to changes in the quantity of money (*CW, VII*: 296).

It does this by addressing the factors which tend to introduce complications into the effects of changes in the quantity of money. We have touched on some of them already. Keynes sums them up as follows

(1) Effective demand will not change in exact proportion to the quantity of money.
(2) Since resources are not homogeneous, there will be diminishing, and not constant, returns as employment gradually increases.
(3) Since resources are not interchangeable, some commodities will reach a condition of inelastic supply whilst there are still unemployed resources available for the production of other commodities.
(4) The wage-unit will tend to rise, before full employment has been reached.
(5) The remunerations of the factors entering into marginal cost will not all change in the same proportion (*CW, VII*: 296).

Keynes stresses that these 'complicating factors' interact with each other. They must not, therefore, be regarded as 'strictly speaking, independent' (*CW, VII*: 297).

Thus Keynes sees the theory of prices as one which explains how all the individual prices in the whole complex of prices are determined by the conditions of supply and demand in the context of differences in the quantity of money. It is clear then that the theory of money denoted in the title of his book, namely, *The General Theory of Employment, Interest and Money*, is to be regarded as synonymous with the theory of prices as he understands it. He stresses that the traditional 'theory of money and prices' or quantity theory in which supply and demand play no part in the determination of price is unsatisfactory because of the implication that the elasticity of supply is zero and that demand is proportional to the quantity of money (*CW, VII*: 292). His aim is 'to bring the theory of prices as a whole back to close contact with the theory of value' (*CW, VII*: 293). That is to say, his purpose is to show that differences in prices as a whole against the background of differences in the quantity of money can be, and indeed must be, explained in the same way as they are explained by the theory of value, namely, by the conditions of supply and demand. In other words, the ultimate objective of the theory of money and prices is to trace out the impact of differences in the quantity of money on the conditions of supply and demand in regard to commodities. The theory of interest, for its part, deals with the impact of differences in the quantity of money on the prices of debts and, therefore, with the determination of the rate of interest. Thus the theory of interest and the theory of money are two facets of the explanation of the rôle of money in the determination of the prices of debts and of commodities respectively.

THE QUANTITY THEORY OF MONEY

Keynes's explanation of the determination of the level of prices as a whole is obviously very different from the traditional quantity theory of money, or the 'crude quantity theory' as he termed it (*CW, VII*: 289).[23] According to this as we have seen an increase in the quantity of money has no effect on output but causes prices to rise in exact proportion to the quantity of money. Its 'great fault' (*CW, VII*: 209) is that 'it does not distinguish between changes in prices which are a function of changes in output, and those which are a function of changes in the wage-unit' (*CW, VII*: 209). He suggests that

The explanation of this omission is, perhaps, to be found in the assumptions that there is no propensity to hoard and that there is always full employment. For in this case, (output) being constant and M_2 being zero, it follows, if we can take V (that is, income-velocity) also as constant, that both the wage-unit and the price-level will be directly proportional to the quantity of money (*CW, VII*: 209).

Following this line of thought Keynes formulates 'a generalised quantity theory of money' (*CW, VII*: 285) which he expresses as follows

> So long as there is unemployment, *employment* will change in the same proportion as the quantity of money; and when there is full employment, *prices* will change in the same proportion as the quantity of money (*CW, VII*: 296).

Several assumptions are required to support this generalized version of the quantity theory. Keynes enumerates them and examines them in the light of his own analysis.

The first is that the rates of remuneration of all the factors of production 'which enter into marginal cost' all change in the same proportion as the wage-unit. This allows the conclusion that 'the general price-level (taking equipment and technique as given) depends partly on the wage-unit and partly on the volume of employment' (*CW, VII*: 295). Accordingly, changes in the quantity of money can be regarded as affecting the price-level through the wage-unit and through employment.

The further assumptions, '(1) that all unemployed resources are homogeneous and interchangeable in their efficiency to produce what is wanted, and (2) that the factors of production entering into marginal cost are content with the same money-wage so long as there is a surplus of them unemployed' (*CW, VII*: 295), permit the conclusion that there are constant returns and an unchanging wage-unit provided there is *any* unemployment. On that basis an increase in the quantity of money

> will have no effect whatever on prices, so long as there is any unemployment, and ... employment will increase in exact proportion to any increase in effective demand brought about by the increase in the quantity of money; whilst as soon as full employment is reached, it will thence-forward be the wage-unit and prices

which will increase in exact proportion to the increase in effective demand (*CW, VII*: 295).

The final assumption required to support the generalized quantity theory is simply that 'effective demand changes in the same proportion as the quantity of money' (*CW, VII*: 295).

As Keynes sees it these assumptions are not plausible because of the 'complications' which we have listed above (page 179). These are self-explanatory but Keynes's discussion of the fifth one, namely, that the remuneration of the factors entering into marginal cost will not all change in the same proportion, calls for a brief comment.

He argues that if this assumption is replaced by the assumption that the proportions may differ and that if the idea of 'a weighted average of the rewards of the factors entering into marginal prime-cost' (*CW, VII*: 302) is used instead of the wage-unit then this unit, or *cost-unit* as he terms it, becomes 'the essential standard of value' (*CW, VII*: 302) in the context of the generalized quantity theory.[24] A sum of money expressed in terms of cost-units furnishes the weighted average of the number of units of all factors, including labour, implicit in that sum. Given the state of technique and equipment the price-level would depend

partly on the cost-unit and partly on the scale of output, increasing, where output increases, *more* than in proportion to any increase in the cost-unit, in accordance with the principle of diminishing returns in the short period (*CW, VII*: 302–3).

The ultimate conclusion to which this line of argument points is that

We have full employment when output has risen to a level at which the marginal return from a representative unit of the factors of production has fallen to the minimum figure at which a quantity of the factors sufficient to produce this output is available (*CW, VII*: 303).

This passage may be interpreted to mean that when the cost-unit, that is 'the weighted average of the rewards of the factors entering into marginal prime-cost', is equal to the value of the output of that set of factors at the margin full employment prevails (*CW, VII*: 302). Any expansion of output beyond that point would mean that its value would be less than the cost-unit at the margin. Accordingly, output would have to become inelastic at that point and so, by definition, there would be full employment.

Keynes concludes his examination of the relationship between the quantity of money and prices with some observations on the nature of this relationship 'in the long run' (*CW, VII*: 306). He suggests, however, that this 'is a question for historical generalisation rather than for pure theory' (*CW, VII*: 306). Looking at the question from the stand-point of his own analysis he considers that

> If there is some tendency to a measure of long-run uniformity in the state of liquidity-preference, there may well be some sort of rough relationship between the national income and the quantity of money required to satisfy liquidity-preference, taken as a mean over periods of pessimism and optimism together. There may be, for example, some fairly stable proportion of the national income more than which people will not readily keep in the shape of idle balances for long periods together, provided the rate of interest exceeds a certain psychological minimum; so that if the quantity of money beyond what is required in the active circulation is in excess of this proportion of the national income, there will be a tendency sooner or later for the rate of interest to fall to the neighbourhood of this minimum. The falling rate of interest will then, *cet. par.*, increase effective demand, and the increasing effective demand will reach one or more of the semi-critical points at which the wage-unit will tend to show a discontinuous rise, with a corresponding effect on prices. The opposite tendencies will set in if the quantity of surplus money is an abnormally low proportion of the national income. Thus the net effect of fluctuations over a period of time will be to establish a mean figure in conformity with the stable proportion between the national income and the quantity of money to which the psychology of the public tends sooner or later to revert (*CW, VII*: 306–7).

10 Conclusion

Keynes's reasoning in *The General Theory* is developed in two stages. Chapters 3 to 17 set out the 'first approximation' (*CW, VII*: 286) while the elaborations of the basic first approximation are dealt with in Chapters 19, 20 and 21.

The first approximation is summarized in Chapters 3 and 18. The summaries in these Chapters differ from each other especially in that the order in which the various elements of the method of reasoning are set out is (more or less) reversed in Chapter 18 as compared with Chapter 3. That brings to mind what Robertson says about the Cambridge equation, namely, that in using it as a method for organizing one's thinking about the monetary matters to which it relates, one can begin at whichever variable seems most appropriate to the problem under consideration (page 21).

SUMMARY

A useful way of envisaging *The General Theory* is to begin by recalling that its purpose is to address the question as to what determines the employment of the available resources in the monetary-entrepreneur economy. The next step is to recall that it is entrepreneurs who employ resources. Hence the method of addressing the question has to be rooted in the firm, the firm being the entrepreneurial entity or unit which consists of the entrepreneur and the resources employed (Kirzner, 1963:149; 1973:27), but in such a way that it can be extended to the economy as a whole in a coherent manner. This involves (i) the adaptation of the theory of the firm so that it explains the determination of employment, while leaving the explanation of the determination of output implicit; (ii) seeing demand both from the seller's and from the buyer's point of view; and (iii) addressing some matters of technique, especially the selection of units of quantity that can be added unambiguously, the identification of what constitutes an income and an output, and the adoption of a plausible and coherent way of dealing with time and with the uncertainty that is inseparable from time.

The matters mentioned in (iii) above are the perplexities that confronted Keynes. Their resolution played an essential part in the method of analysis formulated in *The General Theory*. It is hardly an exaggeration to say that the possibility of addressing the central question depended on the resolution of these perplexities. Only with their resolution was it possible to separate the two aspects of demand from each other, to go from the individual seller and the individual buyer to the economy as a whole, and to establish the exact relationship between an income and an output in any period irrespective of its duration.

The entrepreneur is assumed to seek to maximize profit. Since the entrepreneur operates in time and, therefore, under conditions of uncertainty this is the only plausible assumption that can be made in regard to profit-maximization. As Keynes is dealing with the employment of resources he couches his treatment of the decision to employ them in terms of the proceeds the entrepreneur would expect to receive from the sale of the output produced at different possible scales of the utilization of his capital equipment in conjunction with different possible levels of the employment of labour and in terms of the proceeds that would be required to maximize profit given costs. If there is some particular scale of utilization and corresponding level of employment at which the expected proceeds and the proceeds that would be required to maximize profit coincide, the entrepreneur will operate at that level of employment. That is the basis of the concept of effective demand. It is the corner-stone of the general theory of employment. Its rôle in the analysis is to provide the means of identifying demand as the seller sees it and of identifying the scale on which resources, both capital and labour, are employed.

By separating the two perspectives on demand, the way in which the entrepreneur perceives demand can be dealt with independently of the determinants of demand. This gives a clearly distinguishable supply-side and demand-side as far as the firm is concerned in that the demand facing the firm on the basis of which its decisions are made is the subjective judgement of the entrepreneur as to what demand might be. There is no confusion or ambiguity about this as it is quite distinct from the conditions of demand on the buyer's side. If what the entrepreneur expected to receive were to be what buyers were to spend, the entrepreneur would have achieved the objective of maximizing profit and so the firm would be in equilibrium.

Effective demand denotes the extent to which the firm employs labour, the scale on which it operates its capital equipment and the volume of output it produces. It is a highly comprehensive concept. Although it relates to the supply or production side of Keynes's analytical apparatus, it is aptly named because the entrepreneur has no logical alternative to the demand which will be *expected* to maximize profit as the basis upon which to make decisions regarding the employment of resources and the production of output.

With the aid of the homogeneous unit of quantity, the labour-unit, which Keynes devised on the one hand, and of the naturally homogeneous unit of money on the other, it is possible to add both the proceeds expected by all firms and the number of labour-units they decide to employ so as to obtain supply-side totals for the economy as a whole. Since effective demand is defined in expectational terms it provides the basis for arriving at these totals without ambiguity and without involving any complications by reason of the different lengths of the 'days' from one firm to another.

By deducting user cost from the gross proceeds expected the income (factor incomes and expected profit) which entrepreneurs would expect to generate in producing an output is seen to be equal to the value of that output. Output in this context is made up of the goods and services bought for consumption and devoted to investment.

Keynes makes little of his treatment of the supply-side in *The General Theory*. As mentioned several times his development of the theory of the firm lay in treating it in terms of expectations and thereby being able to distinguish between demand as seen, or imagined, by the entrepreneur from the decisions of buyers to buy. His originality in regard to the supply of output as a whole lay in his being able to deal with it in terms of units of money and of units of labour. In that way the problem of the heterogeneity of output was coped with.

Keynes wished to concentrate on the development of a theory of demand for output as a whole because up to his time no such theory existed. Neither on the demand-side was there anything analogous to the theory of the firm which could be generalized to the economy as a whole and, thereby, serve as the basis on which a theory of the demand for output as a whole could be developed. Relative prices help the consumer to determine how best to apportion what he wishes to spend on the various goods and services on offer. The ultimate limit, apart from borrowing and dissaving, to what he can spend is his income. Since Keynes is primarily concerned with the demand for output as a whole and more specifically with the employment implied in that demand rather than with the demand for particular products he has to concentrate on the relationship between consumption and income. He conceptualizes that relationship in terms of the propensity to consume, which is an aspect of time-preference. There is a 'gap' between income and expenditure for consumption purposes which allows for the possibility that there may be a profit-disequilibrium at the level of the economy as a whole consequent on the further possibility that investment may not be such as would fill the gap at the expected level of income, thereby resulting in a level of income other than that expected when the entrepreneurs' decisions to employ resources are made.

Keynes sees investment, the second, but more volatile, source of demand, as being determined by the subjective estimate of the investor regarding the returns that might be expected over the life of the investment, conceptualized as the marginal efficiency of capital, and by the rate of interest. Expectation again is at the heart of the decision to invest. Once again the uncertainty surrounding all economic activity is brought to the reader's attention. Once again also expectation is the device which enables future returns to be converted into a present phenomenon, namely, the rate of discount, which can be related to another present phenomenon, the rate of interest.

The sums spent on consumption and the money value of what is devoted to investment can be added so as to arrive at total demand in the economy as a whole. Moreover, these sums by being expressed in wage-units are translated into the number of labour-units implied in demand. In that way total effective demand on the supply-side and total consumption and investment on the demand-side are expressed in the same units of quantity.

The equilibrium of the whole system depends on whether or not the 'gap' is filled by a level of investment such that total demand is what entrepreneurs would expect it to be when they make their decisions to employ resources and produce output. Given the marginal efficiency of capital, the volume of investment is limited by the rate of interest.

This leads to the consideration of the nature of the phenomenon of interest and to the analysis of its determination. Interest on money is traced to the second aspect of time-preference, namely, liquidity-preference or the desire of people to have all or part of their wealth immediately available in the form of money. Money is, therefore, to be regarded as an asset and demanded for that reason. It is this particular characteristic of money which distinguishes a monetary economy from a real exchange economy. While it is doubtful if a real exchange economy could exist in practice the concept of a real exchange economy is an indispensable analytical device in the elucidation of the theories of price and distribution.

The rate of interest, or rather the complex of rates of interest, is the obverse of the price of debts which earn a monetary return. Given the quantity of money and the level of income the prices of debts must adjust in such a way that the public is able to satisfy its liquidity-preferences through the choices open to it to hold wealth in terms either of debts or of money. In that way the rates of interest are determined.

The components of the general theory of employment can now be seen to be the principle of effective demand, the propensity to consume, the state of liquidity-preference, the rate of interest and the wage-unit. When the magnitudes associated with these phenomena are in a particular relationship to one another the quantity of employment which entrepreneurs decide upon will be the same as that implied in total demand for consumption and investment. Profit in the economic system as a whole is then at its maximum and the system is, therefore, in equilibrium in the sense that, other things being equal, there is no reason for it to change.

If these conditions prevail the determinate relationship which Keynes calls the investment multiplier will hold between a small increment of investment and the increment of income. The principle or law of the multiplier must, therefore, also be included as an essential component of the general theory of employment.

The foregoing is the core of *The General Theory*. It is essentially what Keynes develops in the first 18 chapters and summarizes in Chapters 3 and 18. But it is, as already observed, only a first approximation. In Chapters 19, 20 and 21 he elaborates on his basic method of reasoning in order to show how the impact of changes in wages and in the quantity of money on the employment of the available resources can be analyzed. In doing so he also shows how enormously complex the economic system is. It is so complex that it is extremely difficult, if not indeed totally impossible, to trace out the effects of any cause in full, and quite impossible to foretell what the consequences of change will be. Keynes stresses that with the expansion in employment accompanying a rise in effective demand, output will not become uniformly inelastic so that the possibility of 'true inflation' while there is still some unemployment has to be allowed for.

RELATIVE STABILITY

Keynes considers that 'an outstanding characteristic' (*CW, VII*: 249) of the economic system as it was in and before his time is that, while the level of activity fluctuated severely, it was not 'violently unstable' (*CW, VII*: 249). He says that the economy 'seems capable of remaining in a chronic condition of sub-normal activity for a considerable period' (*CW, VII*: 249). By this he means that it operates neither at or even near full employment nor collapses altogether. He claims that 'approximately' full employment is rare and short-lived. Our 'normal lot' as he puts it is one 'which is neither desperate nor satisfactory' (*CW, VII*: 250).

This relative stability may be regarded as the actual counterpart of the concept of profit-equilibrium at less than full employment. It arises because the determinants of employment happen to have certain values and characteristics rather than that they have them as a matter of logical necessity. Keynes refers to these values and characteristics as the 'conditions of stability which the foregoing analysis suggests to us as capable of explaining the observed results' (*CW, VII*: 250).

The first condition is that the multiplier must be greater than unity but not very large. He considers this to be a highly plausible hypothesis. The psychology of people is such, as he sees it, that in general and, on the average, a person's consumption fluctuates less than does his income (*CW, VII*: 96). He suggests, moreover, that the same is true of governments 'especially in an age when a progressive increase of unemployment will usually force the State to provide relief out of borrowed funds' (*CW, VII*: 251).

Keynes goes on to argue that 'experience would be extremely different from what it is if the [psychological] law did not hold' (*CW, VII*: 251). If it did not, even a very small increase in investment would lead to a 'cumulative' increase in aggregate demand and consequently in effective demand also until full employment was reached. A decrease in investment would lead to a situation in which no one was employed (*CW, VII*: 252). There may be a range, though a narrow one, 'within which instability does in fact prevail' (*CW, VII*: 252). But outside of this range 'our psychological law must unquestionably hold good' (*CW, VII*: 252). Furthermore the multiplier cannot be very large because if it were 'a given change in the rate of investment would involve a great change (limited only by full or zero employment) in the rate of consumption' (*CW, VII*: 252).

The second condition is that 'a moderate change in the prospective yield of capital assets or in the rate of interest' would not lead to an unlimited change in the rate of investment. This is likely to be the case because of 'the increasing cost of producing a greatly enlarged output from the existing equipment' (CW, *VII*: 252). Hence the cost of newly produced capital assets could be expected to rise considerably if their production were to be greatly expanded. It follows that either a very low or perhaps a zero or even negative rate of interest on the one hand or a very great increase in prospective yields on the other would be required to make it worthwhile to invest in more costly capital assets. If, however, there were very large quantities of unemployed resources available for the production of capital assets their cost of production would not rise as their production was increased and this too could give rise to 'considerable instability within a certain range' (*CW, VII*: 252).

The third condition relates to the stability of prices rather than to the stability of the economic system as such. It is that moderate changes in employment should not be associated with very great changes in money-wages. Keynes considers this in fact to have been the case. He argues indeed that it must be the case because otherwise there would be what he terms 'violent instability in the price level' (*CW, VII*: 253).

The fourth condition underlies the tendency of 'a fluctuation in one direction to reverse itself in due course' (*CW, VII*: 251). Keynes attributes this tendency to the impact of a changed rate of investment on the marginal efficiency of capital 'if it is continued for a period which, measured in years, is not very large' (*CW, VII*: 251). This contention is based on the plausible assumption that

> Capital assets are of various ages, wear out with time and are not all very long-lived; so that if the rate of investment falls below a certain minimum level, it is merely a question of time (failing large fluctuations in other factors) before the marginal efficiency of capital rises sufficiently to bring about a recovery of investment above this minimum. And similarly, of course, if investment rises to a higher figure than formerly, it is only a question of time before the marginal efficiency of capital falls sufficiently to bring about a recession unless there are compensating changes in other factors (*CW, VII*: 253–4).

Keynes's method of identifying the conditions under which the relative stability of the economic system holds is an example of what he understood the purpose of the theory of economics to be. It, as he says, is a 'technique of thinking' by means of which particular aspects of the way in which the economic system behaves can be understood and explained.

THE TRADE CYCLE

The conditions required for the existence of the relative stability of the economic system do not of themselves explain the fluctuations in the level of economic activity usually designated the trade cycle. Keynes takes it for granted that such a cycle exists and attempts to explain it with the aid of the general theory in a manner which again exemplifies what he means by the theory of economics and how it is used as a method of reasoning.

He begins his explanation of the cycle by observing that if his theory of the determination of employment 'at any time' is right, that 'theory must be capable of explaining the phenomena of the trade cycle' (*CW, VII*: 313). The cycle is 'highly complex' (*CW, VII*: 313). He considers it so complex that 'every element' of his analysis 'will be required for its complete explanation' (*CW, VII*: 313). Fluctuations in the propensity to consume, in the state of liquidity-preference, and in the marginal efficiency of capital all play a part in the cycle. Keynes emphasizes that in his view what justifies the use of the term *cycle* to describe the essential character of the fluctuations in economic activity above all else is the 'way in which the marginal efficiency of capital fluctuates' (*CW, VII*: 313). He thinks that

> The trade cycle is best regarded ... as being occasioned by a cyclical change in the marginal efficiency of capital, though complicated and often aggravated by associated changes in the other significant short-period variables of the economic system (*CW, VII*: 313).

A cyclical *movement* is one in which the forces propelling the system in a particular direction have a 'cumulative effect on one another' (*CW, VII*: 314) but eventually they weaken and are replaced by forces which propel it in the opposite direction. In addition 'there is some recognisable degree of regularity in the time-sequence and duration of the upward and downward movements' (*CW, VII*: 314). There is also another aspect of the cycle which must be explained, namely, the *crisis*. What constitutes a crisis is that an upward movement is suddenly replaced by the downward movement whereas the change from the downward to the upward movement takes place gradually.

Though he refers to events in the United Kingdom and in the United States in the 1920s and 1930s Keynes concentrates on what he refers to as 'the case of a typical industrial trade cycle in the nineteenth-century environment' (*CW, VII*: 314). In these cycles

fluctuations in the marginal efficiency of capital had cyclical characteristics for 'certain definite reasons' which were 'by no means unfamiliar either in themselves or as explanations of the trade cycle' (*CW*,
VII: 314–15). Keynes says that his 'only purpose' in his investigation
of the trade cycle is to 'link up' these reasons 'with the preceding
theory' (*CW*, *VII*: 315).

He begins his explanation of the cycle 'with the later stages of the
boom and the onset of the 'crisis'' (*CW*, *VII*: 315). In the case of
durable assets expectations about the future inevitably 'play a dominant part in determining the scale on which new investment is deemed
advisable' (*CW*, *VII*: 315). In the nature of things these expectations
'are subject to sudden and violent changes' (*CW*, *VII*: 315). He
suggests that in the typical case the crisis is due not so much to a
rise in the rate of interest, as is often claimed, but to 'a sudden
collapse in the marginal efficiency of capital' (*CW*, *VII*: 315).

In the later stages of the boom expectations are highly optimistic as to
future yields in spite of the increased quantities of capital goods available and of the rising costs of producing them and of a probable rise in
the rate of interest. Eventually 'disillusion falls upon an over-optimistic
and over-bought market' and it falls 'with sudden and even catastrophic
force' (*CW*, *VII*: 316, *footnote omitted*). A 'sharp increase' in liquidity-
preference is precipitated by the fall in the marginal efficiency of capital
and that brings about a rise in the rate of interest which in turn aggra-
vates the decline in investment. But Keynes contends that liquidity-
preference 'except those manifestations of it which are associated
with increasing trade and speculation, does not increase until *after* the
collapse in the marginal efficiency of capital' (*CW*, *VII*: 316).

It is the collapse in the marginal efficiency of capital 'which renders
the slump so intractable' (*CW*, *VII*: 316). Its recovery takes time
which is of 'a particular order of magnitude' (*CW*, *VII*: 317). Hence
the explanation of the time element in the cycle must be sought 'in the
influences which govern the recovery of the marginal efficiency of
capital' (*CW*, *VII*: 317). The length of life of durable assets 'in relation
to the normal rate of growth in a given epoch' (*CW*, *VII*: 317) and the
carrying-costs of durable assets cause the downward movement to
have 'an order of magnitude which is not fortuitous, which does not
fluctuate between, say, one year this time and ten years next time, but
which shows some regularity of habit between, let us say, three and
five years' (*CW*, *VII*: 317).

At the beginning of the slump there is probably a good deal of
capital the marginal efficiency of which is negligible or even negative.

The interval of time that must elapse before it recovers 'may be a somewhat stable function of the average durability of capital in a given epoch' (*CW, VII*: 318). This is because capital will have to become scarce before the marginal efficiency of capital will increase. This scarcity can only occur in the circumstances prevailing at the start of the slump 'through use, decay and obsolescence' (*CW, VII*: 318). Keynes's claim then is that there *may be* a fairly stable relationship between the length of time it takes capital to become scarce again for these reasons on the one hand and the average durability of capital on the other.

The cessation of investment after the crisis 'will probably lead to an accumulation of surplus stocks of unfinished goods' (*CW, VII*: 318). Keynes claims that the carrying costs of these stocks will 'seldom be less than 10 per cent per annum' (*CW, VII*: 318). The further accumulation of stocks will be restricted and existing stock will be disposed of over a period of 'three to five years at the outside' (*CW, VII*: 318). Their disposal would, of course, be partly dependent on the extent to which their prices fell. The process by which the stocks are disposed of 'represents negative investment' and when it is over 'a manifest relief will be experienced' (*CW, VII*: 318).

Furthermore, the reduction in working capital which necessarily accompanies the reduction of output also represents disinvestment. Once the decline has begun, this aspect of negative investment 'exerts a strong cumulative influence in the downward direction' (*CW, VII*: 318).

A 'serious fall' in the marginal efficiency of capital also has an adverse effect on the propensity to consume. That is because a fall in the marginal efficiency of capital also involves a decline in the value of equities on the stock exchange. Those who are actively engaged in the purchase and sale of shares, especially if they are employing borrowed funds, are very much influenced in respect of their expenditure on consumption by a fall in stock exchange values. Indeed Keynes considers that these 'people are, perhaps, even more influenced in their readiness to spend by rises and falls in the value of their investments than by the state of their incomes' (*CW, VII*: 319). He gives the United States in his time as an example of this phenomenon.

During the downward phase of the cycle when fixed capital and stocks of materials are excessive 'for the time being' and working capital is being reduced 'the schedule of the marginal efficiency of capital may fall so low that it can scarcely be corrected, so as to secure a satisfactory rate of new investment, by any practicable reduction in the rate of interest' (*CW, VII*: 319–20).

Having explained the trade cycle in the light of his own theory Keynes proceeds to examine other theories of the cycle. He does so within the framework provided in *The General Theory*. He begins with the theory that over-investment is characteristic of the boom then goes on to examine the under-consumption theory, the notion that the solution of the trade cycle lies in reducing the supply of labour seeking employment and the idea that the boom should be checked in its early stages by a higher rate of interest. He concludes by discussing theories of the cycle which see fluctuations in agriculture due to changes in weather conditions. He finds particular merit in these latter theories especially for the era in which they were propounded because of the effects that fluctuations in the stocks of agricultural products must have had on the rate of current investment.

OTHER ISSUES

In Chapter 23 of *The General Theory* Keynes again demonstrates how his method of analysis can be used to throw light on a number of issues both historical and theoretical. These are mercantilism, the usury laws, stamped money and theories of under-consumption.

Keynes sets out in his own terms what seems to him to be the 'element of scientific truth in mercantilist doctrine' (*CW, VII*: 335). But before doing so he emphasizes that the advantages claimed for mercantilism 'are avowedly national advantages and are unlikely to benefit the world as a whole' (*CW, VII*: 335).

Growth in wealth is liable to be interrupted by 'the insufficiency of the inducements to new investment' (*CW, VII*: 335). If investment is determined by the 'profit motive alone' (*CW, VII*: 335) the opportunities for domestic investment will ultimately be limited by the rate of interest. The volume of foreign investment 'is necessarily determined by the size of the favourable balance of trade' (*CW, VII*: 335). Hence 'the economic objects, with which it is reasonable for the government to be preoccupied, are the domestic rate of interest and the balance of foreign trade' (*CW, VII*: 335). If the wage-unit, liquidity-preference and banking conventions are stable the rate of interest 'will tend to be governed by the quantity of the precious metals, measured in terms of the wage-unit, available to satisfy the community's desire for liquidity' (*CW, VII*: 336). Since in mercantilist times, foreign loans and the ownership of wealth abroad were 'scarcely practicable' (*CW, VII*: 336) changes in the quantity of the precious metals would depend almost entirely on changes in the balance of trade. Concern with a favourable balance of trade 'served *both* purposes; and was, furthermore, the only available means of promoting them' (*CW, VII:* 336).

At a time when the authorities had no direct control over the domestic rate of interest or the other inducements to home investment, measures to increase the favourable balance of trade were the only *direct* means at their disposal for increasing foreign investment; and, at the same time, the effect of a favourable balance of trade on the influx of the precious metals was their only *indirect* means of reducing the domestic rate of interest and so increasing the inducement to home investment (*CW, VII:* 336).

Keynes points out that the success of this policy is subject to two limitations. The first is that the domestic rate of interest might fall so low that investment might be so great as to increase employment to a level which would lead to a rise in the wage-unit. If that were to happen the increase in costs would have an unfavourable effect on the balance of trade 'so that the effort to increase the latter will have overreached and defeated itself' (*CW, VII:* 336). The second is that the domestic rate of interest might fall compared with rates of interest abroad so that a volume of foreign lending might be stimulated 'which is disproportionate to the favourable balance' (*CW, VII:* 337), thereby leading to an outflow of the precious metals 'sufficient to reverse the advantages previously obtained' (*CW, VII:* 337).

Keynes cites Spain in the latter part of the fifteenth century and in the sixteenth century as an example of a country, the foreign trade of which 'was destroyed by the effect on the wage-unit of an excessive abundance of the precious metals' (*CW, VII:* 337). Great Britain in the early twentieth century is a case where the rate of interest was prevented from falling low enough to ensure full employment because of the 'excessive facilities for foreign lending and the purchase of properties abroad' (*CW, VII:* 337). India 'at all times' has been impoverished by such a strong preference for liquidity 'that even an enormous and chronic influx of the precious metals has been insufficient to bring down the rate of interest to a level which was compatible with the growth of real wealth' (*CW, VII:* 337).

Keynes stresses that a high level of protection is unlikely to lead to a highly favourable balance of trade. Hence he warned that 'a premature conclusion as to the *practical* policy' (*CW, VII:* 338) to which his argument leads should not be drawn. His discussion of mercantilism is not aimed at advocating mercantilist policies but rather at showing that what he considers to be the logic of the mercantilist position corroborates his own analysis particularly in regard to the determination of the rate of interest and of the volume of investment.

Turning specifically to the rate of interest Keynes observes that, in his view, the medieval attempt to distinguish the return on money-loans from the return on 'active investment' (*CW, VII*: 351) was 'an honest intellectual effort to keep separate what the classical theory has inextricably confused together, namely, the rate of interest and the marginal efficiency of capital' (*CW, VII*: 352). It now seems clear, he says, that

> the disquisitions of the schoolmen were directed towards the elucidation of a formula which should allow the schedule of the marginal efficiency of capital to be high, whilst using rule and custom and the moral law to keep down the rate of interest (*CW, VII*: 352).

Again, as in the case of mercantilism, Keynes sees the medieval attitude to usury in terms of his own logic and sees it as a vindication of that logic.

Keynes next deals with Gesell's contribution to the theory of money and interest. He credits Gesell with distinguishing correctly between the rate of interest and the marginal efficiency of capital and with the insight that it is the rate of interest which limits the growth of real capital. He also attributes to Gesell the view that the rate of interest is a monetary phenomenon and that the ownership of money as an asset involves negligible carrying costs and that other assets, such as stocks of commodities, involve carrying costs and yield a return 'because of the standard set by money' (*CW, VII*: 356). But Gesell did not conceive of the idea of liquidity-preference. For that reason he 'constructed only half a theory of the rate of interest' (*CW, VII*: 356). Keynes looks favourably, at least in principle, on the idea that money, in the form of currency notes, should involve carrying costs analogous to the carrying costs of stocks of goods. This view underlies his advocacy of 'stamped' money. Keynes points out, however, that there are many difficulties involved in any attempt to put such a scheme into effect which Gesell did not confront. In particular he failed to see that money is not the only asset that has a liquidity-premium attached to it. Money differs in degree only from other assets in that respect so that if currency notes were to be costly to carry 'a long series of substitutes would step into their shoes – bank-money, debts at call, foreign money, jewellery and the precious metals generally and so forth' (*CW, VII*: 358). It follows that however logical in principle, the practical difficulties to which stamped money would lead could be insurmountable.

Keynes finds much to commend in the various theories of under-consumption advanced by writers from the late sixteenth to the early twentieth centuries. In particular, he quotes Malthus at length and criticizes Ricardo for being 'stone-deaf to what Malthus was saying' (*CW, VII*: 364). He credits Hobson with

> the first explicit statement of the fact that capital is brought into existence not by the propensity to save but in response to the demand resulting from actual and prospective consumption (*CW, VII*: 368).

But Keynes criticizes Hobson for having no independent theory of the rate of interest with the result that he laid too much emphasis on the contention that under-consumption leads to over-investment 'in the sense of unprofitable investment'. What Hobson should have done, in Keynes's view, was to explain that 'a relatively weak propensity to consume helps to cause unemployment by requiring and *not* receiving the accompaniment of a compensating volume of new investment, which...is in general prevented from happening at all by the prospective profit falling below the standard set by the rate of interest' (*CW, VII*: 370).

Keynes's approach to the theories he examines is to identify those elements in them which conform to the logic of his own analysis and to reveal their defects in so far as they do not accord with his logic. By contrast he uses his own method of analysis to *explain* both the relative stability of the economic systems and the trade cycle. Thus he uses his theory as a method of thinking in two ways, namely, as a way of explaining a phenomenon and as a way of assessing another theory.

THEORY NOT POLICY

The last chapter of *The General Theory*, Chapter 24, entitled 'Concluding Notes On The Social Philosophy Towards Which The General Theory Might Lead', is of a different character from the rest of the book. Of it Keynes himself says

Assuredly my last chapter is not a necessary consequence of the previous parts. It brings in all kinds of non-economic factors about which economists as such are entitled, as well as likely, to differ *à l'outrance* amongst themselves (*CW, XXIX*: 231).

It is neither part of the method of analysis formulated in *The General Theory* nor is it an example of the use of that method as a means of understanding and explaining phenomena and theories. Accordingly, it is not considered here.

It is significant that the main examples that Keynes gives of the use or application of the general theory of employment as a technique of thinking relate to major issues arising from the nature of the economic system as a monetary-entrepreneurial one. It is also significant that the 'facts' he deals with are those of common experience rather than facts discovered by detailed historical or statistical research.

There is little or nothing in *The General Theory* to suggest that Keynes saw it as providing a 'model', in the modern sense, which could be used as a basis for the 'management' of the economy. Nor did he see it as providing a means by which economic forecasts could be made.

He does, of course, refer to matters of policy throughout the book. But subsequent to its publication he emphasized, as he had done in the Introduction, that it is a book about theory and not about policy. In the article which he published in 1937 he says

This that I offer is therefore, a theory of why output and employment are so liable to fluctuation. It does not offer a ready-made remedy as to how to avoid these fluctuations and to maintain output at a steady optimum level. But it is, properly speaking, a theory of employment because it explains *why,* in any given circumstances, employment is what it is. Naturally I am interested not only in the diagnosis, but also in the cure; and many pages of my book are devoted to the latter. But I consider that my suggestions for a cure, which, avowedly, are not worked out completely, are on a different plane from the diagnosis. They are not meant to be definitive; they are subject to all sorts of special assumptions and are necessarily related to the particular conditions of the time. But my main reasons for departing from the traditional theory go much deeper than this. They are of a highly general character and are meant to be definitive (*CW, XIV*: 121–2).

The emphasis on the supposed policy implications of *The General Theory* which is generally found in the literature, professional as well as popular, is misplaced and certainly is not in accordance with what Keynes himself said about the book. Nevertheless, it was perhaps inevitable that the book would be interpreted as one on policy in the circumstances of the times. Keynes himself indeed contributed to this interpretation, partly because of the extent to which he discusses 'cures' in the book and partly also because of his active involvement in the debates about policy.

It was natural enough in Keynes's time, especially in view of the experience gained during the war in 'managing' economies, to look to governmental policy in order to overcome what were regarded as deficiencies in the competitive market process. It came to be taken for granted that economic management had to be resorted to so as to achieve the three great objectives of full employment, a stable level of prices, and equilibrium in the balance of payments. A virtual consensus in favour of interventionist measures quickly emerged in the belief that these objectives could be attained. Few doubted that they could. Those few who did oppose interventionist policies, and they were in a very small minority, did so because they thought that intervention could not but make bad worse.

Keynes favoured intervention and thought it could be carried through successfully. There can be no doubt about that. Yet, he was cautious too. He had not 'worked out' how policies aimed at maintaining investment, for example, could be devised and implemented. He warned, as will be recalled, specifically of the danger of an expansionary monetary policy (*CW, VII*: 173).

Moreover, some of his statements which superficially seem to be making a case for governmental activity, on closer inspection, must be seen as making analytical points instead. For example, he says

> Let us assume that steps are taken to ensure that the rate of interest is consistent with the rate of investment which corresponds to full employment. Let us assume, further, that State action enters in as a balancing factor to provide that the growth of capital equipment shall be such as to approach saturation-point at a rate which does not put a disproportionate burden on the standard of life of the present generation (*CW, VII*: 220).

This passage looks like a plea for governmental intervention. Its real purpose, however, is to establish that if the *result* he is talking about were to prevail, the marginal efficiency of capital in equilibrium would be approximately zero and that a quasi-stationary state would come into being 'where changes and progress would result only from changes in technique, taste, population and institutions, with the products of capital selling at a price proportioned to the labour, etc., embodied in them on just the same principles as govern the prices of consumption-goods into which capital-charges enter in an insignificant degree' (*CW, VII*: 220–1).

Those who regarded themselves as Keynes's followers generally lacked the caution of the Master. They tended to ignore his reservations and warnings (many of which, of course, were confined to his private letters and so did not become generally known until the publication of the *Collected Writings*). Many also put aside the subtlety of his arguments and the implications of his insistence on the interdependent nature of all the different elements of the economic system. What now seem like quite naive attempts at 'demand management' were resorted to and very often justified by reference to Keynes. For a time, indeed, they even seemed to work at least to the extent that unemployment seemed no longer to be a problem in western countries from the end of the war to the late 1960's. Inflation and the state of the balance of payments rather than the employment of the available resources seemed to be the predominant problems. These could be seen and, rightly or wrongly, were seen, as the price that had to be paid for the success in eliminating unemployment. That *The General Theory* entered the folklore of economics as a work on policy is hardly surprising in these circumstances. Nor is it surprising that it largely ceased to be seen as a theoretical work in view of the current fashion which equates 'scientific' economics with the use of mathematical and econometric methods and which regards theory expressed in 'literary' form as belonging to the 'pre-scientific' stage of the development of the subject.

KEYNES'S OWN VIEW OF *THE GENERAL THEORY*

In the preface to the French edition of *The General Theory* Keynes, as we have already seen, foretold that historians of economic thought in the future would regard his book as being in the 'classical' tradition. In writing the book, however, he felt himself to be breaking away from that tradition (*CW, VII*: xxxi). Both views are well founded.

Keynes was certainly breaking away from classical theory in a particular way. He came to see that classical theory could not be used to address the questions that concerned him. Attempts to address questions analogous to his, as for example, those relating to the trade cycle, by means of the 'classical' theory were misconceived. Hence what Keynes was doing, as he himself understood it, was breaking away from the misuse of that theory.

He realized that classical theory was the proper theory to use in addressing questions relating to (1) the allocation of expenditure for consumption purposes by a consumer given the amount of money at his disposal for such expenditure, (2) the determination of the pattern or composition of output, and (3) the distribution of income. He saw also that this traditional theory needed to be complemented by a new body of theory if his particular question was to be addressed. Traditional theory simply did not provide the appropriate means for dealing with that question. His new theory and traditional theory, as he knew it, are complementary in that they provide the machinery of thought by means of which issues appropriate to each may be addressed.

Being complementary, the two sets of theories exist independently in their own right. They do not under any circumstances form a synthesis. They are distinct methods elaborated to deal with distinct questions, namely (i) what governs the *employment* of the available resources? and (ii) what governs the *allocation* of the available resources and the *distribution* of output or income?

In terms of Keynes's view of economic theory the notion of a 'neo-classical' synthesis can have no meaning because such a synthesis would imply that traditional theory and Keynes's theory would cease to have any separate validity of their own under certain conditions. The possibility of a neo-classical synthesis implies that theory is to be seen as purely descriptive and, therefore, is inconsistent with the purpose of theory as Keynes understood it. In other words, the notion of a neo-classical synthesis is inconsistent with theory seen as a 'technique of thinking'.

What Keynes would seem to have had in mind when he foretold how historians in the future would perceive *The General Theory* was that the book is very much in the traditional mould in that it was written in order to provide the new piece of the 'apparatus of thought' which Keynes saw was needed. As we have already stressed, it is wholly within the tradition in that respect. That tradition was associated above all with Marshall, but in Keynes's view it went back to Adam Smith himself. More broadly it was part of what he described as the 'Scotch' and 'English' tradition of 'humane science' which he traced back to John Locke and to which he felt he belonged.

Notes

1. *In The Collected Writings of John Maynard Keynes*, abbreviated as *CW* with the volume number following, *The General Theory, CW, VII*.
2. The term 'model' in the sense in which Keynes uses it has a different connotation from the sense in which it is used at present. Nowadays, a 'model' denotes an analytical representation expressed in mathematical notation which may, or may not, be statistically estimated.
3. Keynes is dealing only with the monetary-entrepreneur economy as far as employment is concerned. Therefore, employment given by government and by non-profit organisations as well as by people who employ labour as a consumer service is to be taken to be implied in the 'social structure' to which Keynes refers (*CW, VII*: 245). Accordingly, firms may be seen as the *causa causans* governing employment.
4. Alternatively, the aggregate supply function may be derived by assuming that the firm adds a 'mark-up' to its costs to provide for its profit at each level of output. The relationship between the number of labour-units implied in each level of output and the proceeds that would be required to cover costs and profit would then be the aggregate supply function. Each point on the function would represent a higher level of profit than would be represented by any point below it. Each such point would, therefore, be a potential maximum profit point. Hence all the points, that is, the aggregate supply function would again be the locus of the potential maximum profit levels of employment in the firm. This method of deriving the aggregate supply function requires that 'the expectation of proceeds which will just make it worth the while of the entrepreneur to give that employment' be interpreted to refer to the attainment of a level of proceeds that would include the 'mark-up'.
5. Keynes shows that under certain conditions the slope of the aggregate supply function would be 1, and under other conditions it would be the reciprocal of the money-wage (*CW, VII*: 55–6).
6. If the 'mark-up' method of deriving the aggregate supply function is followed the point of effective demand denotes the higher level of profit the firm expects to be attainable. To the left of the point of intersection the firm would not be able to meet the expected demand implied in the aggregate demand function at the supply-prices and corresponding quantities implied in the aggregate supply function. To the right of the point of intersection the expected proceeds would not be sufficient to cover the expected outlays and the mark-up required.
7. The term 'derived demand' is somewhat misleading as it may easily be misinterpreted as meaning that final demand constitutes the means (as distinct from the purpose) of employing the factors of production.
8. Keynes's concern, as we have emphasized, is with the acquisition of newly produced capital equipment, since it alone is part of current output, rather than with the acquisition of capital equipment in general,

both old and new. An entrepreneur who buys a piece of second-hand equipment is making an investment, from his point of view. But as he is not buying newly produced equipment his purchase is not part of the demand for current output.

9. That an individual entrepreneur might contemplate the purchase of only one unit of a particular asset does not invalidate this analysis.

10. For example: 'Interest is the payment made for the use of money and is dependent on the amount of capital on loan, and the length of time involved' (Allen, 1939: 31).

11. The fact that the types of debt (nowadays often erroneously referred to as 'products') in which banks deal evolve and change over time and that different types of financial institutions are allowed by the monetary authority to provide 'banking' services does not vitiate Keynes's approach. Keynes is dealing with the principle at issue. All that is necessary is that whatever definition of money is adopted be adhered to consistently.

12. The use of money for the transaction of current business and as a store of wealth are two of the three standard functions ascribed to money. The third function, that of unit-of-account, is, of course, not related to the question of actually holding money, since a unit-of-account need neither be a medium-of-exchange which would be held for the purpose of transacting current business, nor a way in which to hold wealth (e.g. the 'ECU', which is merely a notional 'basket' of national currencies, and the guinea).

13. If the price of debts could be foreseen with certainty, lending and borrowing would, of course, still take place. If people and firms had more money than they needed for the purpose of transacting current business they could 'rent' their surplus to those who required cash. The rent they would receive would depend on the strength of the demand for cash on the part of borrowers. If those with surplus cash could use it themselves for investment purposes they would require borrowers to compensate them for the gains they forego by lending. (Keynes's remarks about the medieval schoolmen are relevant in this connection (*CW*, *VII*: 352); also Chapter 10, p. 196). But in these circumstances there would be no advantage in *holding* cash, apart from the convenience of having it for the purpose of effecting current transactions. That means that $q - c + l$ would be zero or nearly zero. In fact, the price of debts cannot be foreseen with certainty. For that reason there are advantages, discussed in the text, in holding money over and above what is required for current purposes. Consequently l is positive. Holders of money will part with it in exchange for debts only if they are compensated for foregoing the advantages of holding it. That compensation is what Keynes identifies as the money-rate of interest as such.

14. In terms of the more familiar notation and taking, for example, the current rates of interest on two debts of $(n + r)$ and n years maturity to be i_1 and i_2, respectively, the present values of £1 discounted over these periods are respectively,

$$£1 * \frac{1}{(1 + i_1)^{n+r}} \quad \text{and} \quad £1 * \frac{1}{(1 + i_2)^{n}}$$

If the debts of n years maturity were to be extended for a further r years at the future rate of interest, i_3, that would prevail on debts of r years maturity n years from now, its present value would be

$$\pounds 1 * \frac{1}{(1 + i_2)^n} * \frac{1}{(1 + i_3)^r}$$

$$i.e. \ \frac{\pounds 1 * \frac{1}{(1+i_2)^n}}{(1 + i_3)^r}$$

If, furthermore, it can be taken that this present value would be equal to the present value of the original debt of $(n + r)$ years maturity discounted at the rate of interest i_1 we have

$$\frac{\pounds 1 * \frac{1}{(1+i_2)^n}}{(1 + i_3)^r} = \pounds 1 * \frac{1}{(1 + i_1)^{n+r}} \tag{1}$$

Dividing the numerator on both sides by $\frac{1}{(1+i_2)^n}$ gives

$$\frac{\pounds 1 * \frac{1}{(1+i_2)^n} / \frac{1}{(1+i_2)^n}}{(1 + i_3)^r} = \pounds 1 * \frac{\frac{1}{(1+i_2)^n}}{(1 + i_1)^{n+r}} \tag{2}$$

$$i.e. \ \pounds 1 * \frac{1}{(1 + i_3)^r} = \frac{\pounds 1 * (1 + i_2)^n}{(1 + i_1)^{n+r}} \tag{3}$$

$$= \frac{\pounds 1 * (1 + i_2)^n}{(1 + i_1)^{n+r}} * \frac{\frac{1}{(1+i_2)^n}}{\frac{1}{(1+i_2)^n}} = \pounds 1 * [\frac{\frac{1}{(1+i_1)^{n+r}}}{(1 + i_2)^n}] \tag{4}$$

$$= \pounds 1 * \frac{[\frac{1}{(1+i_1)^{n+r}}]}{[\frac{(1+i_1)^{n+r}}{(1+i_2)^n} * \frac{1}{(1+i_1)^{n+r}}]} = \pounds 1 * \frac{\frac{1}{(1+i_1)^{n+r}}}{\frac{1}{(1+i_2)^n}} \tag{5}$$

or, in Keynes's less familiar notation where $_nd_r = \frac{_1d_{n+r}}{_1d_n}$, where d denotes debts of £1 deferred $(n + r)$ and n years from the present and r years n years from now. Leaving aside algebraic manipulation, the economic rationale for taking it that the two sides of (1) are equal is the existence of certainty as to the future of the rates of interest. Under these conditions the relationship between the ratio of the present values on the left hand side is one of identity with the present value on the right hand side because the current rates of interest (i_1, i_2) implied in these present values are adjusted to the knowledge of the future rate of interest (i_3) in such a way that there will be neither gain or loss if a debt is realized before it reaches maturity.

15. Keynes takes this to be the normal method of bringing an additional amount of money into being. It is directly associated initially with a lower rate of interest. He points out (*CW, VII: 200*) that if the additional amount of money were to come about in other ways, it would still be associated, albeit less directly, with a lower rate of interest.

Thus, for example, where an addition to the amount of money accrues in the first instance as someone's income, as happens when money consists of gold coins, so that 'changes in M can only result from increased returns to the activities of gold-miners who belong to the economic system under examination', or where changes in the amount of money 'are due to the Government printing money wherewith to meets its current expenditure', it will still be associated with a lower rate of interest (*CW, VII*: 200). In a monetary economy, as we have already noted, money is held to satisfy both the transactions and the speculative motives as well as the precautionary motive. Accordingly, unless special and peculiar assumptions are made it must be accepted as a general principle that an additional amount of money will not be taken up solely to satisfy the transactions and precautionary motives. Some of it will be taken up to satisfy the speculative motive and, by adding to the demand for securities or other assets, will raise their prices and, thereby, lower the rate of interest.

16.   Keynes notes that, even 'if the increased employment ensuing on a fall in the rate of interest leads to an increase of wages, i.e. to an increase in the money value of the wage-unit', or in other words, to a higher value rather than a higher volume of transactions, the result would be similar to the previous case of a higher volume of transactions, unless in this case liquidity-preference were to be measured in terms of wage-units rather than of money (*CW, VII*: 172). Although, as he also notes, it is convenient in some contexts (for example, in regard to the theory of employment as such) to measure liquidity-preference in terms of wage-units it would not be appropriate in this context as to do so would eliminate the very matter of concern from the possibility of consideration (*CW, VII*: 172, also 246).

17.   The current earnings from holding debts are reduced by a fall in the rate of interest. These earnings serve to offset the possibility of a capital loss. The amount of this offset will be 'the difference between the *squares* of the old rate of interest and the new' (*CW, VII*: 202). Keynes illustrates this by pointing out that if the rate of interest on a long-term debt is 4 per cent, it is better to buy this debt unless one expects the long-run rate of interest to rise faster than by 4 per cent of itself annually. Thus, for example, a £100 debt at a rate of interest of 4 per cent should not be purchased if the rate of interest is expected to rise by 25 per cent of itself yearly, because the capital value of the debt would fall to £80, giving a capital loss of £20 after the first year, which, allowing for £4 interest, would yield a net loss of £16. So, with these expectations one would not pay £100 to get £4 yearly when in a short while an £80 outlay would be expected to yield the same yearly return. The debt would be purchased, provided that on the 'balance of probabilities' it is expected that the rate of interest will not rise yearly by more than 4 per cent of itself. Thus in the case of an expected rise of 0.16 per cent yearly (i.e. 4 per cent of itself or 0.04*0.04*100 per cent) in the rate of interest holding a debt of £100 at 4 per cent, rather than cash, would not result in an overall loss because the capital loss of

approximately £4 (£3 $\frac{11}{13}$ to be exact) would be compensated by the interest income (of £4).

18. If we take the case of the combination of *rising* prices and unemployment (stagflation) which, of course, Keynes does not, we find other dilemmas. Entrepreneurs cannot curtail the quantity of money. Neither, for political reasons, can the authorities. Even if it could be curtailed the rate of interest would rise thereby reducing investment and increasing unemployment. Should the authorities try to reduce unemployment by increasing the quantity of money the result is likely to be that the wage-unit would rise as fast as or faster than the quantity of money so that in terms of the wage-unit the quantity of money would remain the same as before or fall. If inflation were to be very rapid there may even be a flight from money to commodities (but without stimulating their production because the schedule of the marginal efficiency of capital would be in a state of collapse) and to other currencies leading ultimately to a breakdown of the monetary system.

19. Keynes points out that if money-wages are inflexible 'such changes in prices as occur' will correspond in the main 'to the diminishing marginal productivity of the existing equipment as the output from it is increased' but that, in addition, 'other considerations' will enter into the determination of "administered" or monopoly prices' (*CW, VII*: 268).

20. Keynes uses the word 'directed' presumably because the aggregate demand function expresses the outlay which the entrepreneur expects to be directed towards him by his customers at the point of effective demand.

21. It is well to bear in mind also that Keynes assumes that the reader accepts that a writer must not be expected to repeat explanations and definitions every time he uses them and that the common-sense of the reader can be relied on to supply them as required (see above, p.33). In an early draft of *The General Theory* Keynes specifically warned that he would frequently drop 'the distinction between "gross investment" and "effective demand based on an expectation of gross investment", leaving the reader to supply the more exact phrase himself... And similarly as regards the distinction between the expected consumption and the actual consumption' (*CW, XIII*: 433).

22. The income and industrial circulations correspond to what Keynes denotes as *income deposits* and *business deposits* in *A Treatise on Money* (*CW, V*: 31).

23. It was in connection with this that Keynes made what is probably his most celebrated and certainly his most misquoted statement. In *A Tract on Monetary Reform* (1923) he said that 'the error often made by careless adherents of the quantity theory' was that 'an arbitrary doubling' of the quantity of money would mean no more than that the cost of living index would also double (*CW, IV*: 64–5). Keynes agreed that 'in the long run' this was 'probably true'. By 'long run' he meant a period of 50 or 60 years. But he pointed out that 'this *long run* is a misleading guide to current affairs' because in 'the *long run* we are all dead'. He added that 'economists set themselves too easy, too useless a

task if in tempestuous seasons they can only tell us that when the storm is long past the ocean is flat again' (*CW, IV:* 65).

24.　The cost-unit changes with each change in the mix of factors employed and with each change in the rates of remuneration of the individual factors. Thus the cost-unit cannot, any more than the wage-unit, be regarded as a deflator.

References

Allen, H.V., *Commercial Arithmetic*. London: Longmans, 1939.

Cannan, E., 'The Application of the Theoretical Apparatus of Supply and Demand to Units of Currency'. originally in *Economic Journal* 31: 453–61, 1921. Reprinted in F.A. Lutz, and L.W. Mints, editors, *Readings in Monetary Theory*: 3–12. New York and London: Garland Publishing, 1983. (1921).

Keynes, John Maynard, *The Collected Writings of John Maynard Keynes, Volume I: Indian Currency and Finance*. London: Macmillan, 1971. (1913).

Keynes, John Maynard, *The Collected Writings of John Maynard Keynes, Volume IV: A Tract on Monetary Reform*. London: Macmillan, 1971. (1923).

Keynes, John Maynard, *The Collected Writings of John Maynard Keynes, Volume V: A Treatise on Money*. London: Macmillan, 1971. (1930).

Keynes, John Maynard, *The Collected Writings of John Maynard Keynes, Volume VII: The General Theory of Employment, Interest and Money*. London: Macmillan, 1973. (1936).

Keynes, John Maynard, *The Collected Writings of John Maynard Keynes, Volume X: Essays in Biography*. London: Macmillan, 1972. (1933).

Keynes, John Maynard. *The Collected Writings of John Maynard Keynes, Volume XII: Economic Articles and Correspondence: Investment and Editorial*. Donald Moggridge, editor. London: Macmillan, 1981.

Keynes, John Maynard. *The Collected Writings of John Maynard Keynes, Volume XIII. The General Theory and After: Part I Preparation*. Donald Moggridge, editor. London: Macmillan, 1973.

Keynes, John Maynard, *The Collected Writings of John Maynard Keynes, Volume XIV: The General Theory and After: Part II Defence and Development*. Donald Moggridge, editor. London: Macmillan, 1973.

Keynes, John Maynard, *The Collected Writings of John Maynard Keynes, Volume XXI: Activities 1931–1939: World Crises and Policies in Britain and America*. Donald Moggridge, editor. London: Macmillan, 1982.

Keynes, John Maynard, *The Collected Writings of John Maynard Keynes, Volume XXIX: The General Theory and After: A Supplement*. London: Macmillan, 1979.

Kirzner, Israel, *Market Theory and the Price System*. Princeton: Van Nostrand, 1963.

Kirzner, Israel M., *Competition and Entrepreneurship*: University of Chicago Press, Chicago and London, 1973.

Marshall, Alfred, 'The Graphic Method of Statistics', Paper at International Statistical Congress, 1885. In A.C. Pigou, 1925: 175–187. (1885).

Marshall, Alfred, 'The Present Position of Economics. Inaugral Lecture, Cambridge, 1885. In A.C. Pigou, 1925: 152–174. (1885).

Marshall, Alfred, *Letters* 19/8/1982, 3/3/1901, 20/12/1901. In A.C. Pigou, 1925: 378–379, 421–423, 425–427.

Marshall, A., *Principles of Economics: An Introductory Volume*. 8th Edition. London: Macmillan, 1920. 9th (Variorum) Edition. London: Macmillan, 1961. (1920).

Pigou, A.C., editor, *Memorials of Alfred Marshall*. Originally published by London: Macmillan, 1925. Reprints of Economic Classics. New York: Augustus M. Kelley, 1966. (1925).

Robertson, D. H., *Lectures on Economic Principles: Volume III*. London: Stable Press, 1959.

Index